Stepping Out

of related interest

Small Steps Forward
Using Games and Activities to Help Your Pre-School Child
with Special Needs
Sarah Newman
ISBN 1 85302 643 3

Helping Children to Build Self-Esteem
A Photocopiable Activities Book
Deborah Plummer
ISBN 1 85302 927 0

Relationship Development Intervention with Young Children
Social and Emotional Development Activities
for Asperger Syndrome, PDD and NLD
Steven E. Gutstein and Rachelle K. Sheely
ISBN 1 84310 714 7

Playing, Laughing and Learning with Children
on the Autistic Spectrum
A Practical Resource of Play Ideas for Parents and Carers
Julia Moor
ISBN 1 84310 060 6

Giggle Time – Establishing the Social Connection
A Program to Develop the Communication Skills of Children
with Autism
Susan Aud Sonders
ISBN 1 84310 719 3

Stepping Out

Using Games and Activities to Help Your Child with Special Needs

Sarah Newman

Illustrated by Jeanie Mellersh

Jessica Kingsley Publishers
London and New York

First published in the United Kingdom in 2004
by Jessica Kingsley Publishers Ltd
116 Pentonville Road
London N1 9JB, England
and
29 West 35th Street, 10th fl.
New York, NY 10001-2299, USA

www.jkp.com

Copyright © Sarah Newman 2004
Illustrations copyright © Jeanie Mellersh 2004

Library of Congress Cataloging in Publication Data
A CIP catalog record for this book is available from the Library of Congress

British Library Cataloguing in Publication Data
A CIP catalogue record for this book is available from the British Library

ISBN 1 84310 110 6

Printed and Bound in Great Britain by
Athenaeum Press, Gateshead, Tyne and Wear

Contents

This book is dedicated to Nick and Billy

Acknowledgements

Among the many parents who talked to me about their experiences my particular thanks go to Ann Baker, Gill Bennet, Andrea Blower, Catherine Bowell, Kay Cooper, Helga Crosland, Suzannah and Mike Fussell, Sue Harvey, Sarah Hicks, Sheila Hummerstone, Cheryl Maher, Claire Muir, Sandra Parker, Glender Phillips, Julie Pursey, Sharon Street, Jacolyn Thomas, Lisa Thomas, Elaine Waterhouse, Lyn White and Deirdre Witherby.

My thanks are also due to the many individuals and professionals who advised and helped, particularly Tim Anstey, rugby coach; Lesley Berry, teacher; Eva Chrispin, Citizens Advice Bureau; Steve Crawley, community nurse; Sue Evans, social worker; Katya Gorman, occupational therapist; Dr Neil Harris, child psychiatrist; Barbara Humphreys, teacher; Ruth Linsley, teacher; Gay Kennard, nursery nurse; Dr Jo Lee, GP; Evelyn New, speech therapist and Kenzie Revington, physiotherapist.

I would like to thank the Makaton Vocabulary Development Project for allowing me to reproduce the signs and symbols on page 112.

My particular thanks go to Michele Francis, teacher; Jenifer Gurd, teacher and Rosie Mitchell, occupational therapist, who were so generous with their time and support.

I would also like to thank Catherine Lindsay, Jo Strudwick and Christine Woolley and my parents, who all helped in different ways.

I would like to thank Jeanie for her illustrations and Nick Mellersh for all this support and computer advice. We both thank all the carers and children, some with special needs and some without, who modelled for the illustrations in the book. Particular thanks go to Martin Lenaerts and New Forest Mencap and to Allison Carter and

Charlie Brown of Nevada City schools district special education department for their help.

My biggest thanks are for David who was wonderfully supportive and encouraging and whose comments and constructive criticism were invaluable. My children were all very keen to hear of progress and even to help with the writing. I am particularly grateful to Christopher who resisted the strong temptation to 'delete Mummy's book out'.

Introduction

I wrote my first book *Small Steps Forward: Using Games and Activities to Help Your Pre-school Child with Special Needs* as a response to finding out that my son, Christopher, had special needs. He was diagnosed with global developmental delay at the age of one and with autism at three. After the initial shock, my response to the news of his problems was to find out what I could do to help him. When I realised that there was very little information for parents in my situation I decided to write my own book.

Christopher is now nine years old and has two younger brothers. He has made huge progress, way beyond our expectations in the first dark days of his diagnosis. We have all moved on a long way, but we continue to face new situations and new issues. I thought it would be helpful to look at children's development while they were at primary school. I wondered initially if there would be anything to say, given that children spend so much of their time at school and I imagined education would cover everything. In fact, on the contrary, you will see that so much of child development happens naturally and normally within the family and at home.

Although my son is autistic I have tried to cover a broad range of learning disabilities. This is partly because many people do not have a diagnosis and partly because even if they do it is still best to look at a child as a unique individual and take time to see what might work for him or her rather than follow the 'usual' route. Also, I believe there is far more that unites children than separates them. Some of the nicest compliments I received for *Small Steps Forward* were from friends who read the book and said they found it helpful even though their children do not have special needs. The point is surely that we are not asking our special needs children to do anything different to ordinary children. They may just need more time to get there and a bit more awareness, understanding and patience on the way.

HOW THIS BOOK IS STRUCTURED

Children with special needs often need more help, stimulation and encouragement to develop skills than other children. In order to know what support they need to reach the next stage, it helps to have an understanding of their stage of development.

This book has been written, therefore, to give you a brief idea of the progression of child development to enable you to see the stage your child is at and where he or she is heading. Once you know the context it is much easier to see what he or she is doing, why and how you can help.

The book starts with a chapter on everyday living with a child with special needs. Chapter 2 gives general information on how to play with your child which is relevant to all aspects of development. In the subsequent chapters, child development is divided into the following areas: cognitive, language, physical, sensory, social and emotional. However, all areas are closely inter-related and such divisions are inevitably rather artificial. Consequently, you will find many cross-references to highlight the inter-connections.

The chapters outline the theory of development chronologically. Some also have very brief outlines of the academic theories which underlie it. Then in the games and activities sections you will find a variety of ways to stimulate your child's progress.

Chapter 9 gives additional practical advice on behaviour management, sleep and toilet training and Chapter 10 looks at choosing a school and making it work for your child as well as the Statutory Assessment procedure. Chapters 11 and 12 give information on support, useful books and voluntary organisations.

This book follows on chronologically from *Small Steps Forward* which looked at early development from birth to around age four (if a child is reaching normal milestones). This book continues from about age four but I have included a very brief description of early development. You could refer back to *Small Steps Forward* if your child is still developing these early skills.

I have deliberately tried not to include references to the age at which children are supposed to achieve certain skills. They are very vague anyway and I don't think it is very helpful. It is more important to understand where your child is developmentally and to be aware of the progress, however small, that he or she is making. However, sometimes it is difficult to get a sense of the passing of time so, for clarity, I have used the terms young child (for skills developing in a normally developing child aged 0–4), middle childhood (5–9) and late childhood (10–12).

HOW TO USE THIS BOOK

I have not written this book to tell you what you *should* be doing with your child. It is designed to give you ideas for games, if you *want* to do something structured. I am sure you don't need any more pressure. There are many times when you just want to have fun with your child in a completely free and relaxed way. On those occasions, leave this book on the shelf.

This book is not meant to be read in one go. Read Chapter 1, Everyday Life, if you want to. Then Chapter 2, What Everyone Needs to Know, and then dip into whichever chapter you need at the time. Remember that each chapter covers years of development so concentrate on the sections relevant to your child at a particular time.

Not all the ideas will work for all children. Use and adapt what you think will work for your child.

This book is a starting point only. For more specialist information and advice use the references and refer to the organisations and books listed in Chapter 12, Resources.

Please note

- I have used parent as shorthand for mother, father or primary carer.
- I have alternated the use of the pronouns 'he' and 'she' in each chapter to represent your child.

- I have included quotes from parents about their experiences. The child's name has usually been changed.

- I have written this book from the standpoint of a family consisting of a mother and father. However, I appreciate this is not always the case and hope that the many lone parents who may be reading this book will have no difficulty adapting the ideas to their circumstances.

- When making toys or playing games, make sure they are safe and appropriate for your child.

- If you are concerned about any area of your child's development seek advice from your GP or health visitor. They should be able to help you or refer you to someone more appropriate.

CHAPTER 1

Everyday Life

When you have a child with special needs, it can feel as if you are on a journey, sometimes moving forwards, sometimes backwards. Occasionally it is plain sailing, at other times an uphill struggle.

When I started writing this book, I thought to myself how I had moved on over the years since my son's first diagnosis. Initially it seemed as if my whole life was bound up in his special needs. There was no other existence. Now, most of the time, although his autism is a significant part of my life and it affects pretty well everything we do as a family, it does not seem to demand my whole attention in the same way. I seem to have found a new perspective on it, and there are now other things in life to think about.

> Every year we go to the Christmas party run by the charity Reach, which has been great for meeting other children and families; but this year we decided that our daughter, at 6, was the oldest child there and that it would probably be the last year. We have moved on and don't need that kind of support now.

> When we first found out about our daughter it seemed like a life sentence but life does return to some kind of normality.

However, there are times when you feel you are in that big black hole again. Something goes wrong and all of a sudden the struggle to deal with it takes over your life. It does not take much – an unkind word, a bad day – to send you over the edge. Then it seems like a long long struggle to get back to normal.

Everything was going fine until one day out of the blue I got a phone call to say that the respite care centre wanted to discharge Steven. I put the phone down and was reduced to a shivering, sobbing wreck with only one topic of conversation for days. It stirred up all sorts of emotions. Are we demanding too much? Is Steven really perfectly OK and is it all in my mind? Do they think I am a liar?

I was preparing tea for five children including my autistic son and everything seemed to be fine as I carefully arranged the plates according to each child's individual requirements – no peas here, Bolognese sauce on the side there, not too much pasta here and so on. Then Tara asked for lemon instead of orange squash. Instead of saying 'yes' or 'no', I lost control and started bashing each plate with my spoon sending spaghetti flying round the kitchen.

Parenting is a hard job at the best of times. As a parent you worry whether you are doing the right thing, you worry about your child's happiness, you worry about his future. No one, least of all your child, tells you that you are doing a good job. Having a child with special needs gives you even more to contend with.

Situations are always changing, children are growing up and you are up against new challenges. You are constantly having to re-evaluate what you are doing. It means that good times rarely last forever – but then again, neither do bad times.

Additionally, children with special needs can be less resilient and less able to cope with change and variety than their peers. It can be as if they are skating on thin ice. There is less flexibility, less leeway for changes or mistakes. Maybe a club is cancelled. Any child would be disappointed but perhaps could be distracted or could understand that the organiser was ill. A child with special needs might be thrown by it and become unsettled and difficult. That will impact on you quite considerably.

THINK OF YOUR OWN NEEDS TOO

Your child is not the only person who has needs. You too have needs which are just as valid. You must accept them and find a way of meeting them so that you too can be fulfilled and happy. If your needs are not being met and you feel isolated, bored, stressed or overwhelmed then the way you live your life, how you feel about your child and how you respond to him and to others will all be affected. We all know that when we are feeling happy and fulfilled we can appreciate the positive things in life and cope with the more difficult aspects. On the other hand, when we are fed up and unhappy, the smallest problem takes on the proportions of a nightmare. Don't feel guilty if you sometimes put your own needs before those of your children. In the wider picture that may be the right thing to do.

Strategies

- *Decide what is important in your life.* Think about what is important in your life and work out a lifestyle that meets your priorities. Be prepared to make changes to your current lifestyle and to tread your own path. One of the good things about having a child with special needs is that it makes you reflect on your core values of what is important – health, time with your children, appreciating achievements and so on. In many ways you have to opt out of the great rat race because having a child with special needs does not fit into society's current concepts of 'having it all' – the perfect family with money, looks, health, etc.

- *Make life as easy for yourself as you can.* Try to think about the causes of stress in your life and how you can eradicate them. Sometimes it is a case of simplifying how you live – getting rid of ornaments that need to be dusted and only get broken, abandoning the allotment because you just don't have time to grow your own vegetables. Maybe you could pay someone to do the chores you don't have time for.

    I employ someone to help me in the summer holidays so we can all get out, do a greater variety of activities and I can give more time to all the children as well as Fiona.

- *Give yourself time off.* Find a way of having some time off from caring for your child so that you can do the things *you* enjoy – perhaps seeing friends, going for a swim or going to an evening class. Use respite care or babysitters, take up any offers from family and friends or get your partner to look after your child for the day or weekend so that you can have a break.

What will work for you will depend enormously on your circumstances, your needs and your child's disability. Don't feel guilty about it because in the end everyone will benefit. Time off gives you a chance to put things in perspective and allows you to see the positive sides. You will feel relaxed and renewed and will be a happier and more positive person and parent who is able to cope better.

> One year we were feeling so buried under the limitations of our three children that we decided that we had to accept that we had to do things separately or we would never be able to do them. So Yasin had a week skiing with friends and I had a few weekends through the year when I met up with friends in London and I even went to Barcelona. It was fantastic to have that freedom and the lack of responsibility and we both came back feeling refreshed, revitalised and exhilarated by our experiences. At some point in the future I am sure we will do the same thing again.

- *Try to keep a reasonable detachment.* Try not to be over-involved with your child – concerned and anxious about every detail. Sometimes you have to take a step back and remember that things are as they are and you cannot live his life for him.

LOOK AFTER RELATIONSHIPS WITHIN YOUR EXTENDED FAMILY

Relationship with your partner

Having a child with special needs adds stress to any relationship because it means you both have to deal with the problems and anxieties it throws up. It will probably mean you have less time and energy to devote to each other and will throw into sharp focus any differences in attitude and in your abilities to cope. It may also mean you have to negotiate a change in your lifestyle and expectations. Some relationships are able to withstand these pressures and some are not.

Strategies

- *Keep lines of communication open.* Make sure you talk about your child and any issues that arise. If you cannot do it informally than make a time to 'talk about the children'.

- *Find time to enjoy things together* without the children. Use respite care, babysitters or family to give you a chance to go out and have fun – perhaps for a drink, a walk or to see a film.

- *Be generous and give support to each other.* If your partner is having a particularly hard time give him or her a weekend off or a night out.

- *Be careful not to get polarised.* You can get into situations where one of you takes a more extreme position on an issue such as managing behaviour, future plans or education and it can force the other to seek to compensate by taking an opposite view. In reality your views may not be so dissimilar. Take time to reflect whether or not your real views are being represented.

Your relationship with your children

All parents worry about balancing the needs of their children. With a child with special needs this issue is even more of a hot potato because you feel either that he is getting the lion's share of attention or that he is being neglected for other more demanding children. Which way it goes will probably depend on his special needs. There is no perfect solution, no right or wrong, no perfect balance. It is probably crazy to think you can partition a day or even a week fairly between all the different claimants. Life does not really work like that.

So much depends on your child's special needs and the impact they have and on the personalities of the children. Some crave a lot of attention while others would not want it anyway. The needs of children change as they get older and they need different treatment at different stages. Sometimes one child and sometimes another will need a period of attention.

It is important to make sure that you are aware of the needs of every member of your family. While it is probably likely that the child with special needs will require more attention in some respects, the balance should never be tipped too far in his direction. Just because your other children don't have special needs doesn't mean everything for them will be plain sailing. Behavioural problems are common in all children and these, if not attended to, may become more of a problem for your family than those posed by your child with special needs.

I found my relationship with my daughter more difficult than with my son who has dyspraxia. I eventually realised that I had been too preoccupied with meeting his needs and had ignored hers. So the pair of us went skiing together for a week which was a great success and heralded a more balanced perspective.

Strategies

- *Put your child's special needs into perspective.* He is just one member of the family and if some activity is going to help him a little but could have a considerable negative effect on the rest of the family don't do it. Think about the whole family.

- *Try to live as normal a life as possible* and do the things that other families do. This is as important for your child with special needs as for his siblings.

- *Make sure you give time and attention to all your children:*

  - Always value the activities and achievements of all the siblings – whether it is a nice picture, a Lego model or learning to ride a bicycle. It is so easy just to ignore their little achievements thinking that there is nothing special about what they have done (after all, they are normal children and should be doing these things anyway). But all children crave such praise.

  - Make time to spend with them by using either respite care or offers of help from family or friends and go and do something special with them that you could not do normally – going to the cinema or shopping for example.

- Make a time during each day which is their
  special time – a story before bed or chatting
  over the washing up.

- Give them the opportunity to pursue a special
  hobby or activity – swimming, riding, sailing,
  music – whatever particularly appeals. It could
  be used to improve self-esteem or be an avenue
  for giving special attention.

- *Consider their strengths and weaknesses* – where they need support
  and help and what might boost their self-esteem.

- *Give siblings their own space* where they can play, their toys will
  be safe and where they can be left in peace if they wish.

- *Encourage siblings to develop their own social life.* Make sure that
  you invite friends round from school or on trips out with you.
  Get grandparents or uncles and aunts to take them out or have
  them to stay. It is not a substitute for time with you, but it is a
  good addition.

- *Give them time not toys.* Siblings want to spend time with a
  parent or parents alone rather than with a toy. Find
  opportunities to take siblings out individually to the cinema,
  shopping or the park so that they feel special.

  Think carefully before making your other children
  'responsible' for their disabled brother or sister. Make sure the
  level of responsibility is appropriate and also that they are
  getting enough time to themselves.

  Encourage them to be as independent as they can so that they
  can have fun and get on with doing things they want to do.

- *Don't have unrealistic expectations of your other children.*
  Understandably, when you are having a tough time with your
  child with special needs, it is very easy to expect the other
  children to just somehow know this and behave like adults.
  Often they do mature very quickly but you must not forget
  that they are still children with their own needs.

I was having a particularly bad day, was very fed up and the children were driving me round the bend. Nick did something vaguely naughty and I completely over-reacted and screamed at him: 'And how old are you?' I expected him to reply '25', instead this terrified little voice said 'four, Mummy' and I just wanted to die.

When siblings are alone with you it can be an opportunity for them to test the boundaries and so you can find precious respite care time spent dealing with behavioural issues with your other children. So be prepared for this and give them lots of attention for good behaviour.

- *Think about the different standards in behaviour you expect of your children.* You may have to allow your child with special needs more freedom than your other children. Children notice different treatment and will comment on how unfair it is. Explain why you have different standards in a way that is positive and understandable to your other children. 'I know Jake makes a mess when he eats but you know he finds it difficult to use his hands carefully and he is trying very hard. It is nice to see how beautifully you can use your knife and fork.'

Why can't I do that?

- *Point out to your children the positive aspects of having a sibling with special needs* – special toys, trips away, people you have met.

- *Make sure you are communicating with your children.* Talk to them honestly, in a way that they can understand, about what is going on and why things are as they are.

- If your children are feeling angry and frustrated because their brother is annoying them or restricting them, accept and acknowledge their feelings, take them seriously even if you cannot do anything about it. Talking things over and sharing feelings helps. After all, you share your problems with friends even if they cannot give you any answers. It still makes you feel better.

Helping your children come to terms with their sibling with special needs

In the same way that having a child with special needs affects your own life, so his siblings' childhoods will be affected. Their family life and their childhood experiences may be curtailed or enhanced, but they will certainly be different from those of others. They will have to think of the issue of disability which other children or people may never have to face up to. They are also bound to be affected by the stresses and additional burdens placed on relationships within the family, particularly between their parents. They may have to deal with the way their peers will handle the information, and the questioning or maybe teasing, mocking or even bullying which may happen at some point.

Children respond very differently to having a sibling with special needs because so much depends on the severity and nature of the disability, the age of the children, their position within the family, their personality and their gender. It is impossible to generalise, especially as the response will change over time. A young child might be very accepting but as he gets older might find it more difficult. Another child might find it very difficult to deal with her sibling's disability when young but as they both mature come to an acceptance.

Siblings also have to try to understand what a disability is and what it actually means. These are quite difficult questions for adults, let alone children, to address. Why has my brother got a disability? How does an extra chromosome give him a learning disability? What does this mean for me if I decide to have children? What kind of society do we live in that bullies or mocks someone like my little brother whom I love?

In response to these questions many siblings grow up to be more caring, accepting, gentle and responsible children. It can be a very positive experience for a child to grow up appreciating how some children have to make huge efforts, how they have to be caring and supportive of others who have problems and how they should not take their own good health for granted. Your children take their cue from you. If you feel positive about your life, love all your children and value their efforts and their achievements, then siblings will have a greater chance of valuing their special needs siblings and will feel valued themselves.

> In the research for this book many parents paid tribute to how their other children had responded to their sibling's special needs and commented on their compassion and consideration. I saw little evidence of it in my pair. However, one day we had a couple of children with special needs to play and I was amazed by how beautifully my children responded. They wanted to play with them in the most natural way – they were so encouraging, supportive and accepting.

Strategies

- *Explain your child's special needs and his behaviour* in a way that has meaning for his siblings, is positive and shows you accept your child. It sets a tone and your children will probably use those explanations for themselves and for others, e.g. 'John will learn to walk, it will just take him a bit longer' or 'Anna loves saying "hello" to babies and so do we. Some mummies like it, others don't; it is nicer when people are friendly, isn't it?'

- *Talk to your children about how they feel,* give them the chance to express their feelings and accept those feelings. Even if you cannot do anything to help them or change the situation itself, it helps them to have their feelings acknowledged and recognised.

- *Give siblings the chance to meet others in their position* so they can talk about similar experiences, maybe talk about how they feel, swap stories of embarrassing incidents, talk about how unreasonable their parents are, and so on. Many local organisations offer whole family activities and there may also be workshops for siblings in your area: ask locally for details.

Sometimes siblings need someone to talk to outside the family because they could not be brutally honest about how they feel to their parents, whom they know are already overloaded with problems. Sometimes a relative or a friend may provide an outlet. Many of the organisations listed in Chapter 12 also offer support to siblings.

Children can get very hurt by comments made by schoolmates and others about their sibling. They can be embarrassed by their sibling's behaviour or disabilities. Talk about it and *give them strategies for how to respond* and suggestions of things to say if people make comments about their sibling.

As children get older they will need to develop their understanding of their sibling's disability. A young child will accept that his sibling with Down's Syndrome takes a bit longer to learn things, later on he will use the term Down's. At secondary school age he may think about the genetics and later on he may be concerned about the implications for his own children.

Talk to your other children about any concerns they may have about their friends' reactions if they were to be invited over. Suggest honest, positive and comprehensible ways for them to explain their sibling's special needs. If necessary, make it easy for your other children by inviting friends over when their sibling is away or by keeping him occupied so that they can play freely.

Grandparents and extended family

Don't forget the needs of grandparents and wider family members. They may have expectations or feelings of guilt to address. Grandparents can be a source of great support and help to parents, both practical and emotional. They often have a very good relationship with their grandchildren because of the special bond of love, and a bit more time without the stresses of daily care. It can be a really positive experience for everyone.

Sometimes families have difficulty communicating with grand-parents about the child's special needs – the nature of them, future plans and so on. Try to keep talking and discussing issues. If you cannot do it informally then try to do it formally by setting a time and place for discussion, for example: 'Let's talk about Milly after supper tonight.'

FAMILY SCRIPTS

Sometimes it can help to take a dispassionate look at the way you do things within the family and to see if it could be changed for the better. You can feel trapped inside expectations and traditions which are not helpful and not of your conscious making. For example, you may feel that your house has to be spotlessly clean and tidy. Does it really need to be? All families set up ways of doing things, patterns of behaviour and expectations, which are passed on to the next generation. Sometimes it helps to take a long, hard look at what is going on within your family to see what you are doing and whether it is really what you want.

MEETING OTHER PARENTS OF CHILDREN WITH SPECIAL NEEDS

All parents spend a lot of time checking up on what other parents are doing with their children. They meet up at the school gate, chat on the phone or over coffee about their child's eating habits, bed wetting, clubs they go to, friendships, performance at school, etc. They do this just to make sure that their children are on the right track and that they, as parents, are doing roughly the right thing.

Parents of children with special needs need these checks as much as anyone else but it can be more difficult to have contact with parents in similar situations. If your child is at your local school then he might be the only one with special needs and that can feel very isolating, especially if other people's expectations and experiences are far away from your own. If your child is at a special school then he may go by bus or taxi and you are unlikely to meet the other parents who may live a long way away from you.

Whilst you may have many really good friends they don't necessarily share the same experiences and concerns that you have about your child's education, behaviour and health. On the contrary, you can sometimes feel you are in a parallel universe where your own experiences bear no relationship to those of other parents, for example when you are talking about holidays or schooling. Meeting other parents of children with special needs gives you a chance to swap stories, laugh about your experiences, get information and support and feel that you are not alone.

Strategies

- *Keep in touch with other parents* you have met in the past through playgroup, opportunity group, portage or other services.

- *Join local support groups* to meet other parents nearby. Many of the major charities have affiliated local branches which are not listed in this book but can be found by contacting the head office, in your local telephone book or on the internet (see Chapter 12 for a list of national organisations).

- If your child is at a special school *join the PTA or the governors* or make sure you attend fund-raising events and ask the head to introduce you to parents of children in your child's class. Ask if any children live nearby and make contact. Find out whom your child plays with and arrange to meet up with his parents.

- If they don't already happen, you could *organise a coffee morning* for parents or a tea party at the end of the school day for children and their parents. Some schools will host such events, perhaps with a guest speaker; or you could hold it in your own house or at a convenient community centre. This gives an opportunity to meet all the parents and share experiences and expertise.

- Women tend to have a much better support network of friends with children with special needs. It is rare for men to share their experiences. As a result it is much easier for women to find support from others than it is for fathers. *Try to arrange whole family activities* for weekends or evenings so that fathers can come as well.

At the school gate

DIAGNOSIS

Many parents have different views on having a diagnosis. Some do not want to have their child 'labelled'. Maybe this is because they are not ready to face up to their child's problems, or maybe they do not want to go down the path of medicalising all personality traits. Some say that there is no problem in having a diagnosis, the only problem is in stereotyping. Some parents feel they only obtained services, information and support once they managed to get a diagnosis. Others, who feel their child has been wrongly diagnosed, have a very different attitude. A lot will depend on your own experiences.

The most important thing to remember is that each child should be considered individually and that while a diagnosis might help to point you in the right direction, it is not prescriptive.

> I found that having a diagnosis helped me come to terms with my daughter's disability, but now I have little truck with anyone suggesting that maybe the diagnosis should be modified because in the end the most important thing is her own individual needs.

DEALING WITH OTHER PEOPLE'S REACTIONS

One point of stress is dealing with other people's reactions every time you go out. Some people say the most terrible things and are extraordinarily judgemental ('That child needs a good smacking'), while others come out with stereotypes and platitudes ('Down's Syndrome children are so loving').

> I find that a comment made one day will not bother me, but the next day it might send me into a frenzy. It is much more a symptom of how I feel — relaxed, happy and enjoying life or stressed and struggling to keep control. Interestingly, when Pete and I go out together we flip at different things, which shows, I suppose, that it is more to do with how you are feeling than what people actually say.

However, along with the insensitive and judgemental remarks you often come across people who are incredibly kind, helpful and considerate and sometimes incredibly knowledgeable and supportive. Not all reactions are bad: more often we are amazed at how fantastic some people are. Nor can you always predict what people are thinking from looking at them.

Strategies

- *Don't make assumptions about people's reactions* — one person may think something is an example of outrageous behaviour, the next will comment on how good it is to see children having fun.

> When we were on holiday in the Wye Valley, we were on top of a viewpoint and a man was there taking photographs on a very expensive-looking camera. Christopher was fascinated but the man turned to him rather gruffly and said: 'That camera cost me a lot of money, if you touch it, I'll throw you over the edge!' It was very difficult to keep Christopher away. Instead, he hovered around asking questions and eventually wound up being photographed and taking pictures himself. The man turned out to be a really friendly guy.

- *Think of your own needs.* If you are finding people's reactions difficult it may be because you are under stress and need more support or you may need to modify what you are doing to make life easier.

- You are in a difficult situation and sometimes things are too much and you will boil over and say things which you regret. You're not perfect. *Forgive yourself* – for your own sanity.

- *Remember the many positive experiences you have.*

Hannah is fascinated by how things work and many people respond really well – we get to look in the cabs of steam trains, she gets to work the tills in shops, swipe credit cards for shop assistants, sit on people's motorbikes – all because people can be so friendly.

- *Have a standard response* which you can deliver in a civil manner for those awkward moments when people are being unpleasant, for example: 'It is generally thought rude to stare' or 'I am sorry my son's behaviour is bit difficult, we find it hard too: he has autism'.

MAKE FULL USE OF SERVICES AND BENEFITS AVAILABLE

Take advantage of any services or benefits that you feel might be helpful and don't feel guilty about it. There will always be other children who have greater needs than yours, but you are not in a position to help them; your duty is to your own child. It is more expensive and more difficult having a child with special needs. They may need more toys or specialist equipment, there may be more breakages and more laundry to do and you may have to travel more to appointments and activities. It is also much more stressful, so take any help you can to alleviate any financial or emotional stress.

We used the disabled pass at Legoland (which allows the families of children with special needs to avoid queuing for rides), only to find people tutting about queue jumping. I used the riposte: 'If you think it is worth having a disabled child 365 days a year just to avoid the queues at Legoland, you're sad.'

Although we are comfortably off, I think of the social security benefits we receive as Mark's breakage and toy allowance. When a window gets smashed or the hoover gets broken I always say to myself that this is what Mark's benefits are for. We also buy more expensive toys for him like grown-up tricycles and trampolines which I would probably not have chosen to buy in other circumstances.

See Chapter 11, Financial and Practical Support, for financial benefits and services that you may be able to access.

DEALING WITH PROFESSIONALS FROM HEALTH, EDUCATION AND SOCIAL SERVICES

Always remember that you, as a parent, know your child best. You must have the confidence and courage to make demands and decisions about him. You know far better than anyone else what he is able to do, what he is not able to do, where he needs help and which strategies are and are not working. The professionals are there to support and help you and your child. Have confidence and tell the professionals what you think because they need to know your views. Professionals too want a good collaborative relationship. A true partnership between parent and professional will generate the best provision.

When they have had a long history of struggle and adversity parents sometimes go to meetings with new professionals with a very defensive/aggressive stance, convinced that the professionals are out to hinder and deny. Give them the benefit of the doubt when you first meet them and approach the meeting positively.

Try to create good relationships with professionals. Inevitably you will get more help, advice and support and it will come much more easily if you communicate well – by talking honestly and by listening to the professionals' views and giving any suggestions a chance. Unfortunately, resources are constrained in most areas and you may have to lobby and hassle for what you need; but you can do this while maintaining friendly relations.

You cannot expect to 'like' all the professionals you deal with, because personalities play a part; but you can expect to have a good professional relationship.

If you are going to an important meeting, think about it beforehand and write down any questions you want to raise. Otherwise you may find you forget everything when you are on the spot. Take someone along to the meeting so that you can get his or her perspective and discuss what was said. Often when you are in a meeting you may understand everything said at the time, but not actually take it in. So after the meeting it is useful to be able to go over the main points with your friend.

THINK POSITIVELY

Try to take time to acknowledge that having a child with special needs brings many positive things into your life – experiences that you have had, people you have met, friends you have made or a new career you have started.

> John has no shyness and talks to everyone he meets. One day the local council were re-tarmacing our road and I took my children outside to watch. The chippings lorry was standing outside our house and the driver was waiting in the sun, bare-chested, tattooed and with pierced nipples. Alarm bells rang because John is obsessed with stomachs and I wondered what he would do when he saw this man. Fortunately, he was too short to appreciate the nipple piercings but he plied the man with beer and chocolate biscuits. After watching me struggle to keep John relatively under control, he commented on what a handful he was and I told him he was autistic, whereupon he told me all about his niece with Williams Syndrome!

CHAPTER 2

What Everyone Needs to Know

INTRODUCTION

This chapter deals with the general issues which are important for all children, whatever the nature of their special needs. It looks at what kinds of things to tackle, how to arrange activities to give you the best chance of success and how to create an environment which will work for your child.

KNOWING YOUR CHILD

The most important thing for you, as a parent, is to have a real understanding and awareness of your child – her abilities, motivations and interests, and how she responds to different experiences whether physical, emotional or sensory. We are all told that as parents we know our child best, and we do. Yet it can sometimes be difficult to be truly objective and dispassionate. Our natural feelings of love and protectiveness can make us underestimate our child's potential and abilities, while our hopes and desires can make us overestimate them. Added to which it is hard not to be influenced by our own preferences and prejudices.

Try to reflect as objectively as possible on what your child is doing and what she is capable of. Sometimes it is helpful to seek the views of a really good friend or professional. If you know your child really well, then it will be easy to see where she should be heading and to provide the right environment and stimulation to help her move on.

EXPECTATIONS

Have high, but realistic, expectations of what your child should achieve and how she should behave. There is a strong link between expectations and motivation. Your expectations will affect how far you stretch her and you have to stretch her to keep her motivated. If you have expectations that are too low she may become bored and demotivated and perform below her abilities. Equally, if you ask her to perform way beyond her abilities she will fail, become despondent and not bother trying any more. From our own experience we know that we like a challenge, something which stretches us to do more than we would normally do but which is within our reach.

High expectations

High expectations (cont.)

When Amina was younger we would all be delighted if she put pen to paper because it was an achievement for her. We would celebrate any scrawl. Now we know she can make marks, we expect her to do more.

It is important that you share expectations with other people who are caring for your child so that there is consistency. It would be very confusing if there were different expectations in different settings. An example would be if it is acceptable for her to use a spoon at home but a knife and fork at school. You want to encourage her to generalise her skills (see 'Generalising skills' in the section on issues affecting children with special needs, below) and operate at the highest levels she can.

MOTIVATING YOUR CHILD

Learning new things such as skills, behaviour or language is often a long and slow process for children (and their parents). Children with special needs often do not have such a strong desire to master skills as other children, nor the drive to explore and experiment. They may find certain activities very hard and would, if left to themselves, avoid them. Parents have to be much more pro-active in stimulating and helping a child with special needs compared to another child.

Make activities interesting and stimulating

It makes a big difference if games are presented in a way that is fun and interesting. Try to think of imaginative ways of introducing ideas and playing games which will intrigue and interest your child. For example, when you are practising using pegs you could get her to pinch them onto a tin or shoe box. It might be more fun to make the face of a clown on a piece of card and put the pegs on as hair. Another child might be more motivated by using pegs to hang out the washing on the line or by making herself look like a hedgehog using pegs as prickles attached to her clothes.

Make activities interesting

Find ways to introduce variety into activities, otherwise you and your child will get bored and lose motivation. Use different materials and toys if you can and try to extend games by introducing new ideas so they can be taken further.

Use your child's interests

Sometimes you can use a child's interests and obsessions as a way into an activity that she would usually avoid.

> Anthony does not see the point of playing catch but he is obsessed with the number eight, so we play catch and he has to catch eight balls in a row and then we can stop.

Try to use your child's interests imaginatively; for instance, if she has a favourite character in a book or a cartoon, you could use that character to create imaginative play situations or you could make your own stories for reading, board games or scrapbooks by taking pictures cut out of books or comics, or generated on computer.

If your child likes a particular toy try to find ways of broadening the way she plays with it. So, for example, if she likes playing with her doll's house you could sometimes encourage her to count items such as rooms, chairs or people, talk about colours, patterns and shapes. You could encourage another child or more children to play with her or when you play try to develop and extend your conversations.

Use praise and encouragement

Use lots of praise and encouragement to show your child how well she has done or how you appreciate the efforts she has made. Make it special and meaningful with lots of words and signs, big smiles and natural gestures to give visual reinforcement to what you are saying.

Make the level of praise appropriate for what has been achieved. The first time your child learns to do something new, such as getting dressed by herself, give her lots of praise, a full-blown song-and-dance routine and phone Granny and tell her all about it. Make her feel really special. The next few times she will need a similar level of praise but after a while gradually tone it down until it is a matter of a quiet 'well done'. You may need to increase the level of praise for an activity if it shows signs of stopping; for example, if she stops dressing herself.

Some children who have low self-esteem are not able to accept praise because they believe they are so worthless. With such children you have to pitch the praise at a relatively low level so that they can accept it and then gradually increase the praise. For example, if your child shows you something she has done, rather than praise it in general just focus on a small element and say 'You have done rather well here.' Make the praise believable and acceptable to her. For more on self-esteem see Chapter 8, Emotional Development.

When you are praising a child try to remember to praise the activity rather than the child herself. This is so she knows what it is that she has done that is good, because it may not be clear. Also aim to give the praise immediately following the activity, not some while later when she has forgotten all about it: 'Well done, that is really good drawing' or 'Good sitting still'.

Be positive and focus on the good rather than the negative. So, if your child has made a real effort to pack her bag for swimming but forgotten her towel, try not to say 'Oh no, you've forgotten your towel' but 'Well done, you have packed your costume, your shampoo and your comb. There's one more thing, to dry you, yes – your towel. Can you find it and put it in your bag?'

Always give your child the benefit of the doubt if you think she is developing a new skill. Sometimes you cannot be absolutely sure because you think it may be a fluke or an accident. Assume it is conscious and encourage and support it. It may turn out to be a new skill; if not, you have not lost anything.

Rewards

Praise is one reward but sometimes it is not enough on its own. In addition, you can offer your child a tangible reward as an incentive for her to practise a new skill or change her behaviour. You can use anything as a reward, as long as it is rewarding to her. The obvious choices are stickers, sweets, biscuits, drinks, fruit, crisps or pocket money. However, more interesting treats might be cuddles, tickles, reading a favourite story, doing the washing up, painting, bubbles, going on the computer for ten minutes, going on the bus, sitting in the front passenger seat of the car, playing with a favourite toy, going swimming or going for a bike ride. Try to think imaginatively about the kind of activities which she finds really motivating or, even better, if possible let your child choose her own reward.

If you use an instant reward like sweets or crisps make sure it is small, immediate and under your control. Once the behaviour is established use the rewards only occasionally because you do not want her to become fixated on the reward. Sometimes you might forget to reward and praise instead, sometimes you might reward her for nothing. As the success becomes more commonplace, so reduce the reward until you drop it because it is no longer necessary. You want to use the reward to get her started and then hope that praise and finally success at the activity alone will be sufficient motivation.

As your child becomes more mature you could bring in deferred rewards. For example, she could build up ticks or stickers on a star chart in order to get a 'bigger' prize later. For more information on star charts see Chapter 9, Additional Practical Advice.

Remember that:

- You eventually want praise or just the enjoyment of the task to be sufficient motivation for your child, so make sure you gradually reduce the reward down to just praise and eventually nothing.

- If you have other children you have to make sure they are rewarded in a similar way. It may not be appropriate to reward one child and not the others. You could think of setting each child his or her own goal.

- If you use sweets, biscuits and drinks consider your child's teeth and health.

Join in

Most children want to do things with other people whether parents, friends or siblings. If you sit down and do something like drawing or painting your child may be more inclined to join in. If you tell her to run off and do something by herself she may not be so keen. By joining in you are also demonstrating to her that this activity is fun and you value it. All evidence suggests that children who grow up in households where the parents read are much more likely to be interested in reading themselves. Children like to copy and emulate their parents or other significant people in their lives. So lead by example.

> I bought the children some wools and canvas to start them off sewing – they were vaguely interested. Later when I started sewing name tags onto their clothes they got much more excited and wanted to help.

It can be even more motivating and fun for children when you reverse roles and you let your child have the 'adult' role – giving the orders or looking after you. For example, you could play games like Simon Says, Follow my Leader or copying games and give your child the opportunity to be in charge sometimes.

Joining in painting

The children loved it when we all had star charts. The children decided their father should have one for cycling to work every day and chose his rewards. He was not impressed with the packet of Chewits that he was awarded for cycling for five days. But he did like the beer he got for ten days.

CREATE THE RIGHT ENVIRONMENT

Think about the physical environment in which you live and what you can do to make it work better for your child, bearing in mind her particular needs.

Seating

A child needs to be able to sit comfortably and securely in order to concentrate on other activities such as eating, dressing or writing. If she is not sitting comfortably her concentration and attention will be spent

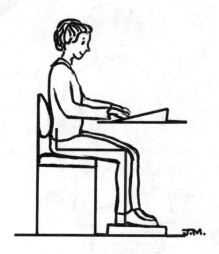

Correct sitting position   *Tripp Trapp chair*

primarily on keeping herself stable rather than on the activity itself. So make sure your child is well positioned. You may need to seek advice from your occupational therapist.

Ideally a child should be sitting at a table with her feet flat on the floor and her thighs and trunk at right angles. With her upper arms down by her side, her elbows should be one inch, or 2 cm, above the work surface. An old-fashioned sloping desk is best, particularly if the child has visual problems because the paper is closer to a 90 degree angle to the eye, making it easier to see.

There are all sorts of options including specialist chairs (available through your occupational therapist) or a low table and chair. There is also a variety of commercially available chairs (including Tripp Trapp) which look rather like conventional dining chairs but have moveable seats and footrests. The positions of these can be changed as the child grows, ensuring that she is always in the optimum position. For children who are very fidgety a good seating position is also important because it is one less thing to distract them.

For some children, for whom balance is not a problem, it can be good to experiment with different sitting positions – on the floor, at a table or kneeling at a coffee table – because using different positions will build up strength in different muscles.

Lighting

All of us need to have good strong lighting but if your child has a visual impairment it is vital to enable her to use and develop the sight she has. You need a good general level of lighting and a lamp for any close work she may do.

Take care to ensure that when you are talking to or playing with her you do not have your back to the light but that your face is well lit so she can see your mouth and expression clearly.

Noise

Children need to develop the ability to tune into the sounds that are important and to screen out irrelevant background noise. For many children with special needs this can be difficult. To help them concentrate on what they are doing it is best to cut out any competing noise from television, radio and music. This is particularly important if your child has any hearing loss or language delay because she will need to give her full attention to what you are saying and other noises will only serve to confuse.

Distractions

It can be hard to keep spaces tidy and clear but if you have a child who is very easily distracted then it is worth trying to keep your house clear of unnecessary clutter. Try to create a space which is calm and ordered.

When you are playing it is a good idea to keep the floor or table-top free from other toys and games so that there is less opportunity for her to be distracted. As you finish one activity clear it back into its box and place it out of sight ready for the next.

For some games, playing at a table rather than on the floor might be best because your child is 'trapped' and less easily distracted and able to escape. You could consider creating a 'work bay' for her in your house like the ones used in special schools. This is a table placed in a bay with high plain walls on three sides giving her a place away from any distractions. This may seem a rather extreme suggestion for the home but it could be modified to a table in a quiet corner of the room where she could play. The work bay idea comes from TEACCH, which is a programme from the USA used with children with autism and communication disorders.[1]

Timing

Try to suggest activities at a time when they are likely to be of interest and your child is in the right frame of mind. There is no point in trying to encourage an over-tired or over-excited child to concentrate on something which she finds tough. It is a particular problem with children who have been quite contained at school all day and are tired. They need to relax and let off steam.

Stimulation

Some children may need a lot of stimulation and may show frustration or anger when they are under-stimulated. They need to have independent access to a range of interesting activities. If your child has limited play skills think about having an environment with lots of sensory stimulation – visual, audio and tactile. See Chapter 6, Sensory Development, for ideas.

Rotating and varying toys

So many children now have huge numbers of toys. It is worth rotating them by putting some away in the loft or high cupboards and then every few months swapping them round so that they feel they are receiving new toys again. Similarly, at Christmas time, if your children get a large influx of new toys it is sometimes a good idea to spirit some

1   TEACCH (Treatment and Education of Autistic and related Communication handicapped Children) can be contacted at Division TEACCH Administration and Research, CB 7180, 310 Medical School Wing E, The University of North Carolina at Chapel Hill, Chapel Hill, North Carolina 27599–7180, USA. Tel: 001 919 966 2173.

away for a few months and bring them out again when your children need something new.

Make sure you have a variety of different types of toys out such as construction toys, puzzles, board games, dressing-up clothes, art and craft materials and pretend play things.

You can borrow toys relatively cheaply from your local branch of the National Association of Toy and Leisure Libraries (see Chapter 12 for contact details) and you can borrow books from libraries and from school. Alternatively, you could try exchanging toys with friends.

HOW TO GO ABOUT TACKLING NEW SKILLS

If you decide you want to help your child learn a new skill like dressing herself, toileting or kicking a ball, make sure she is ready for it. If she is not you will be wasting your time and you'll get very frustrated into the bargain. All activities rely on there being a number of skills in place already – rather like building blocks. It may be that you have to take a step backwards and address the building blocks first before tackling the target skill.

A very extreme example is learning to write. This is very complex and requires a range of skills: a child needs the balance to sit at a table, the hand strength to hold her pencil with the appropriate pressure, the correct grasp to grip her pencil, the shoulder strength to stabilise her arm, the understanding of moving across the page from left to right, the idea that writing is a form of communication and finally the motivation to have a go. You might look at that list and think your child is ready, but you might on the other hand decide that she needs more practice at some of the elements first.

It is sometimes difficult to judge whether or not a child is ready because some children genuinely have difficulties and are perhaps not ready to tackle something, while others may want an easy life and need encouragement and coaxing to try something new.

Break skills down into small steps

Make things easy for your child by breaking skills down into more manageable steps. Rather than expecting her to do the whole thing in one go, aim to get there gradually.

If you wanted to teach your child to ride her bicycle, you could break the skill into different steps – the pedalling action and balance. You would look at ways to teach her the different skills – pedalling a tricycle, then balancing on a scooter, before seeking to combine the two and launching her on her own bike.

For other skills it helps to start from where your child is comfortable and successful and then gradually move forward in small steps. With puzzles, for example, move from simple two-piece puzzles and gradually work up to four-piece, eight-piece, sixteen-piece puzzles and so on. By moving her forward gradually you will find that your child is more likely to maintain her success.

Make things easy

Start off by making the new skill as easy as possible so that your child has the best chance of success. This will then motivate her to continue. As she becomes more competent you can make it more difficult and/or give less help.

Think about the materials you are using. If you are going to practise fastening buttons make sure the buttons are the right size – not too fiddly but not too big for little hands. Very large objects can be as difficult to handle as very tiny ones. Make sure the hole is a good size – not too tight to require a lot of finger strength but not so loose that the button comes undone all the time, as this would be demotivating. Start by dressing a doll or practising on a fastening board then move onto your child's clothes but you should think about where the button is. A button on a cardigan would be okay as long as it was down by her waist not up under her chin. A tight button on her trouser waist or behind her back would not be suitable!

Scaffolding

Scaffolding is a term used to describe what parents, grandparents, adults, siblings and others do naturally to support children in learning new skills. If a child can do a 20-piece puzzle alone she will need help when she first starts tackling a 36-piece puzzle. A parent can help her child in a variety of ways: sitting alongside her as she has a go; offering practical suggestions, reminders or hints; selecting out a few relevant pieces; doing some of the puzzle when she gets stuck; keeping her on task; orientating pieces so that the correct next pieces are easy to spot; giving verbal encouragement, and so on. As the child becomes more competent so the parent can gradually give her less help until she is able to do the puzzle alone.[2]

You will be doing this anyway but it is worth remembering that scaffolding plays an important part in children's learning. When your child wants to tackle something a little beyond what she is capable of doing alone, do not tell her what to do or do it for her; rather let her have a go with you just offering support and help as she needs it.

Forward and backward chaining

One very useful technique for helping children with new skills is forward and backward chaining. Think of skills as a series of small steps and get your child to start or finish the series depending on which is the easiest and/or the most motivating element. Gradually, working forwards or backwards, increase the amount your child does until she can do the whole thing herself.

An example of backward chaining is with buttons. If you are teaching a child to do up her buttons, you would push the button through the hole and then get your child just to give the button the final tug to get it through the button hole and have the satisfaction of finishing the job. Gradually, you would increase the amount she did so that she has to pull more of the button out and finally learn to put it into the hole as well.

An example of forward chaining is building a tower or construction from bricks, Lego or some similar material. You might ask your child to place the first few bricks but you would then continue to make a more elaborate construction. Over time, you would encourage her to do more and more until she could build her own construction by herself.

2   Wood, D. (1998) *How Children Think and Learn* (second edition). Oxford: Blackwell Publishers.

Think carefully about what you are trying to achieve

Because many activities require a number of skills it is worth thinking about what you really want your child to achieve. For instance, you might want your child to learn to put her shoes on. However, your real aim could be to make her independent; in which case you could buy her shoes with Velcro fastenings and teach her to get the shoes on the right feet and do up the fastenings. Alternatively, you may feel she is ready to tie her own laces; in which case you would have to spend time practising tying bows before asking her to be independent.

Another example is that if you want your child to learn to swim, it might be appropriate to pay for individual lessons. However, if you wanted her to enjoy being in a pool and learn to cooperate in a group you might choose group lessons instead.

> I wanted my son to go to tennis lessons but knew that he would have problems in a group class. So I arranged for him to have private tuition first to learn the techniques and then to attend the group course where he could concentrate on the social skills with the security of already knowing many of the techniques. The two together would have been too much.

Don't try to do too much at once

If you have identified a number of skills you want to address, choose the most important and focus on that first. You only have limited time and energy and your child will not want to be the object of too much pressure and scrutiny.

Completing tasks

It is very important that your child gets the idea that she should finish the tasks set for her. Otherwise she will get the impression that it does not matter and she will be more likely to opt out when she gets fed up or finds it difficult. If she does not complete the game, try to finish it off yourself to show that this is important.

ISSUES AFFECTING CHILDREN WITH SPECIAL NEEDS
Give your child longer to respond

When you are talking to your child or playing with her, give her time to respond. Be patient because children with special needs often need longer to respond than you would naturally give them. They often need a long time to process requests, organise movements and form words. You might give up on your child and turn away just as she gives her response. There is an interesting conformity in the amount of time parents allow for children to respond to them and it is often not long enough.[3] Give her extra time and wait for her to respond. Be patient and try not to hurry her on.

Repetition and reinforcement

Children with special needs often need a lot of practice at something before they master it. There is no alternative but to give lots of opportunities to practise skills or to repeat words and signs. Sometimes you look back and think you have spent half your life saying 'Yes, it's Daddy' or playing posting games, but it is worthwhile when she does finally achieve it. Repeat things over and over again.

Also remember that, while children commit knowledge to short-term memory, you have to revisit and reinforce that knowledge over a long period before it is transferred to long-term memory. So even though you may feel your child has 'got' something, it is always worth revisiting it regularly until it is very secure.

3   Cunningham, C. *et al.* (1981) 'Behavioural and linguistic developments in the interaction of normal and retarded children with their mothers.' *Child Development 52,* 60–70. See also Jones, O.H.M. (1977) 'Mother–child communication with pre-linguistic Down Syndrome and normal infants.', in H.R. Schaffer (ed.) *Studies in Mother–Infant Interaction.* London: Academic Press.

Perseverance

Don't be put off if you try a new activity and it is a disaster; keep calm and give it another go. Have confidence that it can get better as it becomes more familiar and more customary.

> When we were told Patrick needed to wear glasses we thought it would be impossible. But we gave it a go and slowly he got used to wearing them for longer and longer periods until they were completely accepted. When he took them off we just put them back on him. If we couldn't we didn't make an issue of it.

Routines and predictability

Children need routines, structure and familiarity to help them to understand what is going on around them, to recognise situations, to know what is expected of them and ultimately to predict what is going to happen. This creates a feeling of security and understanding.

For a child with communication or sensory difficulties routines are particularly important because she may not find it so easy to pick up on other clues. At home establish a basic routine for each day – get up at the same time, get dressed before breakfast, have lunch at 1 p.m. and so on – and stick to it. Keep the environment the same; for example, if your child has a visual impairment do not keep changing the furniture around. When you go shopping use the same shops each time, the same hairdresser, optician, etc. Your child may be able to use her memory and her knowledge of routines to understand what is likely to happen. Not only will it make her feel more secure but it may enable her to gain more independence and freedom with the safety of the familiar and the predictable.

Routine does not have to imply rigidity; you should build in some flexibility. Some children can become fixated on routines and will therefore need some variation to prevent routines becoming too important and obsessive.

Adopt a multi-sensory approach

Traditionally we have tended to rely on children listening to what we say and taking it on board; but it is increasingly recognised that we all learn in different ways, not just through listening. We should therefore try to engage all the child's senses. If your child has a sensory impairment then this is particularly important.

Some of us prefer to learn visually (through what we see), some aurally (through what we hear) and some kinaesthetically (through movement or hands-on experience). It may be that you find, for example, your child learns better through visual methods and that you should therefore use gesture, signs, symbols, pictures, maps and diagrams to reinforce what you are saying. If you want her to do something it might be best to show a picture or photo of the action rather than just say it. Some children can listen to instructions and commands and respond accurately. Other children find that they don't learn just by watching or listening, they need to actually copy the actions, perhaps with you guiding them hand-over-hand. When learning to use a knife and fork, some children learn by being shown what to do (visual), some by being told (aural) and others by being physically guided (kinaesthetic). Remember the useful phrase 'see, hear, do'.

Generalising skills

Children can sometimes learn a new skill but then find it hard to generalise that skill to other situations or places. For example, they may be very good at threading one particular set of beads but may not be able to transfer that skill to other sets. It is important, therefore, that you make sure that your child has the opportunity to use different toys and materials and in a variety of settings. When she goes to school it is particularly important that there is a good dialogue between home and school and that achievements are shared between the two so that you can be sure that she is achieving her best in both situations.

Don't get fixated on one particular skill

Sometimes it is easy to imagine that learning one particular skill, like toilet training, will transform your child's life, but this is not necessarily a helpful way of thinking. You may spend a lot of energy and get frustrated at the lack of progress, while ignoring other important steps that she is making. You will also be overlooking the fact that all skills are inter-related and interwoven. You should not see skills as isolated and separate. A development in one area will have profoundly beneficial effects elsewhere. For example, improved communication skills make it possible to have more mature social interaction. It is also worth remembering that if your child is making significant progress in one area, such as language, she is probably using so much of her energy and concentration that she will not be making much progress elsewhere for the moment.

Age appropriateness

It is vital that children have activities, toys and books which are appropriate to them and their age. Children who are still learning relatively early skills do not want to play with toys designed for babies and pre-schoolers. If a child is looking at a simple story book, she wants to see pictures of a child like her and objects and activities relevant to her. She should not to be looking at pictures of babies or baby toys because they bear no relation to her experiences or self-image. It is relatively easy to find age-appropriate materials using specialist suppliers, digital cameras and computer-generated images. You can make your own easy board games or simple stories based on characters in more grown-up books. Rather than sing nursery rhymes you could sing and dance to the latest pop music.

However, sometimes it is the activity itself which is not appropriate, whatever the materials used, because it is too simple or uninteresting. What is appropriate will depend on the child. For some children it might be boring and demotivating to be doing simple colouring at the age of ten, whereas for others it might be a great achievement.

Some children cling to familiar toys and games because they do not like change. Such children need to be moved on gently. It is a good idea to encourage your child to extend and develop her play by suggesting ideas or offering different materials.

Despite the above remarks, there is no objective standard for what is age appropriate. In our culture, we do not tend to value play although we all do play in our different ways. What one person thinks is appropriate – computer games, soft toys or Captain Scarlet models – the next person might think childish. It is important, therefore, to value play. Respect your child's preferences and let her play at whatever she enjoys, whether it is playing with dolls, colouring pictures or playing in the sand pit.

The issue may therefore really be one of *place* appropriateness rather than age appropriateness. Consider whether the issue is really the activity itself or where it is taking place. For example, if your child takes her teddy to school you may feel that it is not appropriate, because she might be teased. But the issue here is not *having* a teddy – after all many children and indeed adults have teddies – it is the place that is inappropriate, and in this case you need to encourage her to keep her teddy at home.[4]

> My son is ten and loves everything to do with Spiderman. He enjoyed dressing up as Spiderman and then cycling in the lane outside our house. The local kids started to tease him for being babyish so we had to persuade him that he could dress up at home but not when he went out.

Independence

Aim to enable your child to become as independent of you as possible. The more independent she becomes the better it is for everyone. The more she can do for herself and the more she can communicate, socialise and understand the world about her, the more opportunities she will have to learn more, meet people and develop her interests and friendships. It is a virtuous circle. If she remains dependent on you alone then you limit the experiences she has and it is more exhausting for you. The level of independence that children with special needs reach will vary and they may always be dependent on others to some degree. However, the wider her social group is, the greater the opportunities are. At some point, parents have to start looking to the future and the long-term needs of their child. Ways to increase your child's levels of independence are covered fully in Chapter 8, Emotional Development.

---

4   *To Infinity and Beyond: Age Appropriateness in Play and Leisure*, a pamphlet published by Action for Leisure (2000). See Chapter 12, Resources, for contact details.

FOLLOW YOUR CHILD

There is a danger in the way that we, as parents, look at child development: we can become too fixated on learning skills and moving onto the next stage. As well as striving for progress, make sure you enjoy your child and follow her in her play, language and activities. Go along with her, enter her world and copy her. Learn what she is about and accept her as she is. If you are doing something with your child and she does something unexpected do not necessarily correct her, but go along with it and see what happens. See things from her point of view rather than striving always to get her to conform to your own world and expectations.

Gaining independence

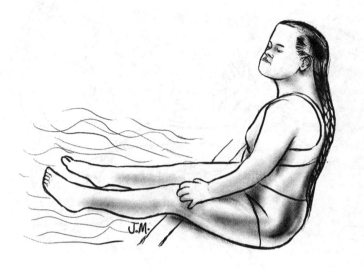

I don't want to go swimming

I don't want to go swimming (cont.)

CHAPTER 3

Cognitive Development

WHAT ARE COGNITIVE SKILLS?

Cognitive skills encompass the complex area of how children think and learn by acquiring, structuring and using knowledge. It includes language, spoken and written, and mathematical skills as well as conceptual and logical thought. Although language is a cognitive skill it is considered separately in Chapter 4.

CHRONOLOGICAL DEVELOPMENT

Children use their senses and movement to actively explore objects and the environment and to gather information on the world around them. They look at objects and their properties, they touch and smell them, they see what happens if they move them, and so on. They make connections between the observations and perceptions they have developed to form an idea or concept. Concepts allow children to take in and process new information, organise their thinking and make predictions. They do this in the following ways:

Matching, selecting and naming

When learning any new concept children always learn in the order of match, select then name. First they see that two objects or concepts are the same, then they have a passive understanding which enables them

57

to select the right one if asked to do so and finally they are able to actively name the object or concept. By putting a name to an object or concept children can classify it and then remember it.

Seeing differences

Children then look at objects for differences – the properties that make them different. For example, what is the difference between an apple and an orange? One is green and one is orange, one has thin edible peel and one has thick inedible skin, etc. Children look for differences based initially on colour (green or red bricks), size (large or small beads) or shape (round or square buttons). Spotting the differences sets things apart and separates them.

Seeing similarities

On the other hand, seeing similarities brings things together. A child might look at an apple and an orange and say they are both fruit. Children see similarities in terms of colour, size, shape and then purpose (a saucepan, mixer and spoon are all kitchen implements).

Classifying

Seeing similarities enables children to classify objects and concepts in different ways, such as foodstuffs into fruit and vegetables, flowers according to colour. Classifications become increasingly sophisticated and open to debate. A slide, skipping rope and ball could all be outside toys, whereas pencils, a book and Lego could be indoor toys, or a child could classify them according to whether he likes them or not or whether he considers them boys' or girls' toys.

Children use the technique of classifying things as a way of taking in new information and making connections – 'What is that?' 'It is a blue tit – a kind of garden bird'. It allows them to structure their knowledge so that it is manageable, usable and easier to remember.

Conservation

One of the early milestones in childhood development is the understanding of object permanence: that an object continues to exist when it can no longer be seen. The next stage is when children learn to 'conserve' number, weight, length and so on. To illustrate what this means, imagine that a child is shown two rows of five coins, equally spaced. He will say that they are the same. If one of the rows is then spread out so it is longer than the other, a young child will say that there are more coins in that row. Only when he is able to 'conserve number' will he be able to say that they are still equal because he will understand that though they look different nothing has actually happened to change the number.

J.M.

Conserving number – rows of coins

Children have to learn that the same is true for volume. A liquid may look different in quantity when poured from one bottle into a differently shaped bottle. Likewise, a substance such as a lump of play dough may look larger or smaller when squashed into a ball or extended into a sausage.

In these situations children have to be able to appreciate more than just the physical appearance, they also have to understand that nothing has changed about the number, weight or length. Using the two pieces of information together makes this such an important milestone. It is also critical for the development of their understanding of mathematics.

Reversibility

Children look at how objects can be transformed by an action and whether or not the action is reversible. For example, in the conservation tasks described above, they learn that the five coins can be placed back into the original position and the number of coins has not actually changed. Addition can be reversed by subtraction, multiplication by division. Water can be frozen to make ice and then warmed up to become water again. However, bread dough, once cooked, cannot be transformed back into dough.

Comparing and sequencing

This is the ability to arrange items in rank order, in terms of their colour, size, age or other attribute. Children typically learn this initially by using a set of nesting beakers, hoops or saucepans.

Scripts

Scripts are familiar routines with some variation. An example would be the sequence of actions involved in getting up and having breakfast or in going to school or to the shops. Children learn them from familiar routines and contexts. Instead of thinking every day when they get up 'What happens now?', they know that they wash, get dressed and have breakfast. It gives them an understanding, which allows them to feel a sense of control over what is happening and is about to happen, and thereby makes them more controllable themselves. It reduces uncertainty, allows children to predict the future and enables them to give attention to unusual things that are happening rather than to the routine itself.

Using symbols (language, visual and written)

Bruner argued that children's thought processes are developed through the different ways they use to represent the experiences they have had.[1] It is by making some kind of symbolic representation of what they have done that they assimilate what they are discovering. It might be through practising a new physical skill, by recalling images in the mind, by drawing pictures, by making models or even just by talking. Later children learn to use written or mathematical language to make these representations.

Sense of time

Children's perception of time develops over a long period. They get a sense of the passing of time from the scripts or routines that make up their lives. For example, a day consists of getting up, going to school, having lunch, more school, coming home, playing, having tea, a bath and bed. Any understanding of the past and future comes by using a timeline that is directly relevant to them. To a child, this afternoon is after his lunch rather than in three hours' time. He might understand the concept of tomorrow by using scripts – after lunch, play, tea, bed and when he wakes up, it is tomorrow.

This is extended gradually until children have a sense of the shape of the week – once they have got into a routine of going to school each day and having weekends off. They learn the shape of the year through talking about seasons, festivals, birthdays and other regular events. They can talk about 'how long until my birthday', 'how long until Christmas' once they have experienced them a few times.

A sense of the past starts with the idea of their own past. They can understand the idea of when they were babies and gradually extend back to when Daddy was young, when Granny was a baby and so on. A sense of the longer passage of time in history comes much later.

1   Bruner, J.S. (1986) *Actual Minds: Possible World.* Cambridge, MA: Harvard University Press.

Telling the time

Children develop a concept of the time of the day from their routines. Lunchtime is at one o'clock, bed-time at eight o'clock and so on. Children gradually learn to tell the time using a conventional clock with numbers (not Roman numerals). Using digital clocks and understanding the 24-hour clock come much later.

Seeing the world from another person's point of view 'decentring'

Young children are egocentric; they think about themselves, what they want and what they can see and are often quite single-minded. Piaget[2] argued that at the age of about seven children learn to view the world from another person's point of view and to consider more than one aspect of a situation at the same time. He called this 'decentring' and believed it to be a critical stage of development. Later research demonstrates that children can think of other people's views at a much earlier age, but at times lapse back into egocentricity. Current research suggests that this development has more to do with lack of processing power rather than any failure of logic. Children just cannot hold onto that much information at one time.

For whatever reason, as children get older they are more aware of other people and the complexity of different issues. They are increasingly able to think of other people's views and weigh up information from a number of sources. As a consequence they become much more amenable and less self-centred.

Theory of mind

A young child believes that everyone thinks as he does and knows what he knows. However, when he is about four years old, he recognises that in fact other people can hold different beliefs from him. This is called having a 'theory of mind'. He sees that other people have ideas about

2   Piaget, J. and Inhelder, B. (1956) *The Child's Conception of Space*. London: Routledge and Kegan Paul.

the world, some of which may not be true (called 'false beliefs'), which explain what people do, think and feel. To illustrate this the example that is often used is of two people who put a sweet in a box. They go out of the room but later Person A comes in and moves the sweet to a different place. A child without a theory of mind will say that Person B will look for the sweet in the different place, but a child with a theory of mind will know that Person B will assume the sweet is in the box where it was left, look there and find it gone. He knows that Person B is labouring under the false belief that the sweet is where he last saw it, i.e. in the box.

Interestingly, second and subsequent children have been shown to gain a theory of mind earlier than first children because they are more exposed to discussions about rights and wrongs and jokes etc., which show up different viewpoints more clearly.

Making rules

Children make sense of the world around them by establishing rules for how things are and how they should be. They go through a phase of being very rigid about these rules – the fruit bowl is always on the table or we must sweep up after lunch. Cries of 'it's not fair' are often heard if the rules are not followed. Rules are used to make sense of a seemingly crazy world. Gradually, children realise through experience that there are exceptions to all rules and that, though most of the time things are done one way, sometimes they are done differently. By finding and accepting exceptions to the rules they are able to become more flexible. However, there is some variation according to personality and some children remain quite rigid in their interpretation of rules.

Thinking

As children mature they develop their ability to think more flexibly and more broadly and to take in different viewpoints. There are a number of reasons for this. Young children cannot hold that much information, which limits their thought processes; but as they mature they are able to hold more. As their language extends they can put together more complex ideas and concepts. Children eventually become able to use language without saying the words out loud: they internalise their language into the thinking process. They also realise that other people have different views. In their social interactions they learn to discuss, cooperate and negotiate with other people to devise solutions to situations that are acceptable to all.

Thinking

Metacognition

This refers to our understanding of our own thought processes. Examples are the awareness that we have or have not understood something, that we have remembered or forgotten something, knowing that we have certain skills and the ability to plan how to do tasks.

Researchers argue that the key change is when a child starts thinking about what he is going to say rather than just saying the first thing that comes to mind. When a child talks to someone they are sharing a context and so the language does not need to be clear. If I say 'It is on the table', the coffee cup makes it obvious to the listener what I mean. However, if I write 'It is on the table', it is not very helpful to a reader unless he already knows what is being referred to. When children start to read and write, they are faced with a situation where there is no shared context and so they are having to use language in a new way. In addition, when children start writing they have to think about what they are going to say, whether it is comprehensible and well expressed and whether it conveys the meaning they intend. They have to be aware of what they are thinking. This awareness leads ultimately to intellectual self-control and then to logical, mathematical, scientific and abstract thought.

PARALLEL DEVELOPMENT
Attention

Attention involves a number of elements: an ability to keep on task, to screen out distractions and to select the relevant from a mass of detail.

Children have a short attention span but can achieve a lot in the short bursts of concentration they are able to give. Sustaining attention over a long period is a learnt behaviour which takes practice and requires support. It does not start until middle childhood and extends gradually over time.

A young child's attention flits around haphazardly and is easily distracted, but as he gets older he is able to direct attention to what is relevant and to stay on track. He learns to give greater attention through joint activities with an adult who is naturally training him to extend his attention by keeping him on target as they share a game or activity together. By extending his attention, a child becomes able to tackle more complex activities which require sustained attention.

Memory

The development of memory is critical for cognitive and linguistic development. We need it to remember and use new vocabulary and grammar, to memorise letters for reading and writing, to remember routines and procedures and to form concepts and develop our understanding of the world.

There are different memories: short-term auditory and visual memory and long-term auditory and visual memory. Children first commit information to their short-term memory and they do this through repetition. After considerable repetition the information is transferred to long-term memory and therefore should be safe, no longer needing practice or repetition.

Young children do remember things naturally and spontaneously through active participation. They recognise faces and objects they have seen before, and they remember events (both good and bad) which have had a large impact and familiar scripts or routines.

Recall is more difficult for children unless they can use strategies to remember things such as rehearsing or categorising. They only develop such strategies in middle childhood because until then they cannot gauge the difficulty of a task. They overestimate their abilities so they do not see the point of using memory strategies. As they get older, however, and they realise how much they can and cannot recall, they start to see the point of memory strategies. They can then be taught common strategies such as rehearsing spellings or a speech, and structuring information into categories so that it is easier to remember.

Memory has been shown to be linked with knowledge and expertise. For example, if you know about cricket you can watch a game and, holding the basic structure in your mind, use your memory to remember the details of the game. If you know nothing about cricket you would just be trying to make sense of what was going on and would be able to remember much less.[3] Knowledge allows you to structure your memory and perceptions. Children are being exposed to new situations all the time and have to make sense of them. As a result they seem to 'remember' less but it has been demonstrated that when children have greater expertise than adults their memory is also better. Child chess players have better memories of moves than non-playing adults.[4]

3   Wood, D. (1998) *How Children Think and Learn* (second edition). Oxford: Blackwell.

4   Chi, M.T.H. (1978) 'Knowledge structures and memory development.' in R.S. Siegler (ed.) *Children's Thinking: What Develops?* Hillsdale, NJ: Lawrence Erlbaum Associates.

Short-term auditory memory

Short-term auditory memory is very important for learning language. It allows us to process and understand spoken language and to produce language ourselves. Words are kept in the short-term memory for a matter of seconds before being either transferred into long-term memory or lost. Short-term memory is often tested by seeing how many digits a child can remember from a spoken sequence.

Visual memory

Visual memory is important for recognising faces, places and symbols, and ultimately for reading and writing. For example children need to be able to remember the difference between 'd' and 'b', or 'p' and 'q'.

Retrieval

Another aspect of memory is the retrieval of information that is stored in the memory. If a child has problems with short-term memory retrieval it tends to show in the difficulties he has in manipulating figures in mental maths; if there are problems with long-term memory it shows in reading, when the word is 'on the tip of his tongue' but he takes longer to retrieve it.

IMAGINATIVE PLAY

Imaginative play is when children use one thing to stand for something else and introduce ideas into a game which come from the imagination. There are many different theories about the purpose of imaginative play. It clearly has important benefits in allowing children to practise and develop skills without fear of failure and to work through ideas, experiences and feelings (hence play therapy). It also allows them to learn about the world and how it works, to explore social situations, rules and relationships and to practise language skills. Further, it is important in enabling children to develop the ability to think abstractly, broadly and flexibly, organise their thoughts and explore ideas of fact and fiction.

Imaginative play usually starts as copying or role play. Children go into the home corner and, using plastic pots and pans, pretend to cook a meal; or they sit in a toy car and pretend to drive. They are copying what they have seen others do rather than using their imagination. Gradually, however, this kind of play develops into imaginative play. A child gets into the toy car and then says he is off to the shops to buy some big sweets or takes a stick and says it is his sword. Imaginative play is personal and creative and is initiated by the child. It takes all sorts of forms: children might use construction toys, dressing-up clothes or objects which are used to symbolise something else (a mat for a magic carpet or a stick for a fairy wand). Their play can be based on experiences they have had; for example, after meeting someone with a camera they might find a stone which becomes their camera and is capable of all sorts of wonderful feats. They might visit the dentist and then come home and play dentists. Sometimes books, TV programmes or films are the catalyst for some imaginary game like cowboys or space travel. Alternatively, children might fantasise about another world.

Imaginative play

Imaginative play tends to become more elaborate as children get older, with a cast of sustained characters or a whole miniature world within a train set or doll's house. Games can continue over days or even weeks.

ACADEMIC THEORIES OF COGNITIVE DEVELOPMENT

Over the last century developmental psychologists have tried to find an explanation for how children learn and think. There is as yet no consensus on this complex issue so I have briefly outlined the different theories below.

Learning theory

This is derived from the work of psychologists such as Pavlov and Skinner.[5] They sought to show that children do things because of the rewards and punishments that parents, teachers and others give. Children learn to hang up their coats because we smile at them and praise them. They learn not to throw their food on the floor because we frown at them or shout.

Skinner looked at how behaviour and learning could be broken down into small steps, each one being rewarded until all the steps together enabled the child to achieve the activity in question. His work provides the theoretical basis for behaviour management techniques – rewarding good behaviour so that it will be repeated and ignoring bad behaviour so it will decrease in frequency (see Chapter 9 for information on behaviour management).

Piaget

Later, Piaget took a radically different view which transformed attitudes to child development. He argued that children learn spontaneously because of an intrinsic desire to explore and master skills for their own sake. He thought they actively shaped their own

5   Pavlov, I.P and Anrep, G.V. (1927) *Conditioned Reflexes.* London: Oxford University Press; Skinner, B.F. (1938) *The Behavior of Organisms: An experimental analysis.* New York: Appleton-Century-Crofts.

learning. They therefore should be provided with the materials and environment which would allow them to explore, experiment and manipulate in an active and hands-on way rather than be taught in a formal style (this method was later called 'discovery learning').

He saw child development as a series of discrete and demonstrable stages:

- *Age 0–2: Sensory-motor period.* A baby builds up a picture of the world through his senses and movement.

- *Age 2–7: Pre-operational period.* During this period children learn to talk about the concepts they have formed, draw them or write them. They cannot think logically or in the abstract (e.g. they can understand the concept of food but not of honesty). They are egocentric and unable to think of things from other people's perspective or think of more than one aspect of a problem at the same time.

- *Age 7–11: Operational period.* Children gain the ability to think more rationally and consider other people's viewpoints. However, they still have a practical rather than an abstract understanding.

- *Age 11+: Formal operational period.* Children develop logical thinking and can think in the abstract. They become aware of their own thought processes and strategies.

He argued that, because children have an innate desire to learn, they move on to the next stage when they are developmentally ready. The adult's role is therefore to provide the materials and help with the transition when the child is ready (this was later called the theory of 'readiness').

Piaget's views had a profound effect on attitudes to child development as the concepts of 'readiness' and 'discovery learning' are widely accepted in nursery and primary schools today.[6] His theories are still much discussed. However, there is a consensus that he underestimated children's abilities because of the way that he used

6   Sylva, K. and Lunt, I. (1982) *Child Development: A First Course.* Oxford: Blackwell Publishers.

language in his tests and, indeed, because of the very nature of these tests. It is also recognised that there are overlaps between the different periods.[7]

Social constructivist theory

Later psychologists, such as Vygotsky and Bruner, have stressed the importance of cultural practices, social interaction, communication and instruction in learning.[8] Vygotsky[9] argued that children learn through social interactions in which parents, adults, older siblings and others support a child in developing his knowledge and skills, a process called 'scaffolding'. The more mature person helps the child by keeping him on task, praising, modelling, breaking up the skill and giving help where necessary. As he gets better at the task less help is given until he can do it alone (see Chapter 2, What Everyone Needs to Know).

He also described the gap between what children can do by themselves and what they can do with help as the 'zone of potential or proximal development'. He argued that children should be given tasks within that zone, tasks which are not too difficult as this is demoralising, nor too easy as this is boring for the child.

Vygotsky also saw that language is important in enabling a child to organise his thought processes. Early language is gradually internalised allowing children to use it to plan, structure and evaluate what they do.

GAMES AND ACTIVITIES

GENERAL GUIDELINES

Give your child time to play actively and engage with different toys and materials to enable him to experiment and explore in a practical way.

7   Donaldson, M. (1987) *Children's Minds*. London: Fontana.

8   Wood, D. (1998) *How Children Think and Learn*. Oxford: Blackwell.

9   Vygotsky, L. (1978) *Mind in Society*. Cambridge MA: Harvard University Press.

Young children learn through direct involvement using all the different senses.

Give him the chance to play with different materials – sand, water, mud, bricks and construction toys.

Let him experiment even if it means he is 'doing it wrong'. Children learn more from their mistakes than by being told how to do it correctly all the time.

Get your child to make a hypothesis and test it out to see if it is true. What happens if we put another brick on here, will it fall down?

Make connections and comparisons with what they have seen and done before. Children can use these memories to make inferences and hypotheses.

Children need real experiences. Going to different places and trying different activities all provide material for children to gain information which they can take on board, and allow them to make sense of the world. It is difficult for young children to get any real sense of a situation merely from photographs, stories or TV programmes; they need to experience things in the flesh.

However, from middle childhood children can start to be 'taught' about things without experiencing them and they will develop an understanding through books, stories, explanations and descriptions.

Matching, selecting and naming games
Matching

Here are some fun games to play which require matching skills:

- Shape sorters, where the child has to put the shape in the matching hole.

- Sticker books where you have to match the sticker to the outline or faint image.

- Snap – using children's cards or, if using playing cards, children can match the colour, suit or number depending on their ability.

- Lotto – using a lotto set, place the cards in a pile and take it in turns to turn over the top card. Players have to match the card to their board. The first to have a line/complete board covered is the winner.

- Pairs or Pelmanism – using children's Snap cards or playing cards, place all the cards face down on the table and take it in turns to turn two cards over. If they match the player takes the pair and has another go. The winner is the player with the most pairs. Start off by using only a few pairs – maybe 12 cards – and gradually increase the number of pairs as your child gets used to the game and his concentration increases. It is easier to place the cards in rows, rather than randomly.

- Old Maid – if you do not have a children's set of cards use ordinary playing cards. You will need to select pairs of numbers – three pairs per player and a black queen. Shuffle and deal the cards. Take it in turns to select a card from the neighbour on your right. As each player makes a pair, he places them down in front of him until the last player is left with the Old Maid or black queen.

- Dominoes – you can get different sets with the traditional dots, numbers, pictures or a combination.

- Card games like Donkey, Eights and Uno. There are many good card game books available which describe the rules of play for these and many other games.

Selecting

Give your child a choice of three things and ask him to select the one you want – the big one, the yellow one, the one shaped like a triangle, etc. You can make it more fun by placing things around the room or the house or make it a running game: 'Run to the picture of the house'.

Naming

A concept is understood when a child can name it – it is red, a car, wet and so on.

Seeing differences

Try the following:

- Spot-the-difference pictures – where there are two pictures and your child has to find the differences between the two.

- Odd-one-out games – where there is a picture of a group of objects and your child has to find the one that is different.

Many children's comics, puzzle and activity books have lots of games which are good for early skills. The Usborne Young Puzzle Books series, published by Usborne Publishing, includes titles such as *Puzzle Town* and *Puzzle Mountain* which are also good.

Seeing differences

Seeing similarities

- Encourage your child to see similarities between objects in everyday life. Start with colour and size before moving on to shape and feel, then the more abstract similarities such as purpose and function.

- Use comics, activity or puzzle books to find pictures of different objects. Get your child to join up the ones that are connected e.g. all the fruits, all the gardening implements.

Seeing similarities

Classifying

- Get your child to sort a mixture of objects into sets, e.g. buttons and beads, according to colour, size or shape.

- Tidying up gives lots of opportunities for classifying, for example:

  - sorting toys into the correct boxes – Duplo, farm animals or dolls' clothes

  - sorting clean washing by person, then into the correct drawer – underwear, shirts, jumpers

  - putting away clean cutlery into the correct compartment – forks, spoons and knives.

Classifying

- Organise objects into subsets according to colour, purpose, size or some other feature; for example, vehicles, animals, sports, musical instruments, food, flowers, fruit, vegetables and buildings.

- Selecting game – put different things around the room, house or garden and get your child to gather the things according to their category.

- Look at pictures and get your child to point to all the red things, things for babies, toys and so on.

- Play the Happy Families card game.

- Make a scrapbook – use old magazines to find pictures of things which are red/big/for eating/furniture/for the garden/old, etc.

- Have a treasure hunt – when you are out give your child a list of things to find – something old, something made of wood, something round, etc.

- Encourage your child to make connections between experiences; for example, comparing playgrounds, supermarkets and so on.

Conservation

- Play with liquids in different sizes and shapes of bottle – pouring liquid from one to another, see which looks bigger, then pour back again.

- Play with modelling material like plasticene or play dough. Roll it into different shapes and squash it up again.

Reversibility

- If you have a spare rubber glove, fill it with water and tie the wrist up tight, freeze it and when it is frozen put it on a plate, cut away the rubber glove to reveal a frozen hand and watch it melt.

- Let your child play with ice cubes. Make ice lollies from fruit juice by placing juice in ice-cube trays each with a cocktail stick and freeze them.

Many cooking activities show irreversibility. See Chapter 5, Physical Development, for ideas.

Point out what can be reversed in everyday life; for example, by adding something or taking it away.

Comparing and sequencing size

- Take any opportunity to arrange things in order from large to small or vice versa. For example, you could use Russian dolls, hoops, beakers, saucepans, containers, cake tins, books, nesting boxes, nest of tables or flowerpots.

Saucepans

- With your child, compare the size of items such as pants, socks and jumpers owned by different members of the family when you are sorting out the laundry, or of shoes when you are lining them up to clean them. Who has the largest, smallest, second largest, etc.? Look at the different sizes of objects around the house, such as plates and cutlery.

- Talk about who is the oldest, next oldest or the shortest, next shortest and so on.

- When you are drawing look at the shades of colouring pencils from the darkest to the lightest.

Scripts

Establish routines in your daily life and stick to them if you can. But remember scripts should have some flexibility in them, so they do not have to mean rigidity. Be careful to build in some variety if your child gets fixated on routines.

Involve your child in everyday practical activities such as going shopping, laying the table or sorting the washing.

Talk your child through scripts and routines beforehand and during the activity to help him to understand what is going on.

Use a visual timetable for reinforcement if it is helpful. (See below.)

Using symbols (physical, language, visual and written)

Children need the opportunity to make representations of their experiences so they can explore ideas, assimilate them in their mind and commit them to memory. How this can be done will depend on your child's abilities and the nature of the experience, but try to use a multi-sensory approach. For example:

Physical

- Play games associated with any new experiences. If you have just watched a horse-riding competition, have a jumping competition in the garden; or if you have been shopping, set up a shop at home.

- Get your child to act out books he has read or experiences he has had.

Touch

- Together with your child, remember the feeling and textures of object and surfaces.

- Make models using junk or clay.

Smell

Remember the smell of places, perfumes, flowers, the sea, coffee grinding, baking bread, sewage farms or manure.

Visual

Look at photographs or postcards of places your child has visited and people he has met.

Hearing

Record a tape with music and sound effects related to any new experiences.

Language

Talk about what your child has done each day and his experiences and feelings.

Drawing

Draw pictures, maps or diagrams together to show journeys, places or activities.

Writing

Encourage your child to write about his experiences. If he is not able to write, you could get him to dictate to you, write single words by hand or on the computer, or select words from a range of flash cards.

Get your child to write a simple diary, send a postcard to someone or make a scrapbook with a combination of pictures and words.

Sophie wrote the following on the computer with help to describe the last day of a weekend break in Wales:

We went for a walk

Car

Tea

Saw ambulance

Long way

Extend experiences by looking up further information in an encyclopaedia, the internet or a CD-ROM.

Sense of time
Sequencing

In order to develop a sense of time children first need to develop a concept of sequencing – of one action following another. To help your child understand sequences of events:

- Establish routines for different activities in your daily life.

- Each day ask your child about his day or an event in the day and the sequence in which things happened.

- Recount familiar stories such as fairy tales, asking what happened next. Or, when you read a book that your child knows, ask him what happens next.

- Create a sequence of pictures or a story, event or routine, cut them up and get your child to put them in the right order.

Sequence of pictures

Understanding the passing of time

When you try to explain the passing of time to your child describe it in terms of events, scripts or routines which are meaningful to him. For example, if he asks how long he has to wait for a party, it may be meaningless to say 'six hours'. Instead, say: 'We will have breakfast, go shopping, have lunch, wash up, then at two o'clock it will be time to go to the party'. Talk in terms of 'sleeps' or going to bed rather than 'nights' which have no meaning to a child.

Visual timetables

Visual timetables are very useful for children who find it difficult to understand time and to cope with situations in which they do not know what is going to happen next. They give children a sense of security and a feeling of control because they can see for themselves how their day is planned and structured. Without a timetable they may feel that seemingly random things are happening to them out of the blue, making them anxious and unhappy.

Visual timetables are used in the TEACCH programme for children with autism and communication disorders. (See Chapter 2, page 44, for contact details.) It is detailed and complex but this idea can be simplified to be used at home.

A timetable might cover a whole day or a few hours depending on your child and it shows the major activities which are going to take place.

Put Velcro on a board or piece of wood to which you can attach objects, photographs or pictures. Alternatively, peg pictures to a piece of string. The timetable should run from top to bottom or left to right.

There are a number of different formats you could use depending on your child, but try to move him up a level when he is ready.

- Use actual objects related to the activity; for example, a fork for a meal or an arm band for swimming.

- Use clear photographs of the actual activity – your child in a swing, your child at his school.

- Use simple line drawings of the activity.

- Use Makaton symbols to show the activity (see Chapter 12, Resources, for contact details).

- Use ordinary words.

Visual timetable

Refer your child to his timetable during the day and as you finish an activity remove the picture. It may seem a bit daunting to start with, but you will quickly find that you only have a limited range of activities so you can create a dozen or so pictures which you can re-use as necessary.

> We used a visual timetable with Jessica for a few years, we drew awful pictures on the back of old business cards and pegged them up on a piece of string attached to a loose block of wood. It was difficult to wake up on a Saturday morning and make up some structure to the day on the spot, but it certainly helped reduce her level of anxiety. Now we can just talk about our plans for the day.

Sense of a day

In your daily routine point out clocks and try to talk about the time as in 'It is one o'clock, time for lunch' or 'It is seven o'clock, time for bed'.

Sense of a week and beyond

- Talk about the days of the week. 'It is Wednesday, bin day.' 'Today it is Friday, swimming lessons.' 'It is Saturday, no school.'

- Draw up a weekly or monthly calendar showing school days, after-school activities and major events and pin it up on a wall

or the fridge. Use photographs, symbols or words as
appropriate.

- Make a 'time line' for your child using a piece of string. Make
  cards for events which are happening over the next few
  months such as festivals, birthdays and holidays. Peg up the
  cards at appropriate intervals on the 'time line'. Take the cards
  down when the event has passed.

- If your child is looking forward to an event like the summer
  holidays or his birthday, cross off the days on a calendar so he
  can see it getting closer.

- Talk about meaningful events which are going to happen in
  the near future and then refer back to them once they have
  been and gone. 'We are going to see Uncle James on
  Wednesday', and a few days later, 'Do you remember, we went
  to see Uncle James last week?'

Sense of minutes

- Talk about time in terms of a few minutes; for example, ten
  minutes until bed-time, five minutes until school.

- Use a kitchen- or oven-timer or an egg-timer to show that
  when it goes off it will be time to go out, clear up or stop
  watching TV.

- Have races against the clock. Time how long it takes to do
  something – get dressed, do an obstacle course or run from
  one side of the playground to the other.

- Set a time limit – say, one minute – and see how many things
  your child can do in that time; for instance, how many times
  he can jump up and down or run to the end of the garden and
  back.

Telling the time

Children learn best in everyday situations so take every opportunity to
point out the time in your daily life. However, there are many books
which show a daily routine with the relevant time or have a clock with
moveable hands.

Use a conventional clock with clear numbers and avoid Roman numerals.

- Start off by pointing out the time when it is on the hour. 'Look, it is eight o'clock – it is time to go.' Show that the small hand shows the hour and the big hand the o'clock.

- Then show your child how to read half hours.

- Once a child can count in fives he can learn five, ten past and so on.

- Learning quarter to and quarter past the hour is the last part as your child needs to have an understanding of the concepts of half and quarter before he can manage this.

Sense of place

Children need a sense of place and of how to get from one place to another. This is a pre-requisite to their gaining independence later. Start with the most familiar place, your own house, and draw a map showing how rooms relate to each other. Do the same thing for your garden, school and then the local community. Try walking to different places from your home and drawing a map of where you go and the landmarks on the way. You can then extend it on to the wider area and beyond as your child's understanding develops.

Seeing the world from another person's point of view

- Encourage your child to take part in imaginative play, perhaps playing the role of someone else – a teacher, Mummy or a bus driver – so he can see a situation from a different perspective.

- In your daily life find opportunities to talk about how people feel and explain why they feel as they do. For example, if you see a child crying, explain that she is in pain because she has cut her hand or worried because she cannot see her daddy and so on.

- As situations occur at home, talk explicitly about why family members behave as they do – because of their beliefs, experiences, interests and plans, etc.

- Use stories and books to talk about characters and their feelings, expectations and motivations.

- Be explicit about how you feel, by talking to your child about your emotions.

- Encourage social interaction – sharing, playing and taking turns all encourage a child to think about other people's views. As play becomes more sophisticated he will have to negotiate with others.

Theory of mind

Try to place your child in situations in which he can see that someone else does not know what he knows:

- Get him to wrap up a present for someone who does not know what is inside.

- Play games such as Hunt the Thimble with objects around the house or garden. If you use mini Easter eggs it is more motivating because he can eat them afterwards. Get your child to hide things for you to find.

- Get your child to make a surprise for tea to show his siblings or parents.

Making rules

Explain to your child what the rules are and why sometimes it is okay to break them. For example: 'We usually go to bed at 8 p.m. but because it is Bonfire Night we are going to stay up later'.

Thinking

- By scaffolding activities with your child – that is, by playing with him to extend what he can do – you will be taking him through strategies for how to do things. He will eventually internalise these spoken strategies into thought.

- Improving spoken language skills will help thought processes because thinking is internalised language.

- Logical thinking is helped by such activities as:

  - sequencing (see above);

  - giving or writing instructions, because the child has to think carefully about the order of instructions and any ambiguity in them;

  - describing how to do things.

- Develop your child's ability to make inferences by picking up on clues. So ask your child what might happen, why did so-and-so think that, etc. in stories that you read and in everyday life.

Metacognition

Talk to your child about his experiences, perceptions and plans. Ask open-ended questions to encourage him to sit back and reflect, rather than closed yes/no questions.

To develop cognitive abilities further children need to develop a different type of language from everyday conversation. They need to be able to structure their thoughts and to do this they need first to develop spoken language. Being able to organise and sustain a narrative and to give and understand information are important skills. So:

- Encourage your child to tell you simple stories – retelling familiar stories, recounting experiences or making them up.

- Give him instructions to follow around the house and ask him to give you simple instructions.

PARALLEL DEVELOPMENT
Attention

Children learn to extend their attention span through joint activities with adults. All children have short attention spans and moods vary, so do not be over-ambitious.

First find a good location. Remove distractions such as radio, music, TV or other people doing more interesting things. Remember, you are trying to keep your child on task by:

- drawing him back to whatever he is supposed to be doing if he begins to lose interest

- encouraging him to focus on the activity and screen out distractions

- helping him find the relevant information in the mass of detail.

Choose an activity which your child finds interesting and motivating but not too difficult. Make sure you start with success, however short, and then extend the time spent doing something very gradually, minute by minute. For example:

- Talk about a subject that interests your child and extend the conversation.

- Play a game that your child likes and extend the game by adding a new idea as his interest fades. If you are playing with a train set you could suggest building a station or a bridge, or a story about a little boy visiting his friend in Oaktown, and so on.

- Play 'Ready, steady, go!' games with cars, balls or marbles and try to extend the time spent.

- Play with bubbles or balloons, gradually increasing the length of the game.

- Do jigsaw puzzles together, starting with simple ones and then using increasingly complex puzzles as your child becomes able to do more.

- Play simple and short board games, such as Dominoes, or card games, such as Pelmanism, using just a few cards. When your child can concentrate for longer, play more complex and longer games such as Snakes and Ladders, Draughts, Connect 4 and Scrabble.

- Involve your child in household activities such as cooking or washing up.

- Look at books together, increasing the time spent on this each time.

- Try lots of short and varied activities, keeping your child focused all the time.

Extending your child's attention span

Memory

Children with special needs require lots and lots of practice and repetition in order to commit skills and information to long-term memory. Even when you feel confident your child has learnt a new skill or word, you should still make sure you return to it occasionally to ensure that it is secure.

Children with Down's Syndrome often have problems with short-term memory which affect their ability to process language. It has been found that it is helpful to work on extending their language through reading because they often have better visual memories.[10]

Present information in an interesting and clear way as it makes it easier to remember.

Reflect on events that have happened, memorable or otherwise:

- Talk about what you have done today, where you went, how and why – a trip to the zoo or a football match. Talk about feelings, emotions and motivations, not just what happened. Draw parallels and make connections with other experiences to aid categorisation.

10   Buckley, S. and Bird, G. (2001) *Speech and Language Development for Children with Down Syndrome (5–11 years)*. Portsmouth: Down Syndrome Education Trust.

- Talk about routines such as going to dance lessons or visiting friends. What usually happens and in what order? Did anything unusual happen today?

- Use visual prompts such as pictures, postcards and photographs, as a source and stimulus for recalling past events.

- Make scrapbooks using photographs of family members, household objects or toys, or of everyday activities such as going shopping or going to the park.

- Do role-play or pretend-play games based on what has happened. For example, if you have been on a train ride, play trains with model trains. You could set up a train carriage using chairs in a line with a driver, guard, passengers and ticket inspector.

- Get your child to draw pictures or a cartoon, or to write a few words about what happened.

When you tell familiar stories, get your child to tell you what happens next. Make deliberate mistakes for him to correct.

Play memory games:

- 'I went to the market and I bought some ____.' Take it in turns to add some item bought shopping with each person memorising what went before. For example: 'I went to the market and I bought some apples.' 'I went to the market and I bought some apples and…some toothpaste.'

- 'The parson's cat is a ____ cat.' Take it in turns to add an adjective to describe the cat with each person memorizing what went before. For example: 'The parson's cat is a fat cat.' 'The parson's cat is a fat…happy cat'.

- Twenty questions – one person thinks of something and says it is either animal, vegetable or mineral and the other people can ask twenty questions to which the answer is 'yes' or 'no' in order to find out what it is.

- Simon Says – give more complex instructions as your child's memory improves and take it in turn to give the instructions.

- Pelmanism or Pairs – see page 73 for details.

- Encourage your child to memorise and tell jokes.

- Encourage your child to sing nursery rhymes and other songs or to recite poems and children's rhymes such as: 'Pardon me for being so rude, it was not me it was my food. It only came to say hello and now it's gone back down below.'

Strategies for memorising

When your child has to 'memorise' formally, suggest he:

- repeats words to himself to memorise them

- rehearses things he is trying to remember – for example, by practising writing spellings or by repeating his poem

- categorises things he is trying to remember.

Short-term auditory memory

For children with problems with short-term auditory memory, try giving a visual prompt. Pictures, symbols and words can be used to accompany spoken instructions.[11]

Stick to routines because they make it easier to remember what to do next.

Use rhymes, rhythms, songs and music because they are an aid to memory. For example, tap out the syllables of words, sing instructions or set the alphabet to music.

Make sure instructions or requests are kept simple and children are not overloaded with information. Check to see if your child has understood before proceeding.

11   Alton, S. (2001) *Children with Downs Syndrome and short term auditory memory*, a pamphlet produced by the DSA. Also refer to the Downs Ed Trust for more information.

Visual memory

Try the following games:

- Kim's game – place a variety of items on a tray (such as a cup, hairbrush, toy, key) and show it to your child. Either he has to try to remember and name them all or you can remove one item and see if he can remember which it was.

- Pelmanism or Pairs, see page 73 for details.

- Get your child to look at a picture for a few minutes, then cover it up and ask questions about it, such as: 'What colour was the dog?' or 'How many children were there?'

Retrieval

Some children with dyslexia and dyspraxia have a problem with information retrieval. It takes a long time for them to 'find' the word or information they need. Make sure you give them plenty of time to say what they want to say or to respond to a question.

Retrieval

IMAGINATIVE PLAY

Some children with special needs find it difficult to play imaginatively, but this is an important skill for cognitive and social development. It is worth trying to encourage imaginative play even if it is very fleeting. Act out a role yourself and encourage your child to take part. Bring in other children if appropriate.

Have different toys and materials to enable your child to play imaginatively, for example:

- clothes and accessories, especially hats
- boxes out of which to make tunnels, dens, houses, boats and cars
- a row of chairs to represent buses, trains or boats
- rugs or sheets to drape for dens and castles
- dolls and teddies to act as characters.

Older children often like to create their own small worlds which they can manipulate and control. Good toys for this include:

- train sets
- car mats
- doll's houses
- sand pits with diggers, animals, cars, houses and buildings
- zoos
- water troughs with boats
- castles and forts with toy soldiers
- construction toys like Lego and K'nex, which allow children to create their own worlds and to make their own objects.

Use novel and everyday experiences as a starting point for imaginative and role play. Choose situations which you think will appeal to your child, such as:

- builders or carpenters making repairs around the house and then presenting a bill
- a post office or bank with forms, envelopes and stamps
- a café taking food orders, and cooking and serving food

- shops with food, shoes, clothes, a till and money
- a home corner with cooking and cleaning equipment
- a hospital with doctors and nurses, a dentist's or a vet's surgery
- a train or bus
- a castle, camp or fort with soldiers
- a builder's yard
- a space station
- a hairdresser's or barber's shop.

READING, WRITING AND NUMBER SKILLS

An important part of cognitive development is learning reading, writing and numeracy. I have not covered these important skills in this book because they are primarily taught in school. Parents can do huge amounts to help their children with these skills in all sorts of ways; by reading with them, playing number games and encouraging them to write their name or little postcards. However, it is best to work in partnership with your child's school because each teacher and each school will have a different approach. Find out from your child's teacher what he is doing at school and what you can do to support him at home. For suggestions of ways in which you can promote a good relationship with school see Chapter 10, Education.

CHAPTER 4

Language Development

WHAT IS LANGUAGE?

Language comprises the ability to express ourselves and to understand what is being said in response. Language is more than just speech. We use words, sign language and pictures to express ourselves but gesture, tone and body language also play an important part in communication. Language is used for communication – for talking to other people, getting what we need and sharing thoughts and feelings – and for thinking, planning, dreaming and so on. Consequently, there are close and complex inter-connections between language, cognitive and social development.

CHRONOLOGICAL DEVELOPMENT

Early development

Babies learn to make eye contact, smile and make different noises such as babbling. They learn to take turns with an adult in their vocalisations and this lays the basis for later conversation. Copying gestures and sounds are also early developments. Children tune in when very young to the sounds which make up their own particular language.

Understanding

Children learn that a picture of an object (say a cup) represents a real object (i.e. a cup) and is not just a collection of marks on a piece of paper. That is, they learn that one thing can symbolise another. They can then go on to understand that a collection of sounds, i.e. a word, can also represent or symbolise an object. They do this because through regular repetition of the same word they eventually make the association between the word they hear and the object they see. For example, when they hear the word 'cup' they learn by repeated association that it is the vessel out of which they drink.

Children cannot understand a word until the concept behind it has meaning. This means that early language is based in the here and now, on concrete objects children can see before them. They usually understand words before they can say them and they reveal this in the way they respond to questions with eye-pointing, finger-pointing or other gestures to show their understanding.

Pre-verbal communication

Children communicate first by crying, smiling and laughing and with their body language (e.g. turning away from something they do not like). They use natural gestures such as eye-pointing when they look at something they want, gesturing with their whole hand, pointing with their fingers or taking an adult's hand to something they want. Adults and children develop a close awareness of what the other is looking at or interested in and direct their communication appropriately. This helps children to understand what is being talked about. For example, a parent might see her child recoil at the sight of a dog and could respond by saying, 'Yes, it is a dog' and then reassure her 'It is all right, it won't hurt you'.[1]

Early language

Children usually learn to use single words first.[2] There is considerable consistency across many cultures in the first words learnt: they are always based in the here-and-now – names of family members, pets,

1   Bruner, J.S. (1983) *Child's Talk: Learning to Use Language*. Oxford: Oxford University Press.

2   Brown, R. (1973) *A First Language: The Early Stages*. Cambridge, MA: Harvard University Press.

A natural gesture

food and familiar objects. Children next learn words which get them what they need, such as 'more' and 'no'.

Children go on to combine two words together, three words and so on until they are able to produce whole sentences. They focus on the meaningful, information-carrying words (such as 'eat', 'ice-cream') and ignore the function words (such as 'the' and 'a').

They continue to make mistakes when they speak but can use quite complex grammar and a wide vocabulary to continue conversations. They start filling in the function words like 'the' and 'a', and prepositions like 'in', 'on' and 'under'.

The combinations reflect the level of cognitive understanding. Children learn to talk about the size, shape and colour of objects as they begin to have an understanding of these concepts – 'big bus', 'round ball' and 'red jumper'.

Elements of language

Language is composed of the following elements:

Vocabulary/semantics

'Vocabulary' is the words we use and their associated meaning. A child's vocabulary grows as she gets older.

Initially, children understand words in terms of physical appearance and attributes; for example, a drink is cold or a person has cold hands. Later they understand that a person can be described as cold.[3] These changes in the way children think about words and their meanings happen as children think about other areas of existence beyond the spatial, such as the psychological.

Grammar/syntax

'Grammar' is the set of rules that governs our use of language so that it is understandable to everyone. Grammatical structures are learnt as children gain the necessary concepts. For example:

- Past and future tenses are learnt as children gain an understanding of time; for example, 'I went to the shops' or 'I will go to school tomorrow'.

- Plurals come as children learn about numbers.

- Questions such as who, where, what, why and how come as children develop their understanding of the world.

- 'No' is one of the first words children learn, but getting 'no' and 'not' right in sentences takes some time: children may say 'No, I no want cheese' before learning 'No, I do not want cheese'.

- 'The' and 'a' are used from early on but are often inter-changed and not mastered properly until late childhood.[4]

- Understanding of the passive voice comes slowly. Children use their knowledge of the world to make sense of 'the ladder was

3   Asch, S.E. and Nerlove, H. (1960) 'The development of double function terms in children: An exploratory analysis.' In B. Kaplan and S. Wapner (eds) *Perspectives in Psychological Theory: Essays in Honor of Heinz Werner.* New York: International Universities Press.

4   Maratsos, M.P. (1976) *The Use of Definite and Indefinite Reference in Young Children.* Cambridge: Cambridge University Press.

carried by the fireman' before they really understand the use of the passive.

Pragmatics

'Pragmatics' is the understanding that there are different ways of saying something and that the most appropriate expression varies according to the social context, the position of the person to whom you are talking and what you are trying to say. You might say 'Oy! Buzz off' to your mate but not to your grandmother.

We tell young children to say 'please' and 'thank you' but as they get older they realise it is politer to say 'Would you mind telling me the time, please' rather than 'Tell me the time, please'. They become able to judge appropriate levels of politeness according to the situation and the status of the person being asked.

Intonation

'Intonation' is the rise and fall of the voice, which carries meaning. For example 'biscuit' and 'biscuit?' would be said differently. Also, if someone says something sarcastically the tone is different to that used in a sincere remark. Children learn to understand this tone and therefore to pick up on sarcasm and humour.

Articulation/voice

'Articulation' is the sounds made by air passing over vibrating vocal cords. The first sounds children learn are usually *m, n, b* and *d*. Children have more difficulty with sounds like *f, v, s, ch, r* and *sh*. Children often transpose sounds within longer words, so *elephant* may be said as 'ephelant' and *hospital* as 'hostibul', because they have difficulty with some sound combinations.

Children can often hear the subtle differences in words but cannot necessarily pronounce them accurately each time. This is because they need considerable control of their lips and tongue, and this takes time to develop.

Non-verbal communication

Even when we are adults with fully developed speech we continue to derive much of the meaning of what people say from non-verbal forms of communication such as context, body language and gesture. A shrug, raised eyebrow, sneer or smile can be more communicative than words.

Thinking about the language she uses

The next stage of development is when children are able to think beyond the literal meaning of what has been said. They start to have an awareness of language itself which enables them to be much more sophisticated in the way they use it and how they interpret it.

The ability to focus on language and reflect on it starts when children develop an awareness of rhymes. They might say 'Cat and hat – oh, they rhyme'. Reading and writing develop this thinking further because they make children think about sounds, their choice of words and grammar. For example, when a child reads a sentence inaccurately the bad grammar can alert her to her mistake. She might read 'We was going to the shops' but realise it does not sound right and go back and correct it to 'We were going to the shops'. Children also start asking what a word means because they can isolate individual words within a sentence.

As they begin to write, children realise that the same sound can have different meanings such as *for* and *four*. This understanding enables them to understand the double meanings which make some jokes funny. 'What is black and white and red (read) all over?' 'A newspaper.' 'How do you get two whales (to Wales) in a mini?' 'Down the M4.'

They also have to decide on the best way of saying something and this requires quite sophisticated thinking about language. Young children may ask if a word is right or wrong; as they get older, they may ask which word is the most appropriate.

Ambiguity and clarification

When children are very young they cannot respond to ambiguous statements by asking for clarification. Instead, they make a choice based on what they understand; and if that fails they try a different choice. If a child were asked to 'pass the jug' and she did not know the meaning of the word 'jug' she might try passing a glass, and when that proved incorrect try a different item until either she got lucky or the speaker explained what he or she meant. Only when they are older and have a greater awareness of language will children seek clarification and perhaps ask: 'Do you mean the red one or the blue one?' Children have to learn to be both listeners and speakers.

Young children also take what people say very literally and cannot see the distinction between what someone says and what they actually mean. For example, 'Is anyone else hot?' could really mean 'Can I open the window?' but to a child it is a simple question.

Beyond everyday conversation

Vygotsky and Bruner[5] argued that children need interaction with adults to develop their language beyond the everyday and that they do this through narratives and giving and understanding information, as described below.

Narratives

Children learn over a period of time to tell stories, linking actions and ideas beyond simple sentences. If a young child is shown a story in pictures, she will talk about each picture in isolation; as she matures, she will see it as a story with a main character. Later still she is able to link the elements, using pronouns appropriately and words like 'so' and 'then' to sequence the pictures.[6]

Giving and understanding information

By giving and understanding information, children have to sequence actions, think logically, infer how much people know and so on.

5   Vygotsky, L.S. (1986) *Thought and Language*. Cambridge, MA: MIT Press; Bruner, J.S. (1983) *Child's Talk: Learning to Use Language*. Oxford: Oxford University Press.

6   Karmiloff-Smith, A. (1986) 'Some fundamental aspects of language development after age five.' In P. Fletcher and M. Garman (eds) *Language Aquisition* (second edition). Cambridge: Cambridge University Press.

Thinking – internalised language

When adults support children by giving guidance and help as they do a new activity, it not only helps them to learn the skill itself but also how to learn, plan and organise themselves. When a child is doing a jigsaw puzzle an adult might say: 'Try this piece, turn it round a bit, that is it'. Later, children talk to themselves in a similar way as they play. They tell themselves how to do it: 'Does it go here, I will try this piece' and so on. Although most of us talk to ourselves occasionally, perhaps when we have to concentrate on something difficult, this language is generally internalised into an inner language and is a means to direct oneself and to exert self-control.

Understanding language with no context

When children are young they learn language from the here-and-now, from games and routines, from the constant labelling of things that they can see and from experiences they have. As they get older they learn that language can be used independently of objects and people to describe concepts – things that are absent or invisible. From hearing simple stories or talking about experiences they have had or are going to have they can extend their experiences and reflect on them. This

Thinking

enables them to use their language to think, imagine, solve problems and hypothesise.[7]

PARALLEL DEVELOPMENT
Attention span

Language develops as the attention span of children increases. They start with short sentences and as they are able to increase their attention span they can then extend their sentences, making them more complex and linking them together into an argument or a narrative.

Young children are very easily distracted, flitting from one activity to the next depending on what seems the most interesting. They learn to cope with distractions and interruptions by screening out anything irrelevant. By doing this they now become difficult to distract. Eventually they become able to switch between two activities – playing a game and then stopping to listen to instructions before turning back. Later they are able to cope with both activities at the same time. See also Chapter 3, Cognitive Development, for more information on attention.

Functions of language

Language is used for more than just communication. When children are young they use their language, however limited, to tell you things ('look aeroplane') and to make requests ('more milk'). But as they mature so they use language to develop their understanding of the world ('Why is the sky blue?'), to express their thoughts and feelings and to describe what is in their imagination. They need to develop an intellectual language to remember, organise and classify information and to use with abstract ideas. Inner language enables them to talk to themselves – out loud when they are young and internally as they get older.

7   Wells, C.G. (1985) *Language Development in the Pre-School Years.* Cambridge: Cambridge University Press.

DIFFERENT SETTINGS FOR COMMUNICATION

Different language and functions are required in different settings. Parents or close adults actively seek to understand what a child is trying to communicate by using clues and context. At home children ask most of the questions. Most of the conversations are one-to-one, or within such small groups that parents can pick up on whether their child has understood and respond appropriately. Parents and children can negotiate and clarify meanings and contexts if one is not sure what the other is talking about.

When talking to peers communication is different because both children have to make sure the other understands what they are talking about, but they do not necessarily share meanings and context.

Language is quite different in the classroom and is often not truly communicative. Most talking and questioning is done by the teacher and many of the questions are 'pseudo' or 'display' questions where the teacher knows perfectly well what the answer is and the emphasis is on giving the correct answer (e.g. 'Where do birds lay their eggs?' – 'In a nest'). Most communication comes from the adult to the child rather than the other way round. Children are not often actively encouraged to ask spontaneous questions and many questions are closed such as 'What is 2+2?' Closed questions have a simple, straightforward, correct or incorrect answer, whereas open questions require thought and discussion. Children also naturally switch off when the language used is beyond them and in a large class it may not be possible for a teacher to make sure that all the children are following what is being said. This is often seen as a failure of the child, who is not 'paying attention', whereas in fact it may be a reflection on the classroom language.

There is also the issue of shared meanings. Some questions have a number of answers but only one is correct according to the intention of the teacher. The child might not know the 'right' answer because she has not shared the context. For example, the head might say in assembly 'What day is it today?' and the children might come up with all sorts of correct answers, such as 'My birthday', 'Friday' or 'Sports day'. However, what the head wanted to hear was that it was the last day of term.

When a teacher, or indeed anyone, speaks in a class she is not using perfectly formed grammatical sentences in a structured discourse.

Instead, she will start, stop, start again, get side-tracked and start again. If children do not understand she may try a different form of words. It makes it very hard for them to follow the thread.

ACADEMIC THEORIES OF LANGUAGE DEVELOPMENT

Developmental psychologists have debated how children learn language over many years and, as yet, there is no consensus; so I have outlined the different theories below. You can follow up the references I have given if you wish to find out more about these theories.

Learning theory

In the first half of the twentieth century it was thought that children learnt language through a process of rewards and reinforcement by parents and other adults. For example, a child says 'Mama' and her parents show their pleasure with smiles, hugs and by repeating the word back, thereby encouraging her to use it again.

Chomsky

In the 1950s and 1960s Chomsky[8] introduced his theory that rather than being 'taught' language children 'acquire' it through an innate process which means they are tuned into hearing and learning language. He argued that children acquire the 'rules' of language, which allow them to experiment and be creative with words and structures. This enables children not just to copy what they have heard but also to make up their own unique sentences.

Vygotsky and Bruner

Subsequently, Vygotsky,[9] Bruner[10] and others have argued that social interaction is also important in the development of language. From birth a child interacts with her mother, who is gradually and subtly

8   Chomsky, N. (1965) *Aspects of the Theory of Syntax.* Cambridge, MA: MIT Press.

extending her daughter's language. She does this by first accepting any vocalisation and then gradually guiding it to become more accurate (the process Bruner calls 'scaffolding'). Also, later in their development children need interaction and support from adults to develop their powers of verbal reasoning which over time become internalised to allow them to think, plan and hypothesise.

LANGUAGE ISSUES AND GAMES AND ACTIVITIES

Being able to communicate is the most important skill children learn. It allows them to live in the real world, to make contact with people, to understand what is happening, to have social interaction, to have some control and to express themselves. You have to find a way of enabling your child to communicate even if it is at a very simple level. We know instinctively how important communication is. Many parents talk about the magic of their child's first word. One of the most enduring memories I have of my son is the day he put his hand out to request Round and Round the Garden. This natural gesture was the first time he had ever reached out to us and all those months and months of endless tickling games were made worthwhile.

Don't be hung up on your child talking; the most important thing is for her to communicate. After all, speech is only one aspect of language anyway and we all use body language, gesture, facial expression and eye movements to express ourselves. There are now many successful schemes for using signs, symbols, words and pictures for communicating with children with special needs. Once communication has started many children go on to use spoken language. Find the most appropriate means to get your child communicating. Ideas are listed below.

I find it extraordinary to look back and think that Christopher now talks constantly and, if not perfectly, with amazing

9   Vygotsky, L.S. (1986) *Thought and Language*. Cambridge, MA: MIT Press.

10   Bruner, J.S. (1983) *Child's Talk: Learning to Use Language*. Oxford: Oxford University Press.

sophistication. He did not speak until he was five or six years old, but had used Makaton to build up a vocabulary of over a hundred words.

Language development is so heavily bound up with other skills, notably social and cognitive, that it is impossible to see it in isolation. Rather than concentrating on the specifics of language, it is probably more helpful for your child if you concentrate on those other skills.

This chapter covers broad issues of language development and points readers to relevant sections elsewhere in the book. If you want help on very specific aspects of language development there are many useful books listed in Chapter 12, Resources. Also, more important, talk to your child's teacher and speech and language therapist. Ask for suggestions and advice.

This chapter is applicable to children with learning difficulties rather than children with specific language processing disorders. These are highly specific and need to be addressed by your speech and language therapist.

GENERAL GUIDELINES FOR EARLY LANGUAGE DEVELOPMENT

Children have to have a reason for communicating. Observe your child and see what her interests are and use them to motivate her to communicate.

> I asked Terwase's mum to bring into school some of his favourite toys. We put them in a box and he loves these things so much that he is keen to communicate with pictures to get them. His mum knows him so well that she found the right motivators for him.

Communication comes from social interaction. Find the time to play with your child and share activities together. Involve her in everyday household activities like cooking tea, tidying the laundry, washing the car or cleaning the house. It is through these shared experiences that so much is learnt, including language.

Talking to your child

- Make sure you have her attention and eye contact if possible.

- Speak clearly and simply using natural intonation. Make sure that your language is appropriate to her level of understanding. If she is using two words make sure you use sentences with just two or three information-carrying words. Say 'No banging' rather than 'Didn't I just tell you that you should not bang on the table?' Use more complicated language as she makes progress, preferably keeping one step ahead to encourage her to move on. Remember, children naturally tune out when they are listening to language which is beyond their comprehension.

- Repetition and consistency is very important. Repeat things as often as you can so that she learns the association between the object and the sound. It may take a very long time, with seemingly constant repetition of simple words and ideas, but it is really important that you persist. Try to be consistent with the words you use for objects; for example, decide on your family word for toilet/loo/lavatory/bathroom.

- Talk about things she is seeing and experiencing as you speak. Give her the language for what she is doing: 'You are having a bath'.

- Follow her focus of attention and her interests – talk about the things which you can see she is interested in, looking at or wants. She is more likely to learn words around subjects which are motivating and exciting to her. Later on, it may be more abstract subjects in which she has an interest.

- Encourage her to use context, clues and routines to help her understand what is being said. Children rely a great deal on these to understand language. They may be able to pick out a few words they know but may then use other clues to make sense of what is said.

- Use natural gestures as much as you can to aid understanding – pointing, indicating and shaking your head.

Follow her focus of attention

- Use facial expressions and tones of voice to show your moods; make sure your expressions match your words.

- Listening is an important part of communication for both parents and children. See Chapter 6, Sensory Development, for ideas on this.

- Give your child time to respond to you and then give her extra time. It cannot be stressed enough that children with special needs require a longer period to reply because of processing problems.

When your child responds

- Always respond immediately and positively to her efforts to communicate. You need to acknowledge what she has said, that you understand it and that you value the communication. And if you are not absolutely sure she is trying to communicate, give her the benefit of the doubt. Do what she has asked if you can or continue the conversation. If you do not understand, seek clarification – 'Do you mean the book or the box?' – and don't be afraid to revert back to pictures or signs so she can tell you what she means. If you ignore her she will not be so inclined to try again.

- Be over the top in your response to your child's efforts. Respond to any conversation by extending and taking it forward by introducing a new idea or pointing something out. If she says 'Look bus', say 'Yes, it is a bus. It has stopped' or 'It's a red bus' or 'It's our bus. Run!' Keep the language one step ahead of your child's abilities, so you can introduce new language, ideas or structures.

- Don't correct pronunciation or what she has said as that is very discouraging for her. If you have understood her then she has succeeded in communicating. Praise or acknowledge what she has said and then just repeat it back to her correctly. For example, 'Look Mummy, ambliance', 'Yes, it's an ambulance'.

- Have patience and give your undivided attention at least some of the time.

If your child has a hearing impairment but no other special needs, consult a speech therapist or adviser for the hearing impaired for the best approach to communication development.

Pre-verbal communication

If your child is at an age when you would expect some language but she is not yet communicating, it may be that she does not see the point. She needs to have an awareness of other people and a relationship with them (even if it is an understanding that they supply food and toys). She also needs the cognitive abilities to see that a word represents an object.

You may still need to work on the early skills of making eye contact and taking turns.

Below I have outlined two communication systems which are widely used – one using pictures, the other signs – which can help children. Many of the children who use these systems go on to develop speech but, in the meantime, they can use them even at a basic level to ask for things they want, to make choices, to be more independent and then later to point out what they see or hear, or how they feel. The positive consequences of this are clear in terms of their feeling in control (they can say 'yes' or 'no'), improved behaviour because they are not so frustrated and the start of social interaction.

Picture Exchange Communication System

The Picture Exchange Communication System (PECS) was developed in the USA for autistic children who have no language. Children learn to communicate by presenting a picture of what they want to an adult.

First you have to identify what it is that your child likes so much that she will be motivated to use the system. This is usually food, drink, toys or books. Make a photograph or a line drawing of that item and then next time she wants it ensure that she presents the picture before the item is given. You will need the help of another adult to introduce your child to PECS. When your child is expressing her desire for a drink, perhaps by reaching out for one at tea time, one adult physically helps the child to pick up the picture of the drink and places it in the hand of the other adult who has the drink. This triggers the response 'You want a drink' and then the drink is immediately given to the child. Repeat this at appropriate opportunities until you child gets the idea that if she presents the picture of a drink she will get a drink. Reduce the prompt until she is using the picture by herself. Then you can gradually put yourself in a position further away from her so that she has to come to you to make the request using the picture.

Over time another picture is added and then another and so on. The pictures are attached using Velcro to a board in an accessible place or held in a file which the child takes round with her as a 'verbal memory'. Gradually, more pictures are added and the child is enabled to make two-word combinations – 'want biscuit', or 'see ball' and more.

Usually it is best to start with photographs of objects, then you may be able to move on to line drawings (your own or computer-generated), symbols and finally words.

When the child presents the picture, the adult models spoken language back. Say she gives a picture of a drink, you would say 'You want a drink' and go and get it for her.

The idea of PECS is that it is highly rewarding and does not require the language skills of speaking or the motor skills of signing. One of its advantages is that the pictures are permanent, unlike a word or a sign, which are gone in a flash; the child has more time to consider them. Another is that the pictures can be highly personal; for example, you can have a photograph of your child's doll or favourite brand of orange juice, if it is important.[11]

Signing systems

Children with communication difficulties are often introduced to Makaton or Signalong which are signing systems in which normal language is accompanied by a sign. The signs are derived from British Sign Language but sometimes they have been simplified and enlarged to make them more appropriate for children. The idea behind these systems is to give children a visual communication tool and enable them to communicate with signs if they cannot yet say the words. As children learn to speak they naturally drop the signs.

Only the really important words are signed, so, for example, if you were to say 'the man is eating' you would just sign 'eat'; but then you might expand it to 'man' and 'eat'.

Some children use signs for a short period before speaking and others use them for longer. There are some children for whom the system has no benefits. Some schools continue to use signs with children who have spoken language as a way of giving visual support to more complex words and ideas.

Makaton and Signalong are based on the same idea but have a slightly different approach. Find out which system is used by local schools and speech therapists in your area and use the same one. For contact details for Makaton and Signalong see Chapter 12, Resources.

Play for early language development

Language development should keep pace with the child's social and cognitive development, unless there are associated physical problems. As she understands a new concept, so she will learn the word. If she understands the idea of 'blue' the word will have meaning; if not, it is just a sound. Use language which is within her understanding. So much

11   Frost, L. and Bondy, A. (1994) *The Picture Exchange Communication System Training Manual.* Cherry Hill, NJ: PECS Inc. Contact Pyramid Educational Consultants, listed in Chapter 12, for more details.

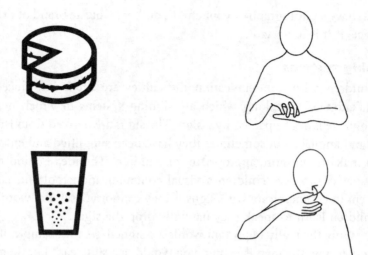

Makaton symbols and signs for cake and drink
Reproduced with permission from the MVDP (registered charity no 287782. Tel: 01276 61390).

of language is about social interaction that you may need to look at encouraging social contact as well.

Whatever your child's level of language, try to keep your own language at the same level or one step ahead. Encourage others to interact with her at this level.

Keep the language appropriate to her age rather than using baby expressions.

Do not introduce your child to 'please' and 'thank you' until she has a reasonable vocabulary (of about 100 words and the ability to use two words together). Please and thank you are not important for communication. It is much more communicative to be able to say 'drink' or 'biscuit' than 'please', which on its own is meaningless. Concentrate on important communicative vocabulary first, and only when she is ready encourage your child to add 'please' and 'thank you'.

Language will arise naturally as you play and interact with your child. You must make time to play games she enjoys, share activities and talk about them as you do them. There are no quick fixes with language development for a child who has difficulties. You need patience, imagination and motivation to find a way of engaging with her. If you can find a way of engaging her interest then you are more likely to see a desire to communicate and, therefore, a development in her language. It does not really matter what it is as long as you can share it with your child – tickling, construction toys or dolls. However, here are some ideas which you might find helpful:

- Talk about what you can see and give her a narrative of what is happening so that she learns the language for what she is doing at that moment. Examples are when you are doing everyday activities, walking around the town, doing the housework, cooking, gardening, washing the car or in the shops talking about what you can see. Verbs or action words are more important than nouns or names because they are far more useful. Names can only be used for labelling.

- Try art activities such as painting and drawing pictures – you can draw pictures to talk about or just share the activity, talking as you paint about the materials, colours and shapes.

- Pretend play is a good way of extending conversations and vocabulary because it gives a different context in which to talk. For example, you could set up a little town in the sand pit, play in the home corner or use dressing-up clothes to play at hospitals. Ideas for imaginative play can be found in Chapter 3, Cognitive Development.

- Use puppets or soft toys to play different characters.

- Get your child to direct you around in a game; it can be very motivating.

In our family we have had endless conversations about cars, petrol stations, tankers, crashes and breakdowns but it has enabled my son to communicate and to develop his language skills and understanding of the world.

- At the beginning and end of each day talk about what you are going to do and have done so that your child can gain an understanding of past and future. Use photographs or pictures, or draw a cartoon version of the sequence of events. This also helps children develop a sense of their own identity and personal history.

- Look at books together. Make sure the books are at the right level in terms of language and content for her and make sure they are visually appealing with good clear expressive pictures. Stories with repetition are particularly good for encouraging language, for example 'Goldilocks and the three bears' and 'Jack and the beanstalk'.

- Start with books showing photographs or clear pictures of familiar objects which you can label and talk about. Make your own books with photographs of your own house, members of the family, toys and so on.

- Then try very simple books showing people doing things, such as a child eating or a man running.

- Move on to simple stories with few words but lots of colourful, appealing and clear pictures. These should show everyday routines like going to school or the park. The stories should also be meaningful – that is, they should be within your child's experience.

- Then try books with more complex language and stories as her language and understanding develop. Look at books which are more imaginative and deal with situations and stories outside her experience.

- Vary the ways you look at books to encourage language and interaction:

  - Read them normally.

  - Talk about the pictures: 'What is that?', 'What colour is the ball?', 'Where is the car?', 'Which cake would you like?', 'Do you think the monster is scary?'

  - Tell the story in your own words to make it easier for her to understand.

  - Encourage her to anticipate what is going to happen next.

  - Get her to talk about the pictures or to tell the story.

Genuine communication

As your child makes progress with her language, make sure that there is a need for *genuine* communication; that is that there is a real exchange of information and that you are not just 'testing' your child. All children will grow wise to tasks if they are pointless; for example, asking a child to describe a picture when you can see it yourself is not real communication. Even expecting your child to ask for a biscuit when it is on a plate in front of her is more about social manners than communication. That is a more advanced level of communication than you should be concentrating on at this stage.

- Give her a reason to communicate. Put things she wants out of reach so she has to ask you for them.

- Make games meaningful. If you want her to describe things to you make sure they are hidden behind a screen or in a box so you cannot see them.

- Don't anticipate her needs all the time because then there is no need for communication.

- Give her choices so she has to communicate what she wants. 'Which would you like?' 'What shall we do now?'

Sentences and beyond

Taking things literally

Some children take language very literally and find it difficult to understand metaphors and similes or to pick up on the mixed messages of irony, sarcasm and humour. This is partly a cognitive issue because, as children get older, they become aware of the complexity of situations and are able to see different angles on issues instead of taking them at face value. It is also a social issue of being aware of other people and their feelings and emotions. It can become a social problem for your child if she does not pick up on jokes or cannot read her friends' body language. See the relevant sections in Chapter 7, Social Development: Understanding the feelings of others (p.222), and Social rules and social skills (p.229).

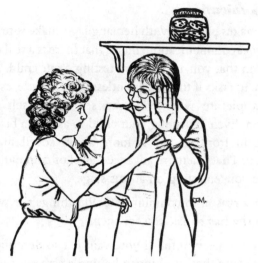

Give your child a reason to communicate

Be aware of these issues and think about the language you are using and the potential for misunderstandings. If it is particularly important to get information across without confusion, make sure you use unambiguous language.

You may have to teach metaphors explicitly. 'Let's call it a day on the gardening front' means 'Let's stop gardening'.

Give her strategies for getting more information if she does not understand what someone says because of the use of a metaphor. Remind her to ask for clarification. Model seeking more information e.g. 'Do you mean baked beans or green beans?' or 'I don't understand. Could you explain that to me?'

Say something completely outrageous to your child to show her how to recognise teasing. Encourage her to think about what you are saying and to look for clues in your expression. You can gradually make your teasing slightly less obvious.

Grammar and syntax

Children pick up grammatical rules from hearing language and using it. For example some children have problems with pronouns because of their lack of awareness of themselves and their connection with others. Problems are usually highly specific and you should get good advice from your child's teacher or speech therapist.

Non-verbal communication

Pragmatics

Some children have difficulties with pragmatics, or the use of language appropriate to the social situation. It can get them into difficulties with their friends if they don't understand slang words or with adults and teachers if they use playground slang.

Adults are very tuned into young children and pick up on their efforts to communicate. But as children get older adults expect them to be able to initiate conversations, by getting the attention of their listener and making themselves understood. Often they say things like 'Mummy, you know what?', to get attention. However, some children have problems with getting attention and grab hands and faces instead of using language. They do not understand how much other people know or do not know, how much they share their context. They can launch into conversations with statements or questions like 'What colour is your lever?' which can leave the listener a bit stumped.

These are often issues about social skills rather than language skills, and all children take time to learn them. The way to help may be through looking at social skills and awareness, perhaps using turn-taking games or Social Stories. See Chapter 7, Social Development, for ideas.

Children also need language to entertain their friends and family. You can help your child to tell and understand jokes. Buy a children's joke book, copy out a few jokes, cut up the questions and answers and get your child to match the question with the answer. This encourages her to think about the language. Increase the number of jokes and then play games like Pelmanism or bingo with the jokes.

Obsessive conversations

As their language skills improve some children may gain a repertoire of subjects which they discuss obsessively. These provide safe territory where they feel socially and emotionally secure. Although these can be a positive way of learning they do need to be controlled.

- Move your child on gently if possible by extending and broadening the conversation.

- Limit discussion of obsessions to a certain time and place. For example, set aside ten minutes at bed-time or after tea and give her your undivided attention.

- Insist you talk about something else first and use the discussion of obsessions as a reward.

- Suggest 'You tell me' when you get fed up of explaining for the nth time how you buy petrol.

- Sometimes, obsessive conversations are a way of gaining reassurance. Try to work out what the underlying anxiety might be and deal with that instead.

Beyond everyday conversation

Children need to develop their language beyond everyday conversations if they are to move on to the higher levels required in secondary educational settings. You can help your child to do this by the following:

- In general conversation make sure you ask open-ended questions, not just closed questions where there is one correct answer. If you ask 'Did you enjoy the party?' a child can just say 'yes' or 'no', while 'What did you do at the party?' might get a fuller response.

- Talk broadly and discursively about general issues of concern and interest, such as items in the news, how to treat people or poverty. Give your child an opportunity to express her views on subjects for which there is no right or wrong. Research has shown that parents who ask open-ended questions encourage their children to reflect and this encourages intellectual self-control.[12]

- Encourage her to listen to and read more challenging stories, which are longer and more complex with fewer pictures. She will have to be more reliant on her language abilities to understand what is going on.

- Talk to her about the stories she has read, what and who is being portrayed to develop her language and to ensure that she has understood it all.

Thinking – internalised language

Before children learn to obey their own commands (i.e. to exercise self-control) they first learn to obey other people's commands. So play games in which you give directions for your child to follow and then reverse roles so you do what your child says. For example:

- Play Simon Says.

- Play a find-the-picture game – pin pictures (say of a car, mushroom, cat and fish) in different places in the room or the garden and when you name a particular picture she has to run to the correct picture.

- Get her to run around the room or garden to music. When you stop the music give her a command, such as run, walk or hop, until the music starts again.

- Play a traffic-lights game in which you have three pieces of paper coloured red, yellow and green. Your child has to do

12   Sigel, I.E. and McGillicuddy-Delisi, I. (1988) *Parents as Teachers of their Children in the Development of Oral and Written Language: Readings in Developmental and Applied Linguistics.* Norwood, NJ: Ablex.

different actions according to the colour you hold up or say. Green may mean 'run', yellow 'walk' and red 'stop'.

- Make sure you talk her through how to do activities, thereby modelling the thought processes you usually internalise. See Chapter 2, What Everyone Needs to Know, the section on Scaffolding, for more details.

- Play a game to keep things in her mind. Children have to learn to keep words in their head, so sing songs where a word is replaced by a gesture and the word is therefore internalised. Examples are Head, Shoulders, Knees and Toes, John Brown's baby and Underneath the Spreading Chestnut Tree.

Playing Simon Says

PARALLEL DEVELOPMENT
Functions of language

We use language for many purposes. It is very important that all children, even if they have limited language, are encouraged to use that language across all areas of functionality and not just to label things. Just a few words can be used to request things ('me ice-cream'), comment on things ('look dog'), refuse things (when offered a biscuit, a child can say 'no, apple'), ask about things ('Where Daddy?') or request attention ('Mummy?').

To develop language for these other functions see the section Understanding and expressing emotions in Chapter 8, Emotional Development; the sections on memory and classifying in Chapter 3, Cognitive Development, and the sections on negotiating in Chapter 7, Social Development.

Attention span

See Chapter 3, Cognitive Development, for ideas for games and activities.

CHAPTER 5

Physical Development

What is physical development?

'Physical development' means all aspects of controlling the body, its muscles and movement. The chapter has been subdivided into a section on gross motor skills, which covers all the movements of the larger limbs, and one on fine motor skills, which covers the delicate and precise movements of hands and fingers.

GROSS MOTOR SKILLS

THE THEORY

Early development

A baby first learns to control his head and then his spine, so that he can roll over and sit up. His control then extends to his hips and legs, enabling him to crawl, stand and walk.

Two rules govern the sequence of development from birth:

- cephalocaudal – which means that development proceeds from head to toe
- proximodistal – which means that development proceeds from inner to outer parts of the body.

Children first learn to perform an action using large movements and gradually refine them over time so that the movements become smaller and more specific. Think of a young child clumsily catching a ball using both arms and his chest. Over time he learns to catch it with just his hands then, finally, with one hand.

Strength

As children get bigger and their muscles develop their strength will also develop. Children initially need to play with light equipment which is easy to handle – not too big but not too small – and then as their strength and ability improve they are able to use heavier equipment.

Children's bones are soft and so their bodies are more pliable. As they grow older their bones become harder and stronger. Weight -bearing exercises, such as running and walking, are crucial to the development of strong bones in legs and hips, and it is good for children to learn to enjoy these activities as they can prevent conditions like osteoporosis in later life.

Walking

When children start to walk their legs are far apart and they fall over easily whenever they bump into anything or the surface becomes uneven. However, with practice their feet come closer together, and they walk with a good gait, moving from heel to toe. As their balance improves they can walk along a narrow line or a bench without falling off. As they get stronger and have more stamina they can walk further and faster.

Running

As children speed up their walking, they learn to run. They need strength and stamina to run faster and for longer. They also learn to stop and start and change direction as they run round obstacles or dodge people.

Jumping

Children learn to jump up in the air, and then off a low object like a log or the bottom stair. They learn to jump forwards, backwards and sideways. Then they learn to jump over something like a low rope. As they develop their awareness of where their feet are in space and of their body position, they gain the confidence to jump higher and further, landing more elegantly on the balls of their feet.

Climbing

Children first walk up and down stairs by putting two feet on one step and then as they gain balance by placing one foot on each step. They then climb up and down ladders, climbing frames, trees and wall bars to reach considerable heights.

Hopping and skipping

Children first balance on one foot for a moment. Then they learn gradually to extend the time. Eventually they are able to balance with their eyes closed. They learn to walk on tiptoe, run lightly on their toes, hop on one leg and skip without a rope. They learn to skip with a rope by themselves and later to skip with two others turning the rope.

Cycling

Children learn to pedal a tricycle and then later to cycle a two-wheeler, which requires the ability to pedal and maintain balance at the same time.

Kicking balls

Children start by kicking a stationary ball; then they learn to kick a ball when it is rolled towards them. They learn to run keeping a ball under some control and then later to be able to dribble the ball in and out of cones and other obstacles. They learn to kick with increasing strength and accuracy and, as they get stronger, to kick increasingly heavier balls.

Throwing and catching balls

Children can initially catch large balls which are thrown from a close distance. They use the whole length of their arms to catch the ball and hug it into their chest. With practice they learn to use just their hands to catch balls and they bend their arms to absorb the impact. As their coordination improves they are able to catch more accurately, to use smaller and bouncier balls and, sometimes, to use one hand only.

When throwing balls children first learn to throw a ball down towards the ground. They then learn to throw the ball from the shoulder but with their feet close together. The final stage is to stand sideways, with the throwing arm right back, transferring the weight onto the front leg as the arm comes through. With practice children learn to throw further and more accurately to other people or at a target.

Children learn to bounce balls on the ground, at first large balls, using two hands, and later smaller balls, using one hand.

Racket games

Using short-handled rackets children learn to hit a ball which is thrown to them. With practice they can build up the rallies so that they can hit a succession of balls and gradually develop more strength and accuracy both in receiving and in placing the ball.

Sensory skills that influence gross motor skills

There are many perceptual skills which have a strong influence on gross motor skills. These include hand–eye and foot–eye coordination, body awareness and spatial awareness, which are covered in Chapter 6, Sensory Development.

GAMES AND ACTIVITIES

GENERAL GUIDELINES

Give lots of praise to children who find physical activities difficult compared to their peers and who consequently may have low self-esteem. This is particularly true for children with dyspraxia.

When playing racing games, rather than competing against each other, which can be very demotivating for those who always lose, have races against the clock.

Simon Says is a wonderful game for practising all sorts of physical skills; for example, for learning left and right. You can make it easy or difficult depending on the commands given. Make sure the commands are clear and achievable.

Action songs and party games are good ways of practising skills in a fun and relaxing environment. Examples are:

- Underneath the Spreading Chestnut Tree
- Hokey Cokey
- Head, Shoulders, Knees and Toes
- Musical Bumps, Chairs, Statues or Mats
- Ring-a-ring-a-roses
- The Farmer's in his Den
- In and out the Dusty Bluebells
- Tall as a House, Small as a Mouse

Play copying games so that your child has to mirror you as you practise certain skills, for example raising one leg, stretching out a hand or touching your toes.

Swimming is a great form of exercise for children with special needs. See page 141.

Use playgrounds and play equipment. Going on see-saws, slides, swings, chain bridges and climbing frames helps to develop balance, hand–foot coordination and spatial awareness.

Strength

Some children have increased muscle tone: the muscles become too tight and limbs cannot be fully extended (hypertonia). It is important that this is addressed to prevent later joint contractures. Children need to do stretches to extend and relax the muscles so they can be used fully.

Other children have decreased muscle tone: the muscles are too weak and ligaments lax (hypotonia) and they need to be made stronger by doing strengthening exercises.

Swimming is a good form of exercise for general strengthening. Floating in the water supported by floats and kicking is particularly good for hips and quads, especially if your child is wearing flippers.

Trampolining is also good for improving strength, particularly in the muscles around the hips. It is often known as rebound therapy.

Gradually make some physical activities more difficult to build up strength; for example, by using heavier balls for throwing or kicking, walking further or cycling up steeper hills.

Hypotonia

Stretches and strengthening exercises

Some children need to do strengthening exercises, especially for their quads, abdominal muscles and back extensors if they are hypertonic, and stretches for their hamstrings, Achilles tendons, hip flexors and adductors if they are hypotonic. There are all sorts of different exercises to do, so talk to your physiotherapist about the best ones for your child.

Physio balls can now be bought relatively cheaply and often come with explanatory sheets of exercises. They can make exercises more fun for children.

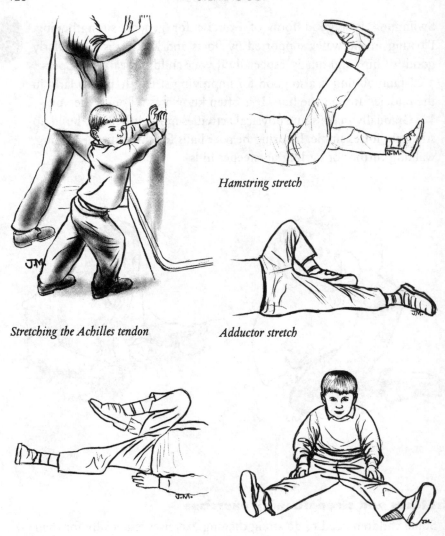

Hamstring stretch

Stretching the Achilles tendon   *Adductor stretch*

Hip flexor stretch   *Another hamstring stretch*

Walking

Watch your child walking and make sure that he has a good gait
(putting his foot down heel to toe with an equal stride pattern). If he
does not and is perhaps walking on his tiptoes or with knocked knees,
this may indicate that there is a problem with his hip/knee/foot

alignment and he could be in pain. This also has implications for his future health. Make an appointment to see a physiotherapist or podiatrist who can check if there is any problem.

Try different walking games to encourage good balance and feet placement:

- Get your child to keep his balance while walking along a line on the ground (draw one using chalk or use the markings on a playground). Use a combination of straight lines and lines that go round corners.

- Practise walking on low walls, beams, kerbs, planks or fallen logs.

- Walk across stepping stones, rocks or boulders or make your own steps using mats.

- Play the Bear Game in which he must not tread on the cracks in the pavement otherwise the bear will get him. Alternatively, play a game where you must step on the lines or only on certain coloured tiles, perhaps.

- Have paper chases or make flour trails to follow.

- Sing songs and rhymes as you walk such as 'The grand old duke of York' or 'We are soldiers marching along'.

Develop stamina and strength by gradually extending the distance your child walks and by varying the surface and gradient. A rough terrain – for example, stones, rocks and sand – is much more difficult than a nice smooth tarmaced path and it is more difficult going up and down hill than keeping to the level. Get him to practise walking on his heels or on his toes.

Going for walks

Sometimes it can be difficult to motivate children to walk. You can always find something to use as a reward when you reach your destination such as a drink or tickles or a treat. However, here are some ideas for making walks more interesting for your child:

- Play Hide-and-Seek or Chase.

- Take a camera or binoculars and use them.

- Play 'I spy' games or take an 'I spy' book.

- Take a treasure bag for collecting bits and pieces.

- Have a list of things to find on the way – tick them off as you go along. They can be tangible objects that you know will be en route, such as a bridge or a bus, or conceptual, such as something red or something square.

- If you can find water you could play Pooh Sticks, building dams, sailing paper boats, fishing nets, paddling or skimming stones.

- Take a ball for throwing or kicking, a Frisbee, kite or model plane.

- Make a picnic.

- Dress up – he could pretend to be an Indian chief or a soldier and make the walk become a game.

- Pretend to be trains, cars or planes having races.

- Use a timer and estimate how long the walk will take.

- Make miniature gardens and landscapes using stones, weeds, sticks and other found objects.

- Draw a map together either before you go or as you go along.

- Take a sketch pad and pencil and get him to draw what he sees.

- Have a focus for your walk which he particularly likes – a petrol station, café, train station or the shops.

Balance

Play musical statues but encourage your child to take up a variety of positions when the music stops, maybe standing on one leg or stretching out his arms.

Set up an obstacle course in the garden which requires him to use his balance. You could have a section which requires walking on a line or holding a pose while you count to ten.

Walking in water, either in a swimming pool or paddling on the beach, is harder work than normal walking because you have to cope with the drag of the water and also keep your balance.

Fill a paddling pool so he can splash, jump, kick and generally run around.

Good activities for balance are:

- space hoppers
- scooters
- pogo sticks
- stilts
- roller blades or roller skates
- skateboards
- Twister
- bikes
- horse riding
- yoga.

Running

Try the following games to encourage your child to run, thereby developing his speed, strength and stamina:

- Get him to run both ways in a circle and in a figure of eight.
- Use a playground and pitch markings to get him to run along straight lines and turn corners.
- Play a traffic-lights game. You call out commands: red for 'stop', yellow for 'walk' and green for 'run fast'.
- Play a game where he has to run to a named location or a picture on the wall.
- Encourage him to bounce on a trampoline or trampette as these improve stamina, bone density and strength.
- Practise running both on even ground and up and down hills.
- Have family running races against the clock or against each other. If children are different ages or abilities you could give some a handicap such as starting ten seconds later or running farther.

- Have family relay races.
- Play What's the Time Mr Wolf? in which one person is the wolf and stands at one end of the garden, and the others approach him shouting 'What's the time Mr Wolf?' If he shouts 'one o'clock' then the children take one step towards him, if 'five o'clock' then five steps and so on. When he shouts 'dinner-time!' everyone runs back to the start and whoever the wolf catches is the next wolf.
- Play Hide-and-Seek.

Dodging games

The following games all encourage children to dodge and manoeuvre, change speed and direction, stop and start:

- Play Chase. One person chases another until he catches him and they then swap roles.

  To motivate Christopher I used to get him to chase me and when he caught me I would tickle him, otherwise he could not see the point of the game.

- Play Tag in which one or two people are 'it' and there are two or more safe bases. Children have to run from one base to another and if one is caught he becomes 'it'.
- A fun variation is Chain Tag if you have a lot of children. If you are caught you hold hands with the catcher, making a chain until there is only one person left. He starts the next chain.
- Stick-in-the-mud is a version of Tag. If you get caught you have to stand still with your legs apart until someone crawls between your legs to 'free' you.
- British Bulldog is a game where children start on one side of the playground and have to run to the other side, with a few children in the middle trying to catch them. If they get caught they join the children in the middle trying to catch the others until only one person is left.

- Children run around in whatever direction they want and when you blow a whistle or give a shout everyone has to change direction.

Jumping, hopping and skipping

Encourage your child to jump in all the different ways – on the spot, forwards, backwards and sideways, up high or from a high to a low place.

- Play High Jump in the garden by jumping over a rope which you make progressively higher.
- Make a horse-jumping course using flower pots and sticks, and compete against the clock.
- Play Long Jump in the garden, in a large sand pit or on the beach, by jumping across two ropes on the ground which you gradually place further apart. Alternatively mark a launch spot on the grass and measure how far your child jumps.
- Practise jumping on something and jumping off something, such as the bottom of the stairs or a low wall.
- Hang something up high for your child to jump up to reach.
- Jump across stepping stones by setting out a course for your child to jump from one mat, hoop or chalk circle to the next.

For hopping try:

- encouraging your child to hop on each leg in turn, going both ways in a circle and in a figure of eight;
- using playground markings and getting him to hop along a straight line and turn a corner;
- doing playground games like Hopscotch, French skipping/Elastics and skipping when the end of the rope is held by two others.

Encourage your child to skip as you are walking home, or play skipping music or sing songs for him to skip to.

To practise all the skills, set up a trail in a playground. Get your child to walk from one spot to the next, then run for a bit, then hop, skip and finally jump right back to the beginning.

Climbing

Encourage your child to extend his climbing abilities by climbing stairs, ladders to slides, climbing frames, obstacle courses and trees.

Cycling

Cycling is a great activity for children as it can bring feelings of exhilaration, freedom and fun.

Cycling a tricycle

If your child has outgrown conventional tricycles you can still buy them from specialist manufacturers (see Chapter 12, Resources). However, they are not cheap so it is worth making enquiries about second-hand trikes in the cycling press, among local parents whose children have outgrown their trikes, via schools or to your occupational therapist.

Children need to get the idea that they can pedal their tricycles to make them move. To begin with you may have to push them along with their feet on the pedals so that they can feel the sensation of pedalling. For children who find pedalling difficult because their feet keep slipping you can get straps which hold the foot onto the pedal (rather like toe clips). Then they have to learn to steer and to control the speed.

Pedalling a go-cart

Cycling on two wheels

To be able to cycle a two-wheeler children need to combine pedalling with balancing. It is best to separate out these two skills and get your child to practise them individually before combining them. Give him the opportunity to pedal a tricycle or a bike with stabilisers so he gets used to pedalling.

To give him a sense of balance take the pedals off his bike (they should unscrew quite easily) and get him to scoot around on it, using his feet like paddles. He will develop a sense of balance by learning to free-wheel with his legs off the ground when he has built up enough momentum. Two-wheel scooters are also good for building up a sense of balance. Stabilisers allow children to use their bicycles but they do not really give children a feeling for balance.

When he is confident at pedalling and can also use his pedal-free scooter-bike put the pedals back on and spend some time practising cycling. Support the seat and run alongside him, relaxing your support as you feel him balance properly. It is always easier to practise on a large, empty, smoothly tarmaced area. A school playground or a closed car park are ideal. Try starting on a slight incline to give your child momentum.

When children learn to ride a bike they need to feel very secure, i.e. that they can put their feet firmly on the ground to stop. So make sure your child has a bike which is small enough. Resist the temptation to buy bicycles which are too big, offering 'room for growth', as these will hinder learning to ride.

Initially, children stop their bikes by using their feet rather than having the confidence and ability to rely on their brakes. Make sure that the brakes are not so tight that they cannot be used by small hands.

Once children have mastered cycling they will probably need to move on to bigger bikes quite quickly as a small bike is difficult to steer.

If your child is not able to cycle independently on the roads, trailer bikes or tandems are a good way of giving him the idea of how to cycle and are relatively safe. There are some good traffic-free cycle routes around the country which are attractive and safer for children.[1]

If your child has physical difficulties, contact your occupational therapist, RADAR, specialist cycle manufacturers or specialist voluntary organisations for advice on making adaptations. See Chapter 12, Resources, for contact details. There are a number of country parks and voluntary organisations which hire out specially adapted bikes. Ask locally for details.

Kicking balls

Try any kicking and football games, for example:

- kick at targets (using the left then the right foot) e.g. at a post, a goal or to a person

- dribble round obstacles set up in the garden

- kick, run after the ball, then kick again

- kick towards a wall and then kick the rebound, and so on

- keepy ups.

---

1   To find good cycle routes in your area, including many traffic-free rides, contact Sustrans, 35 King Street, Bristol.

Foot–eye coordination

Try any games which make your child think about the placing of his feet:

- running – first to the left, then stop, then change direction to the right
- jumping – on the spot then to the left, right, forwards and backwards
- hopping (first left leg, then right leg) and Hopscotch;
- star jumps
- trampolining
- skipping – use rhymes and games to accompany the action
- French skipping – using elastic
- using markings on a playground set up a route for hopping, skipping and jumping
- avoiding cracks in the pavement or stepping on the blue tiles only
- all climbing activities require foot–eye coordination so practise on stairs, ladders, trees or climbing frames

Foot–eye coordination

- set up obstacle courses in the garden – running around obstacles, climbing up the slide and sliding down, through the hoop, over a fence and five star jumps. Alternatively, use the park equipment and establish a route around the equipment. Get everyone to race against the clock to see who is the winner

- using computer games with a special floor mat to teach dance routines.

Throwing and catching balls
Rolling balls

- Sit on the floor and roll a ball between you.
- Play skittles or *boule*.
- Create a wall or tower out of children's bricks and then roll balls at it to knock it down.

Throwing

Think about the size and relative hardness of the ball. Initially, use bean-bags or a softish ball which is not too big to handle but also not too small and fiddly.

- Encourage your child to throw his ball first directly in front of him and then to the left and then the right.

- Encourage him to throw bean-bags (rather than balls, which will tend to bounce out) into a hoop or bucket, or balls into a paddling pool to make a splash. As he improves get him to do five in a row or move the hoop or bucket further away.

- Play Hoop-la or Deck Quoits.
- Play Pooh Sticks.
- Get him to throw balls to hit a target such as a tree trunk.
- Throw stones into the sea or river, or try and hit a target.
- Skim stones.
- Shoot balls into a basketball or netball hoop.

Catching

Make it easy for your child to begin with by using largish soft balls, Kosh balls or bean-bags which will not bounce out of his hands. Gradually, make it more difficult by using smaller and harder balls.

Be careful how you place the ball. Start off by ensuring success, aiming the ball carefully and softly so that he can catch it. It takes a lot of practice to be able to anticipate where the ball is going and to move into position. Gradually make throwing and catching games more difficult, by using smaller and harder balls and making him move more to catch the ball.

You could try the following ideas:

- Bounce a ball on the ground for him to catch.

- Get your child to bounce a ball on a hard surface and catch it.

- Count the number of times he throws and catches the ball without dropping it.

- Play Piggy-in-the-middle.

- If you have a group of people, get everyone to stand in a circle. The person with the ball names someone in the circle and throws it to him or her.

- Bounce balls against walls.

- Play netball or basketball.

Racket games

An easy way to begin is to use balloons because they move very slowly. Pat a balloon backwards and forwards with your child. You could use a light racket. Then you could try using a light racket with a short handle and a large, soft ball. Also try:

- using a suction bat and ball

- using a bat and ball on a post

- playing French cricket, cricket, rounders or softball

- playing tennis, badminton or squash.

Hand–eye coordination

Any of the above ball games will help with hand–eye coordination. You could also try the following ideas:

- Get your child to help you to wash things, such as the car, his bicycle or the windows, using a sponge. With a bucket of water he could wash some plastic toys or pots.

- Get him to 'paint' the house, the shed or his bicycle with an old paintbrush and a bucket of water. You could add some food colouring to the water to make it more interesting.

- Play clapping games with your child, for example 'The sailor went to sea, sea, sea'.

Hand–eye coordination also involves fine motor skills which are described below.

PHYSICAL ACTIVITIES

The importance of physical exercise

Give your child lots of opportunities to get out and play in as physical a way as he is able. Find something active that he enjoys and encourage him in that, but don't expect him necessarily to be a brilliant all-rounder. Physical exercise is really important not only in terms of practising skills, but also for health and self-esteem.

Physical exercise is important

Find a way of giving him adequate exercise each day – staying after school to use the playground, regularly playing in the garden or a nearby park, taking a longer walking route home from school, buying a trampoline, going to a soft play centre, having swimming lessons, taking bikes or a ball out, and so on.

Many children have huge amounts of energy and although they may be mentally tired from school they need to let off steam physically. When children are zooming around they are learning important skills such as spatial awareness, coordination and balance.

Children can get a lot of exercise and have a lot of fun playing, walking, going to the park or on their bikes. But there are also lots of different sports and physical activities which they might enjoy and which could be very beneficial. You can organise some yourself, such as swimming or badminton. Others, such as gymnastics or rugby, involve joining a club.

Many sports are competitive from an early age so it is worth finding out about the attitude of the club you are considering – do they make sure everyone plays or do only the best get picked? Do they concentrate on exams and badges or is it more about having fun? Make sure the level of competitiveness is appropriate for your child. Also think about his level of ability. Some children do not mind that they are not the best but others might find it demotivating. For some activities your child might be happy in an ordinary club, for others it might be more appropriate to find one specifically for children with special needs. See Chapter 7, Social Development, for further information.

Swimming

Swimming is an excellent activity in many different ways. Physically, it is a good form of exercise for virtually every part of the body, the natural buoyancy of the water giving support and enabling children to develop strength and control. Also, the special breathing required in swimming pushes children to breathe deeply in a way which is highly beneficial.

Swimming also has a therapeutic value for children. They can play and splash, whizz down slides or relax, floating and feeling the support of the water.

It is great fun for children to play in the water and it is one of the few activities that parents and children can share together. Parents are not distracted by other jobs or activities and can devote themselves wholeheartedly to playing with their children – splashing, tickling, chasing, giving rides or racing.

It is also one of the activities where children with special needs can feel on an equal footing with their peers. Many of the fun activities in a pool can be done by anyone – jumping in, splashing each other and chasing. It can be a really good social experience because there is little social etiquette, no right and wrong and, within a familiar pool, some children can be largely independent.

Gaining water confidence

The most important thing for a young child is for him to be confident in the water – able to move around, get his face wet, put his head under the water and jump in and out. If he is confident it will be easier to learn to swim. Be sensitive to him and encourage him gently to do more. Have fun in the water and try the following ideas:

Moving around

Encourage your child to:

- walk, jump and move in a controlled way
- play Chase – walking in the shallow end or swimming
- walk backwards and forwards
- push boats, floats and toys around
- fetch toys
- throw and fetch balls – a simple version of water polo
- play Follow my Leader
- sing songs with actions, such as 'Here we go round the mulberry bush', 'The wheels on the bus', Simon Says, Hokey Cokey, 'If you're happy and you know it'. Use appropriate actions including 'jump up and down', 'wash our face', 'go under water', and so on.

Floating

- Get him to float on his back, lying still.
- Use large floats for him to lie on his front and back.

Floating on his front

Floating on his back

Encourage your child to get his face wet

- Blow bubbles or talk to 'the fish' in the pool.
- Sing nursery rhymes which involve dropping down in the water, such as Ring-a-ring-a-roses.
- In the shallow end have races – blowing balls across the pool, pushing them with the top of your head.
- Help him to swim through hoops.

Getting her face wet

Going under water

- Pick up weighted hoops from the bottom of the pool.
- Get him to swim through your legs.

Splashing games

- Kicking is good for hips and quads.

Jumping in

- Put him on the side of the pool and sing 'Humpty Dumpty' for him to jump in.

Learning to swim

Swimming with parents should always be fun. However, you may feel that it is more appropriate to send him to swimming lessons, so that he can learn to swim and develop his strokes. Swimming is a life skill and once it is learnt it will stay with him for ever. You could try individual lessons or group lessons if he can operate within a small group. The Amateur Swimming Association has national levels of achievement and schemes for children with disabilities.

Trampolining

This is an excellent form of exercise. It is good for strengthening limbs, developing muscle tone, stamina and coordination. It also helps children improve their reactions, spatial awareness, body awareness and height and depth perception.

Horse riding

Riding is a unique form of exercise which is both good physical exercise and therapeutic. It is good for posture and balance, because the child is constantly being forced to readjust his position according to the movement of the horse. It is particularly good for legs because the movement of the horse provides massage, warmth and movement for the child.

Some children are particularly motivated by the contact with the horse and, for children who have mobility problems, it is wonderful to be mobile with the horse being their legs.

Children can either ride with local stables and pony clubs or there are Riding for the Disabled Association groups which teach children with special needs in weekly sessions.

Gymnastics and ballet classes

These are good ways of getting your child to practise all sorts of physical skills such as coordination, balance and body awareness.

Dance clubs

These clubs can be a good means of encouraging your child to be physically active and practise skills requiring coordination and spatial and body awareness. They tend to focus on having fun and enjoying moving to music.

Music and movement classes

For younger children these are a non-competitive and fun way of encouraging listening, music and motor skills.

Yoga and pilates

There are now yoga classes for children but most are for the 11 to 18 age group. If you enjoy yoga yourself you could try doing yoga with your child at home. There are some useful books for practising yoga with children[2] which show you how to act out stories, getting into the appropriate position for different characters. Pilates is very good for encouraging core stability, but children may have problems coping with the discipline of isolating certain muscle groups.

Football

There are many children's football clubs. Football is a very skilful sport requiring speed, stamina, strength and good foot–eye skills. It is a great form of exercise and socially important for many young boys.

Mini rugby

The Rugby Union has a network of clubs which offer rugby for children. There is a structured system based on age. The under sevens play a version of rugby called Tag Rugby with no tackling. As the children get older different techniques are introduced, including tackling and scrums. The system is very strict about children moving up with their age group. Sessions comprise warming up, skills practice including team play and a warm down.

Rugby skills are running and dodging, passing, catching and placing the ball and communication with team-mates. There is a strong emphasis on teamwork and discipline and coaches work with their teams to ensure that everyone has a chance.

2   Kesikachar, T. and Khasla, S.K. (1998) *Fly Like a Butterfly: Yoga for Children.* New York: Sterling Juvenile Books; Sumar, S. (1998) *Yoga for the Special Child: A Therapeutic Approach for Infants and Children with Down Syndrome, Cerebral Palsy and Learning Difficulties.* Buckingham, VA: Special Yoga Publications; and Luby, T. (1998) *Children's Book of Yoga: Games and Exercises Mimic Plants and Animals and Objects.* Santa Fe, NM:Clear Light Publications.

Racket sports

Racket sports are good for developing hand–eye coordination and tend to be sociable activities which are easily organised. Many tennis clubs offer coaching and clubs for children. Short tennis is widely available through tennis clubs and recreation centres.

A badminton set is cheap and great fun in even quite a small garden.

There is a children's version of squash which can be played with shortened rackets and a bouncier ball.

FINE MOTOR SKILLS

THE THEORY

EARLY DEVELOPMENT

Fine motor skills are the delicate and precise movements of the hands and fingers. Development starts when a baby learns to bat at objects with his hand and then to grasp them using his whole hand. Later, babies learn to release the objects, eventually enabling them to place and post them where they wish.

HAND FUNCTION DEVELOPMENT

Pincer grasp

Children initially use a raking movement to pick things up by moving their thumb and hand together. This is refined over time until they can use their thumb and forefinger together in a precise and small pincer movement. This enables them to place bricks or to pick up tiny objects such as stickers, raisins or pins.

Using two hands together

Children have to use their two hands together (bi-manual manipulation) for a variety of tasks; for example, holding a cup with one hand and pouring with another, or moving a piece of paper to cut out a shape. For writing it is also important that they can hold the paper in place with one hand while writing with the other.

Wrist rotation and extension

Children learn to twist and turn knobs and handles. They need to gain strength to twist stiff handles and precision to twist small ones. They also need to be able to move their wrists up and down (extend and flex) to draw on a blackboard, for example, move their hands from side to side to twist a knob and rotate the hand, turning the palm up and down to toss a coin.

Finger coordination

Children learn to point and poke with their index fingers. However, they have to develop strength in all their fingers and subsequently the ability to move them separately so that they can, for example, press buttons, play the recorder or the piano or type on a keyboard.

In-hand manipulation

Children develop the ability to hold small objects in the palm of the hand and to manipulate them into the right position using their fingers. Examples of this are picking up a pen and turning it round in the hand to get it in the right position for writing, or manoeuv ring coins from within the hand for a ticket machine.

Hand strength

Children develop their hand strength which allows them to cut stiffer paper, use knives and separate snap-together toys such as Lego. This is also important for developing the right pressure for writing.

Hand–eye coordination

Children need to be able to use their hands and vision together to maintain eye contact with what they are doing so that they can interpret what they see and respond physically to it with increasingly precise movements.

Left- or right-handed?

Hand–eye coordination

To learn to write children have to decide which is their dominant hand. It is usually fairly obvious whether they are left-handed or right-handed.

Sensory skills that influence fine motor skills

There are many sensory skills which have a strong influence on fine motor skills. These include sensation, spatial awareness, perception and body awareness, which are covered in Chapter 6, Sensory Development.

FUNCTIONAL SKILLS

Daily living skills, including cooking and writing, require a combination of the above skills such as hand strength, hand–eye coordination, in-hand manipulation, pincer grasp and spatial awareness. Children need to practise their skills so that they can refine them and increase their strength and accuracy. This enables them to use smaller tools and materials. There are two aspects to functional skills – daily living skills, for taking care of ourselves, and using different tools, for drawing, writing and making things.

Daily living skills
Feeding

Initially, children drink from a lidded cup, then from an open cup without spilling the contents. They learn to finger-feed and then to feed themselves with a loaded spoon. They then develop the ability to scoop food for themselves. They move on to stab food with a fork and later to use a spoon and fork together before finally being able to use a knife and fork.

Dressing and undressing

Undressing is easier for children than dressing. Young children pull off hats and socks and shrug off coats and cardigans. Later they can pull off pants and trousers and finally jumpers and shirts.

Early on, children help when they are being dressed by putting their arms in sleeves and legs in trousers. They start learning to dress by themselves by putting on hats, then, with practice, they become able to put on cardigans and shirts followed by pants, trousers and skirts. Socks and shoes are the most difficult.

A tricky aspect of dressing is doing up and undoing fastenings. Children have to learn to fasten toggles, buttons, buckles and zips and then tie laces.

Washing and toileting

Children learn to wash and dry their hands and faces, wash themselves in the bath and dry themselves afterwards, clean their teeth and wash their hair. They also learn toileting skills which are covered in Chapter 9, Additional Practical Advice.

Tool use
Using scissors

This requires a pincer action. Children first make a few snips with scissors to cut through narrow strips but gradually are able to sustain cutting across a whole piece of paper, then to cut between wide tram lines and then to keep more closely to a straight line. With practice they can cut accurately along curved lines and round shapes, turning the paper as they do.

Threading and sewing

Children learn to sew by practising their threading, lacing and sewing skills over many years. They first learn to thread large beads using a stick, then using a lace with a stiff end, then using smaller beads and a thinner lace. Then they start to sew using a sewing card or canvas and finally are able to manage conventional sewing with a fine needle and thread and ordinary fabric.

Pen control

Children first grasp a pen with their whole fist ('palmar grip'), then they grip the pen higher up before changing their grip to use only a few fingers and hold the pen further down. Finally a tripod grip is established using the thumb and two fingers.

Initially, children write using a 'static tripod' grip with the whole arm moving as the child writes. The 'dynamic tripod' grip is when the wrist is stabilised, i.e. the wrist itself does not move and the movement is all in the hand. But it takes many years of practice before children can write with the tiny, almost imperceptible finger movements of an adult when writing.

GAMES AND ACTIVITIES

GENERAL GUIDELINES
Positioning

For all fine motor skills the position of the child is crucial. If he is badly positioned he will not be able to do many of the things described below. Always consider his position. For advice on seating see Chapter 2, What Everyone Needs to Know. If your child has physical disabilities it might be helpful to consult his occupational therapist for advice.

Body stability

Body stability requires a combination of strength and balance to enable your child to keep one part of his body still while another part moves. When throwing a ball he needs to keep his legs and lower body still and just move his shoulder and arm. When taking a photo he needs to keep his whole body and the camera perfectly still and just move his finger to press the button. When getting dressed he needs to keep still and balanced while putting one leg into his trousers.

Shoulder strength and stability to aid hand control

Children need to have strength in their shoulders to keep them stable and still in order to be able to use their hands for fine and intricate movements. Without shoulder strength their hands would be wobbly and their movements uncontrolled. Try the following ideas to improve your child's shoulder strength:

- Doing any kind of crawling activity, such as through tunnels, into dens and on play equipment.
- Playing on monkey bars at the park.
- Playing wheelbarrows – where you or another child holds him by the legs as he walks on his hands.
- Performing handstands and cartwheels.
- Pushing and pulling pushchairs, prams, trolleys, wheelbarrows, wagons and carts.
- Transporting objects of different size.
- Lifting trays.
- Placing objects such as toys or crockery on shelves or in cupboards.
- Doing household chores, including tidying things away and laying and clearing the table.

- Raking and digging in the garden.
- Doing pouring activities using jugs, bottles or a watering can.

Exercises

- Get your child to kneel on all fours, stretch out his left leg and right arm and balance. Get him to repeat the exercise using his opposite arm and leg.

- Get your child to do push ups. Get him to lie face down on the floor with his hands under his shoulders and then to push his head and upper body up.

HAND FUNCTION DEVELOPMENT

Pincer grasp

Having a good pincer grasp is really important. Any games and activities which encourage your child to use the pincer grasp are helpful. Some examples are:

- jigsaw puzzles
- construction toys such as Duplo, Lego, K'Nex, Meccano and train sets
- building towers with wooden blocks, beakers, buttons or coins
- posting games
- Fuzzy Felt
- stickers – make pictures, cards or invitations or put them in sticker books
- making collages using small objects such as pasta, beads or sequins
- marble runs. You can also run marbles or small cars down slopes such as cardboard tubes, pieces of wood or the back of a tray
- board games using spinners rather than dice. Travel versions of board games are especially good because they have smaller pieces
- spinning tops

- board games with small counters which have to be moved; for example, Snakes and Ladders, Ludo and Dominoes
- card games such as Pelmanism, Pairs, Snap, Beggar My Neighbour and Lotto
- threading activities
- picking up small bits of food such as peas, raisins, crisps and chocolate buttons
- decorating cakes and small buns – ice them and then give the children sweets such as hundreds and thousands and Smarties to place on the cakes
- Cat's Cradle
- peg boards – making pictures or patterns with pegs
- pegging out washing
- putting clothes pegs around the edge of a tin
- putting clothing pegs on his own clothes to make himself look like a hedgehog
- hammer nails in a board at intervals and then get your child to stretch coloured rubber bands over the nails to make patterns.

Using two hands together

Though your child will probably have a preference for using one hand over the other, encourage him to do activities which use both his hands. Examples are:

- tearing paper to make a collage
- threading activities – these require both hands
- pull-apart and push-together toys, such as Duplo, Sticklebricks and Lego
- playing musical instruments, such as cymbals, drums and tambourines
- cooking activities in which your child has to hold a bowl and stir or pour
- origami

- cutting out shapes with scissors
- playing cards – Snap, Old Maid, Happy Families
- pouring something from one container to another, and other similar water and sand games
- using a spoon and fork or knife and fork to eat
- folding activities such as putting clothes away or folding pyjamas
- using a dustpan and brush.

Note that many of the above are covered in the Craft ideas and Cooking sections below.

If your child has a weak side make sure he is in a stable position when doing activities. Encourage him to use his weak hand to assist; for example, holding a bowl or the paper.

Wrist rotation and extension

Try the following ideas (but bear in mind the size of the objects and how stiff they are – some can be very difficult):

- winding up toys like cars, trains and jack in the boxes
- putting on and taking off tops and lids from jars, bottles and containers
- turning door handles, control knobs on children's tape recorders and on some pop-up toys
- spinning tops, hoops and balls
- opening tin cans
- turning keys
- turning over cards in memory games such as Pelmanism
- writing on a blackboard or wall – this extends the wrist
- spreading jam, soft butter or margarine on bread.

Finger coordination

It is important to develop a strong index finger, particularly for writing, and to be able to use all the fingers individually. Get your child to do the following:

- Sing action songs involving finger movements such as Incy Wincy Spider, Here is the Church and Here is the Steeple, Tommy thumb, Two Little Dicky Birds Sitting on a Wall and One Finger one Thumb Keep Moving.

- Follow mazes with his index finger.

- Do finger painting or draw patterns in shaving foam, misted-up windows or sand with his index finger.

- Play with cornflour mixed with water and encourage him to use his index finger to make patterns.

- Press buttons, such as light switches, and dial telephone numbers.

- Use finger puppets.

- Play Simon Says but just using finger actions, for example: 'Simon Says point this finger' or 'Simon Says make this shape'.

- Play with play dough, pastry or other modelling material (see recipes later in this chapter).

- Count using his fingers in turn.

- Sing counting songs such as 'One, two, three, four, five, once I caught a fish alive'.

- Work on computer keyboards.

- Play musical instruments like the recorder, keyboards and piano.

In-hand manipulation

- Give your child counters, money or marbles and ask him to give you one, say the red one or the 10p piece. This means that he has to manipulate them in his hand to get one in the right place to give to you. Start with just one item and gradually increase the number as he gets better.

Play with play dough

- Get him to pick up a pencil and turn it over in his hand.
- Play card games which require him to hold his cards in his hand.
- Give him a handful of money to hold in his hand and encourage him to sort out the right change to put money into car-park ticket machines, train ticket machines or vending machines.

Hand strength

Hand strength increases gradually with practice as children tackle harder and stiffer materials. You could try the following ideas with your child:

- Use pegs to hang out the washing or pinch on a tin.
- Scrunch paper to make balls for kicking or throwing or to make collages.
- Tear paper; the more sheets of paper you have, the more difficult it is, so build them up gradually.
- Play with construction toys like Lego or Sticklebricks which require some strength to separate.

- Play with play dough or other modelling materials or do cooking activities involving rolling, pinching and squeezing.

- Play Tug-of-war with a tube, stick or rope.

- Play with squeezy toys – use washing-up liquid bottles to blow bubbles in water.

- Get your child to use hole punchers – to punch holes in paper maybe for lacing – or buy a shaped puncher to make designs.

Left- or right-handed?

Usually your child's preference for the left or right hand is obvious because he naturally uses one hand to pick up a pencil or a spoon or to place a brick. If most of the time he uses one hand, even though sometimes he may use the other, you are safe to assume it is the dominant hand. It is best to let your child determine his own dominance. If you have significant concerns contact your occupational therapist for advice.

Hand–eye coordination

All the activities listed in this chapter will help your child's hand–eye coordination. Also see the games listed above in Gross Motor Skills.

FUNCTIONAL SKILLS
Daily living skills
Feeding

It is important that your child is able to feed himself as well as possible, for the sake of his independence and also because it is important if he is to become socially acceptable. Remember that meal-times are a particularly difficult time to practise new skills because children are often so hungry they will more interested in eating than anything else. Also, as a parent, you can feel under pressure because you may have spent a long time cooking the food or because of others' expectations, which can make you more anxious and stressed.

- Try to practise the skills away from meal-times when he is not hungry and the pressure is off you.

- Make sure he is in a good sitting position.

- Start with foods which stay on the spoon more easily so he has a good chance of success.

- Experiment with different cups, bowls, angled spoons and forks. Try wide-handled, indented cutlery such as Caring Cutlery, which is available from high-street chemists. There are lots of different types of cutlery on the market and your occupational therapist can advise on more specialist equipment which is available from the companies listed in Chapter 12, Resources. Ultimately, however, you may expect him to eat using conventional crockery and cutlery.

- Make sure the plate or bowl is stable and does not keep moving around. You could try Dycem, a non-slip mat which will keep everything in one place. It is available through specialist suppliers, or from some camping shops and chandlers because it is used to stop things slipping in caravans and on boats.

- Do not try to do too much at once but tackle it slowly, aiming to improve the first half-dozen mouthfuls of each meal or just one course of one meal. When this is successful you can try to extend it to the whole meal. Alternatively, you may need to satisfy his hunger a little first before asking him to eat nicely.

Using a spoon

- Get your child to practise scooping sand in the sand pit.

- Try different cooking activities such as scooping cake mix into a cake tin.

- Get him to help in the garden filling pots with soil or compost and digging in the ground.

- Allow him to play with rice, beans or pulses, scooping them from one container to another.

Using a spoon and fork

Once your child can use a spoon and a fork individually encourage him to use them both together.

Spreading with a knife

- Make it easy to begin with by using soft spreads like margarine and jam.
- Practise by spreading glue with a spatula.

Using a knife and fork

- Start by getting your child to hold the item to be cut with his hand and cutting with the other then, when he is confident, encourage him to use a fork rather than his hand to keep it still.
- Practise with play dough or clay.
- Use cooking activities, such as making fruit salads or chopping vegetables or slicing biscuit dough.
- Begin with soft food such as eggs and vegetables. It requires considerable strength to cut tough foods like meat.
- Try using indented cutlery, which has a groove for the forefingers. This is available widely through high-street chemists which stock equipment for the disabled.

Keeping clean

Some children with special needs may not be particularly motivated by a need for social acceptance, so you may have to help your child to keep his face and clothes clean. Giving him gentle prompts encourage him to:

- not overload his spoon
- slow down as he eats
- use a napkin
- lick around his mouth to see if he feels clean or not, so that he can recognise the feeling without having to be prompted.

Get him to check his face in a mirror after each meal.

You may also have to use rewards like stickers, star charts or a tiny treat at the end of the meal to encourage him.

Dressing and undressing

Think of your child's position when dressing. If he is hopping around on one leg trying to get his trousers on, it is not surprising he is having problems. Get him to sit down on the floor, on the edge of the bed or on a small chair. He will find it easier to concentrate on the process itself and will not have to worry about supporting himself or keeping his balance.

Problems with dressing and undressing are often linked to a physical difficulty which is highly specific and requires an approach unique to each child. In such a case consult your occupational therapist for advice. If, on the other hand, your child has problems because of poor fine motor skills, the following ideas may help:

- Break all skills into achievable parts and build the whole skill up slowly.

- Use forward and backward chaining as described in Chapter 2, What Everyone Needs to Know.

- Start with undressing as it is easier than dressing.

- Play dressing-up with big clothes in a fun way.

- If your child has a problem with sequencing and so finds it difficult to get the right order for putting on his clothes, draw a series of pictures for him to follow, lay out his clothes from left to right and get him to start at the left side.

- Practise at times when there is no pressure. Often in the morning everyone is in a rush to get to school and in the evening everyone is tired and irritable.

- If independence is important make dressing as easy as possible for your child. Buy pull-on trousers and skirts, trousers with slides rather than buttons at the waist, jumpers with wide openings over the head, T-shirts or polo shirts rather than buttoned shirts and shoes with Velcro fastenings or curly laces rather than conventional laces. If your child has a school shirt with buttons which he has to wear but cannot manage, try sewing buttons on the outside to look as if they are done up but sew Velcro on the inside as the actual fastening.

Sequence of getting dressed

- Make sure he is able to be just as independent at school. Do not do up the buttons on his polo shirt if he cannot then undo them to change for PE lessons.
- To help your child tell the front from the back of his clothes choose clothes with a patterned front, and always sew his label in the back or embroider a dot or a strip in the back of his clothes.
- To help him tell the left from the right shoe:
    - point out that the Velcro is on the outside
    - write 'left' and 'right' in the shoes if this is meaningful
    - talk about how the shoes feel
    - draw a dot or write the child's name on the inner side of each shoe so they meet if on correctly
    - draw the shoe outlines in the correct position on a piece of card, so your child can put them in the right place before putting them on.

Fastenings

Attach a variety of fastenings, such as zips and buttons, onto boards which are solid and do not move around. Then get your child to practise on these fastenings. There are also commercial dolls available which have different fastenings like buckles, toggles, zips and Velcro.

Buttons

- Practise posting games using smaller and smaller holes, such as putting money in slots of ticket machines or in piggy banks.
- Use forward and backward chaining to break down the skill.
- Sew buttons on with shearing elastic so that they have more give.

Zips

- Use backward chaining to teach your child how to use a zip.
- Put a ribbon or a fob, rather like a key ring, through the zip end so your child has something chunky to hold onto which will make it easier.

Shoe laces

Teach your child to tie shoe laces in two stages: the knot and the bow. First, practise the knot element with a variety of materials such as the handles of plastic bags, string on parcels or a dressing-gown belt. When he feels confident get him to practise on his shoe but have him sitting at a table, with his shoe on the table, where his position will be more comfortable.

There are different ways to tie laces so decide on one method and stick to it. Don't confuse your child with different approaches.

- Use wide laces.
- Practise using two laces of different colours which are tied together to form one long lace, so each end is a different colour to make it clearer.
- Try the hand-over-hand method, when you guide your child's hand by holding it with your own.
- Talk your child through what to do. Sit directly behind him otherwise you may both get terribly confused.

Tool use
Pouring

- During water play in the bath or paddling pool give your child lots of jugs, pots, beakers and funnels for pouring. Do the same with dry sand in the sand pit or bucket, or on a plastic sheet.

- Ask him to water indoor and outdoor plant pots with a small and not-too-full watering can or jug.

- Encourage him to help you cook and ask him to pour ingredients from one bowl to another.

Using scissors

There is a range of different types of scissors available which might help when you introduce your child to scissors. For example, there are scissors which adults use with a child, loop scissors which have a spring action and left- and right-handed scissors. You may be able to borrow these from your occupational therapist before buying them from a specialist supplier such as Peta (UK) Ltd (see Chapter 12, Resources, for contact details).

Think about the weight of the paper you give. It should be neither so flimsy that it is difficult to control nor so thick that it requires considerable strength to cut.

- Start with thin strips of paper so your child needs to make only one snip to cut the piece in two. Gradually increase the width so that he needs to make several snips to cut the paper in half.

- Draw thick lines for him to cut along – initially straight ones, then some with curves and bends.

- Get him to cut out pictures from magazines or from old birthday cards to make a picture or a collage.

- Try getting him to cut doilies and snowflakes by folding up a piece of paper into a square and snipping shapes from the edges. Get your child to take small snips out of the folded edges. Open up the paper to reveal a lacy pattern and stick it up on the window.

- Make birthday or Christmas cards or present tags together by cutting out pictures from old cards and sticking them on a new piece of stiff card.

- Get him to cut coloured paper into small pieces and make a mosaic picture.

- Try making folded people. Fold up a piece of paper like a concertina, draw the outline of a person holding his hands out at the edge of the paper and ask your child to cut round the figure carefully. He should open it up to reveal a long line of people.

Threading

Start threading practice with a stiff wire and chunky beads or cotton reels with a large hole. Gradually make it more difficult by using a lace with a stiff end, smaller beads and so on. Bags of beads for threading are available from toy shops to make necklaces, bracelets, snakes and worms. You can also paint wide pasta such as macaroni and, once it is dry, thread it to make jewellery.

Sewing

Make a spider's web. Draw the shape of a spider's web on thick card, punch holes at the corners and then get your child to sew the shape using wool with sellotape wrapped around one end to make it stiff.

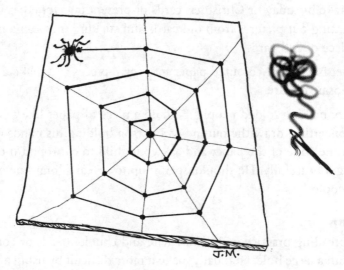

Sewing a spider's web

Mount a favourite picture on card and punch holes round the edge for
him to sew and decorate.

From a needlework or craft supplier you can buy a small piece of
canvas or Binca which you can cut into even smaller squares. Get some
large tapestry needles with blunt ends and a selection of knitting wool.
Thread and knot the wool so the wool will not come off the needle.
Encourage your child to make random stitches showing which side of
the canvas the needle has to come through. He could then progress to
large running stitches, smaller ones and cross-stitches. You can supply
different colours to make different patterns. Once your child has had
enough, cut the thread and re-use the canvas another time.

Pen control

Mark making

Encourage your child to make marks using any kind of media that
appeals, such as:

- chalking on boards or on the patio
- finger painting
- making patterns in sand – wet or dry, on misted-up windows
- making patterns in shaving foam

- writing on magnetic boards which you can then clear
- using window pens.

Give him crayons, pencils and pens which are easy to hold. Chunky pens are better than thin ones for small hands and triangular shapes are particularly good. Your child might find a triangular pencil grip helpful.

Use pens which make marks easily and avoid those pens which have to be held at a certain angle to work. Soft pencils, crayons, chalks and felt-tips are the best.

It is good to get your child to work on an easel or on a piece of paper pinned to the wall because it makes him open up his wrist in a good writing position. If he is working on a flat surface he may keep his wrist very bent which is not good.

All activities which use the pincer grip are good for developing the tripod grip for holding a pen; such as threading, pegs, Lego and puzzles. See the section Pincer grasp above for further ideas.

When writing or drawing on paper, make sure the paper is at the correct angle. It should be at an angle to the table edge and away from the body to give your child room to move his elbow. This is especially important if he is left-handed.

Also, the paper should be anchored so that it does not move around as your child tries to write. Often paper slides on slippery desks. Encourage your child to hold it still with one hand. You could stick Blutack on the corners of the paper to anchor it to the table. Alternatively, use Dycem, which is a non-slip mat for holding things in position. See Chapter 12, Resources, for stockists or try camping shops or chandlers. It is available in coloured or clear form. The clear form is less obvious, which is good for the self-conscious child but, because it is less visible, it is more difficult for him to see and manipulate. Thin Dycem is good for anchoring paper for writing, while the thick version holds heavier items such as plates and cups at meal-times or bowls and items for cooking and craft activities.

Drawing development

Encourage your child to make any kinds of mark – drawing shapes, lines or whatever. He will not start to write until he can control his mark-making, copy simple shapes and draw simple pictures.

Practise simple forms such as lines, crosses and circles by drawing shapes and encouraging him to copy them.

Encourage him to draw pictures of people, houses, trains and cars.

Pre-writing games

Try games which require your child to follow patterns to give him the idea of copying shapes. For example:

- playing with beads threaded on wires
- playing with road-map floor mats and train sets in which your child traces journeys by pushing a car or train around
- doing mazes
- using stencils
- tracing.

Increasing control

Games which make children start and stop in the right place are good for developing control. These include:

- joining up two pictures on a page. For example, draw two cars and get your child to draw a line to connect them, or do the same with drawings of a dog and his dinner
- drawing lines within two parallel lines
- drawing circles
- dot-to-dot pictures – use a book or make you own
- doing mazes with a pen
- tracing pictures
- using stencils to draw interesting shapes.

Colouring

Colouring is also good for developing pen control because your child has to learn to start and stop in the right place if he is to keep his colouring within the lines of the picture.

- Start with simple, appealing pictures which are not too big, and encourage him to keep his colouring within the lines.

Make the lines thick so it is easier for him to keep within the lines.

- Have reasonable pictures which are not too fiddly or too big. Reduce the size and increase the complexity of the pictures as he gets better.

- You could try raising the edge of the picture by gluing string around it so that he cannot go over the edge. This is particularly useful if your child has a visual impairment.

CRAFT IDEAS

All craft activities are fun for children because they allow them to be creative and experimental with different materials, exploring shape, form and texture.

Give your child open-ended opportunities to be truly creative not just to reproduce someone else's ideas. Allow him to explore different materials and activities where there is no right or wrong way of doing things. Remember, the pleasure is usually more in the process itself than in the final product. Although with some activities you may wish to support him so that he produces something reasonable, such as a card to send to Granny for her birthday, at other times let him do his own thing.

Think of the practical issues. If you are doing very messy artwork cover your table top with newspaper and make sure he wears an apron. Keep a route clear to a sink for him to wash his hands.

If he has a very short attention span it may feel as if he has been creative for five minutes and left you with fifty minutes of clearing-up to do. Make sure you are ready for this and give yourself plenty of time to clear up all the mess!

Some children and adults love messy play and are happy to get stuck in, handling paint and glue; whereas other children are more uncomfortable with it or do not like the sensations. Start where your child is comfortable and very gradually encourage him to get more actively involved.

Below are some general ideas for craft activities. There are some lovely books with all sorts of wonderful ideas available from shops and libraries; for example, *Children's Arts and Crafts* by N. Bartlett, published by Australian Women's Weekly. Dorling Kindersley produce a wide range of children's activity books. Two useful series are the *Fun Figures, Fun Movers* series by M. Grater, published by Macdonald, and the Usborne playtime series including *I Can Draw* and *I Can Cut and Stick.*

Drawing and painting activities

Give your child opportunities to practise with different media such as chalks, finger paint, felt-tips, blow paint and poster paint, using different brushes and papers. Let him choose what he wants.

Encourage him to draw different things, perhaps objects, people and scenes in the house or out and about. Get him to draw something from his imagination like an alien, or something from memory such as a trip to the zoo or on a boat.

It is sometimes fun to do a communal picture, particularly if he is not so keen on drawing. Get a very large piece of paper, decide on your theme (space, beach, underwater, street scene, zoo, farm, etc.) and let everyone add their own ideas. Use a combination of paint, stencils, pens and collage.

We used stencils to draw and colour pictures of cars and lorries, stuck them to a long piece of computer paper and added people, signposts and traffic lights to make a huge traffic jam which we stuck up around the room. We also made a sea scene with dolphins and jelly fish, boats and divers and painted pictures of stars, planets and rockets on black paper for a space scene.

Other ideas

- *Finger painting* – easy, tactile and fun.
- *Blob pictures* – put blobs of paint on a large piece of paper. Get your child to roll marbles or run toy cars through the paint leaving tracks in different colours.
- *Mirror pictures* – fold a piece of paper in half and then open it up again. Get your child to paint one side with generous blobs and strokes of paint. Close the paper up and then open it out

to make a mirror painting. You could cut the paper into an interesting shape first such as a butterfly.

- *Magic painting* – paint water on 'magic paper' and the colour will appear.

- *String pictures* – put paint in a pot, and attach a peg to a length of string (about 10 inches or 30 cm long). Get him to hold the peg, dangle the string in the pot to cover it with paint and then use it to make patterns on the paper.

- *Bubble painting* – place a small amount of washing-up liquid and water in an old yoghurt pot, then add some paint. Place the pot on an old tray. Using a straw, get your child to blow into the paint mixture until the bubbles are coming over the top of the pot. Place a piece of paper gently over the top of the pot and the pattern of bubbles will transfer to the paper. You can place a number of pots with different colours of paint together for a variety of colours.

- *Shaving foam pictures* – mix shaving foam with some paint on a tray. Encourage your child to make patterns or shapes in the foam. You can take a print by pressing a piece of blank paper on top.

- *Marbling* – add special marbling inks to a tray of water, swirl them into patterns and then lay a piece of paper gently on top. When you remove it, you will find the colours have transferred.

- *Wax pictures* – cover a piece of paper with wax crayons of different colours and then scratch a picture into the wax.

- *Stencils and tracing* – are good for practising controlled movements.

Print making

Use sponge shapes, leaves or any found objects to make prints. Make potato prints by cutting shapes out of potatoes, foam or rubber.

Stamping

You can buy a range of stamps from toy and art shops to make pictures or decorate cards.

Sticking

Glitter

Glitter is very appealing to children. Use glitter

- on black paper to make fireworks pictures
- to decorate Christmas cards or for decorations
- to make crowns
- to decorate bookmarks.

Collage

You can use all kinds of materials to make collages:

- paper – tissue, sweet wrappers, pictures from magazines, card, glitter
- fabric – ribbons, felt, scraps of material (furry, silky, shiny), beads and sequins
- dried food – rice, beans, pulses, pasta, oats, crushed eggshells, tea, hundreds and thousands (pulses and pasta look good on black paper)
- found objects – leaves, flowers, twigs, sand and small stones.

Use the materials mentioned above for different collages. You could:

- make an abstract design or geometric pattern
- make a picture by filling in an outline of an object (animal, house, train) or create a scene (townscape, beach scene, space)
- make a montage with pictures ripped or cut from magazines
- make a mosaic by ripping up or cutting little bits of scrap paper. Draw an outline on a piece of paper of something like a car, a train or a dinosaur and then get your child to glue and stick the bits of paper to fill in the picture
- make patterns and pictures by sticking string on paper.

Origami

Try simple origami (Japanese paper-folding) to make interesting shapes and objects.

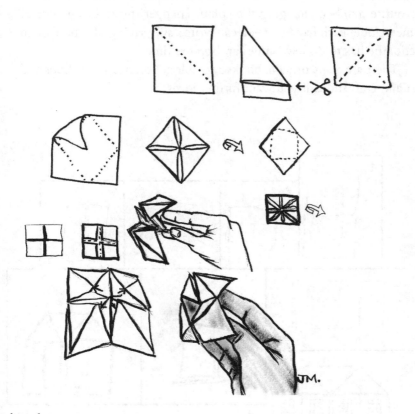

Colour changer

Colour changer or fortune teller

- Start with a square of paper about 8 inches or 21 cm cut from ordinary A4 paper.

- Crease the paper in half diagonally and in half again, open it up and you should see the centre of the square marked.

- Fold the corners into the centre.

- Turn it over and fold the corners into the centre again.

- Turn it over and put your fingers under the flaps.

- You can get your child to colour in the centre in such a way as to make it change colour when he moves it.

Alternatively, he could make a fortune teller by colouring some segments and writing numbers on others. He can then ask a friend his favourite number, changing the colour changer the right number of times. Under each flap he or you can write a silly saying like 'boo' or an action he has to do like 'smile' or 'hop ten times'.

There are many origami books available at libraries, bookshops and art and craft shops if you want further ideas.

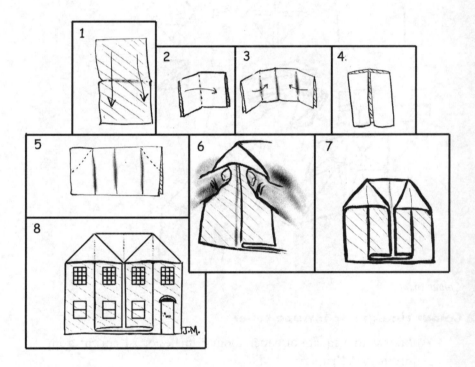

Making a paper house

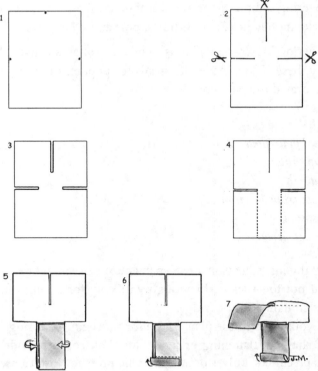
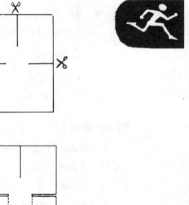

Making a helicopter

Modelling

Junk models

Get your child to make three-dimensional models from old boxes, cartons, loo rolls etc. He could cover them with papier mâché and then paint them. The TV programme and books *Art Attack*, published by Dorling Kindersley, have many inspiring ideas.

Papier mâché

To make papier mâché mix a paste from a combination of flour and water or wallpaper paste and water until quite thick. Rip up bits of newspaper, then get your child to glue and stick the paper on to the model. You can use papier mâché for all sorts of craft activities such as:

- covering models made from junk so that they can be painted

- covering old plastic bottles, cardboard tubes and cartons to make money boxes, desk-tidies, pots and containers

- covering blown-up balloons to make a spherical shape. When dry these can be made into heads for puppets or cut in half and decorated to make bowls.

Play dough

> 2 cups plain flour
> 2 cups water
> 1 cup salt
> 4 tbsps cream of tartar
> 4 tbsps oil
> food colouring

Place all the ingredients in a saucepan and stir over a gentle heat until firm and not too sticky. This dough will keep for a long time in an air-tight container in the fridge.

Get your child to use play dough for squeezing, pressing, rolling, cutting, shaping, flattening or modelling. You could provide rolling pins, shape cutters, knives or an old garlic press for him to use.

Clay

Clay needs to be kept in an air-tight container otherwise it dries out very easily. You can get air-hardening clay or clay that has to be baked in the oven. Once dry it can be painted.

Plasticene

This is good for older children as it has a firmer texture and is therefore harder to manipulate. It is clean to use but can easily become hard so it is best stored in a warm place.

Salt dough

> 2 cups plain flour
> 1 cup salt
> 1 tbsp oil
> ½ cup water
> food colouring

Mix all the ingredients together. If the dough is too wet add some more flour. Knead the dough for four or five minutes.

Get your child to make models and then leave them to harden in a warm dry place. Once dry, he can paint or varnish the models.

Cornflour – gloop

Mix up cornflour with water in a bowl. This has an amazing quality. It looks hard but feels soft and can be stretched into strings and different shapes. Let your child play with it on a tray.

Woodwork

If you have small tools encourage your child to do simple carpentry and make models of swords and bits of 'furniture' or bird tables out of off-cuts.

Fabric crafts

Use an old sock to make a glove puppet with its eyes, mouth, ears and so on made from different bits and bobs (buttons, felt and fabric scraps, ribbons and braid). You can also stuff old socks to make worms or snakes.

Make pompoms by wrapping wool round cardboard circular cut-outs. You need two cardboard circles with a smallish circle cut out of the centre of each. Put the two cut-outs together and get your child to wind the wool round. Keep the cut-outs small and the wool thick otherwise they take a long time and he might lose interest. Use the pompoms as tassels on hats, to make chickens with a head and body and pipe cleaner legs or to throw as soft balls.

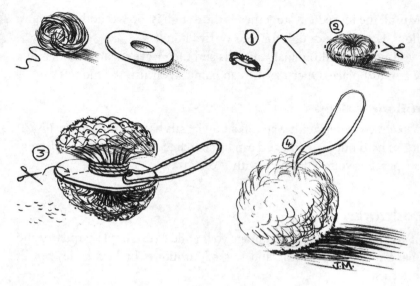

Making a pompom

COOKING

Cooking is a good way for children to practise fine motor skills by doing a little chopping, stirring, spooning, whisking and pouring. It is also great for children in many other ways. Most important, it is a vital life skill which will make them more independent as they get older. It is a practical way to see maths and science in action, good for practising social skills of turn-taking and sharing and, I hope, a positive sensory experience as the end product tastes great.

The following recipes are only suggestions, you probably have your own favourite recipes. More important, your child may have things he likes to eat and therefore cook.

He can be as involved as he wants to be. He may just enjoy a bit of stirring and pouring with lots of licking at the end. On the other hand, you might be able to get him to anticipate what you need, read the recipe himself and ultimately do the whole thing with a minimum of support.

Although my children enjoy cooking I find it can be rather stressful. I have a small kitchen. With three children standing on chairs at the worktop, I find I can't get into the cupboards or drawers or reach anything and it all gets a bit hairy. I need to be well organised. Sometimes I find it easier to use the dining table instead – particularly for icing buns or birthday cakes or for kneading bread. It can be easier to give everyone their own bowl, utensils and ingredients and let them get on with it by themselves. Other times we use teamwork – one does the weighing, the next does the pouring, the next the stirring and so on.

Some children find it very frustrating to wait for things to set, rise or cook so it is best to make things which can be eaten immediately such as fruit salad, sandwiches, iced buns and Rice Krispie cakes.

The following children's cookery books are full of recipes for food which children like to eat. The pictures are appealing and the recipes are explained in detail for children and their supporting parents:

Contini, M. and Irvine, P. (1999) *Easy Peasy*. London: Ebury Press.
Wilkes, A. (1994) *The Children's Step by Step Cook Book*. London: Dorling Kindersley Children's Books.
Gow, E-L. (2001) *Kids Cook Book*. London: Ebury Press.

Recipes
Victoria sandwich cake

110g/4oz butter
110g/4oz sugar
2 eggs
110g/4oz self-raising flour, sifted

Cream the butter and sugar together with an electric whisk or wooden spoon until pale and fluffy. Beat the eggs together and then gradually beat into the butter and sugar.

Fold in the flour with a metal spoon. Divide the mixture between two 7 inch/18 cm cake tins which have been greased and lined. Cook for 25–30 minutes on 170°C/325°F/gas mark 3. When cool, sandwich the cakes together with jam and sprinkle the top with icing sugar.

Fairy cakes

Use the above recipe but put a spoonful of mixture in bun cases placed in patty tins.

Glacé icing

100g/4oz icing sugar
food colouring (optional)

Sift the icing sugar into a bowl and add enough water to make the icing thick enough to coat the back of a spoon. Add colouring if you wish.

You can ice small fairy cakes or just plain biscuits. Give your child a bowl of icing with a spoon and knife and any decorations such as sprinkles, Smarties, raisins or sweets that you have, to make patterns or faces.

Scones

240g/8oz self-raising flour
60g/2oz butter or margarine
1 egg
60g/2oz currants
30g/1oz sugar
a little milk

Rub the flour and butter together with your fingertips until it looks like breadcrumbs. Add the sugar, currants and egg and mix together. Add as much milk as necessary for the mixture to come together into a dough. Roll the pastry out so that it is about 2 cm or 1 inch high. Cut into circles using pastry cutters or an upturned mug or glass and place on a greased baking tray. Brush the tops with a little milk. Cook for 10–15 minutes on 190°C/375°F/gas mark 5 until golden brown. Serve with butter or jam and cream.

Refrigerator biscuits

50g/2oz sugar
100g/4oz butter or margarine
150g/6oz self-raising flour
1 egg

Mix all the ingredients together to a sticky dough. Refrigerate for an hour until firm. Then roll out the dough until 1 cm or ½ inch thick and cut out biscuits using pastry cutters. Place on a greased baking sheet. Cook for 15 minutes at 190°C/375°F/gas mark 5.

You can add 1 tbsp of cocoa powder, the grated peel of one orange or 1 tbsp of coffee essence to the basic ingredients.

Fruit salad

Get your child to chop up a selection of fruit that he likes such as apples, grapes, bananas, oranges and kiwi and to mix them in a bowl. Pour on some apple juice to sweeten it.

Pastry

> *100g/4oz plain flour*
> *50g/2oz fat – butter, margarine or lard (or a combination)*

Place the flour in a large bowl and rub the fat in with your fingertips until it resembles breadcrumbs. Add enough water to make the pastry come together into a dough. If you have time, leave it to rest in the fridge for 20 minutes, and then roll it out on a floured surface.

Get your child to roll out the pastry and makes shapes with pastry cutters. Alternatively use it to make jam tartlets. Roll out the pastry, cut out circles and then line patty tins. Place a spoonful of jam or lemon curd in each pastry case. Cook for 15–20 minuites at 200°C/400°F/gas mark 6.

To make mince pies, line the patty tins as above, put a spoonful of mincemeat in each one and top with a circle of pastry. Press the edges together, prick with a fork and brush with milk. Cook for 15–20 minutes at 200°C/400°F/gas mark 6.

Bread

700g / 1½ 1b plain or strong flour
salt to taste
10g / ½oz lard or butter
1 tsp sugar
425ml / ¾pt warm water
2 tsps dried yeast

Dissolve the sugar in the water and sprinkle the yeast on top. Leave until it is frothy (about ten minutes). Rub the lard into the flour and salt. Mix in the yeast liquid.

Work to a firm dough and then turn out onto a floured surface and knead for ten minutes. Cover and leave in a warm place to rise until it doubles in size (one hour in a warm place). Turn the dough out and flatten to knock out the air bubbles. Knead till firm. Grease two 1 lb loaf tins. Divide the dough in half. Stretch each piece out to the width of the loaf tin and then fold in three. Place the seam underneath and place in tins. Cover and leave to rise until the dough comes to the top of the tin. Place in the oven at 230°C/450°F/gas mark 8 for 30–40 minutes. Turn out and cool on a wire rack.

Coleslaw

Use a combination of:
white cabbage
carrots
apples
mayonnaise or salad cream

Get your child to grate the vegetables and mix them up with the mayonnaise or salad cream.

GARDENING

Gardening uses gross motor skills for digging and raking, fine motor skills for planting and also develops cognitive skills.

Encourage your child to help you in the garden with everyday activities such as raking the lawn or fallen leaves, digging and watering or pruning back bushes with secateurs or loppers.

Children love digging and shovelling. You could get your child to help fill seed trays, pots and tubs with compost ready for planting. Get him to dig out compost or mulch into a wheelbarrow and move it around the garden. If you have any gravel in your garden, he may enjoy digging it up and moving it around.

Your child can water seeds, look after and prick out the seedlings and plant out the plants. Good flowers for children to grow from seed are annuals, which grow and flower in one year. Sunflowers, nasturtiums, sweet peas, cornflowers, statice and marigolds all grow quickly and are pretty foolproof.

Give your child his own garden plot to grow his own flowers and vegetables, weed and water. For size and rapid growth try cardoons (cynara), sunflowers, red hot poker (kniphofia) and buddleias (which are also good for butterflies).

Grow vegetables. Easy vegetables are potatoes which are also fun to dig up. A few strawberry plants, including alpine strawberries, are popular amongst most children.

Grow mustard and cress on newspaper or cotton wool, keep it damp and watch it grow.

Plant bulbs in a pot and keep them watered on a windowsill. Daffodils and hyacinths make a good show.

CHAPTER 6

Sensory Development

WHAT IS SENSORY DEVELOPMENT?

Children use all their senses to gain information about the world which they then use in all sorts of ways. There is such a strong interplay between all the senses and all areas of development that you will find many cross-references in this chapter. In addition to looking at each of the senses in turn, we will also look at sensory awareness and perception.

VISION

Vision is the most important of the senses and plays an important part in learning about the world, about language and social interaction.

Early development
Binocular vision

Each eye records an image and transmits it to the brain which then turns the two images into a single one. In order for this to be achieved both eyes have to aim at the same point otherwise children have blurred or double vision. This can affect their ability to read and do close-up work.

Tracking

Tracking is the skill which enables the eyes to move in a controlled and sequential manner, which is required for following a moving object or a line of text.

Focusing

Focusing is the ability to see an image clearly and sharply, and to change quickly between looking at objects nearby and looking at some far away and still see them in focus.

Hand–eye coordination

Children learn to use visual information together with their fine motor skills so that they can do precise activities, for example, manipulating objects or colouring a small area without going over the lines.

Visual perception

Visual perception is the ability to analyse and give meaning to what is seen. It includes:

- *Visual discrimination* – seeing differences between similar objects or forms.

- *Visual memory* – remembering visual forms such as faces or words. For more information see Chapter 3, Cognitive Development.

- *Visual closure* – working out what something is, even if only part of it can be seen. This ability enables children to recognise a word without processing every letter individually.

- *Visual form constancy* – seeing and recognising a form even though it has changed size, direction or orientation. This enables a child to recognise an object when viewed from a different angle.

- *Visual figure ground* – searching out an object from a mass of detail; for example, picking out socks from a pile of clothes.

HEARING

Sounds enter the outer ear, and pass through the ear canal to the ear drum and then to the middle ear. Finally they reach the inner ear where they are turned into electrical impulses which are sent to the brain via the auditory nerve. Any deficit in any of these parts can lead to a hearing loss.

Early development

Babies' hearing and understanding of what they are hearing develops with age. They learn to discriminate between sounds, recognise them and locate where they are coming from. They learn that certain sounds are words and carry meaning. Children are first able to hear high frequency noises and later on low frequency noises.

Listening

Listening is an acquired skill which enables children to select the important sounds and to screen out others, such as the hum of the washing machine, other people's conversations, the TV or radio.

TASTE

Young children have a preference for sweet foods but acquire a taste for more savoury foods as they become introduced to them.

TOUCH

Children use touch to get information about things around them. As they mature, they tend to rely on information from other senses, particularly visual, rather than on touch. However, they still use touch when they cannot see something; for example, when trying to find a watch on the bedside table in the dark or getting a tissue out of a pocket. Another aspect of touch is protective. Children learn to move their hands away from something which they sense to be dangerous. It is important for their safety that children can discriminate between hot and cold, sharp and blunt and so on.

SMELL

Babies use their sense of smell to find their mother's milk and they can distinguish between strong smells. As they get older they learn to distinguish between smells and decide on their favourites. The sense of smell tends to be under-used, and clearly not as developed as it is in some animals, but it is an important factor in taste.

SENSORY AWARENESS

Children use the information from all their senses to develop a constant awareness of where they are and what is happening around them.

Body awareness

Information from receptors in the muscles and joints tell the brain where joints have moved and where the body is in space; this bypasses the need for one to look to learn this. The body can then make adjustments to position as needed. A child needs this understanding so that when she does a somersault she knows her head is under her trunk and that, with her eyes closed, she knows where her limbs are.

There are three elements to body awareness:

Body awareness

- *kinesthesia* – knowing where your body and limbs are in space (e.g. knowing that you are high up on a climbing frame)
- *proprioception* – knowing where your joints are in space (e.g. knowing that your elbow is raised when throwing a ball)
- *vestibular system* – knowing the position of your head in relation to gravity (e.g. knowing your head is upside down when doing a cartwheel).

Learning left and right

Children become aware that their body has two sides which, over time, they become able to label left and right. They need to be able to use both sides of the body together crossing their left hand to the right side and vice versa (crossing the mid-line).

Spatial awareness

Children develop an ability to understand and interpret the spatial relationship between themselves and other people, between themselves and objects around them, and between one object and another. This ability enables a child to know to duck her head if she is going through a low doorway, to know that the milk is closer to her sister sitting at the other end of the table than it is to her and to draw representations on paper.

Sensation

There is a constant feedback between movement and sensation so that children can adjust their movements; for example, when they walk down the stairs in the dark and misjudge the number of steps. Trying to do anything with gloves on, or with frozen or numb hands, shows how difficult it is to do things with impaired sensation.

GAMES AND ACTIVITIES

Remember that all children benefit from learning in a multi-sensory way because the information that children gather all comes through their senses. A multi-sensory approach is particularly important if your child has a sensory impairment of any kind (see the section Adopt a multi-sensory approach, in Chapter 2).

SENSORY OR TACTILE DEFENSIVENESS

Tolerance of certain sensations varies from person to person. Some children are very sensitive to smells, touch or sounds. You must respect the feelings of your child because certain sensations may be causing her intense irritation, discomfort or even pain. Make sure she is comfortable with the sensory input, whether it is the noise levels or the feel of craft materials. Then try very gradually to develop her tolerance. If she is particularly sensitive, contact your occupational therapist for a sensory profile.

> Jade kept stripping off all her clothes at any opportunity and in the most inappropriate places. When she changed schools, she no longer had to wear uniform. Because she could wear her own clothes she chose ones she found comfortable and stopped stripping off.

> I find we have to be careful of Sam's tolerance of certain sensations. We took him to a children's concert because he likes live music, but we could not get him even to sit in his seat because he was overwhelmed by the noise and atmosphere in the concert hall.

VISION
General advice for helping children with a visual impairment

Make the most of any vision your child has. The RNIB[1] suggests

- using big toys, which are easier to see and handle
- playing with colourful toys. Bear in mind that the eyes work on contrast. Also fluorescent colours are good, as is shiny or holographic paper

1   RNIB and Play Matters/NATLL (1987) *Look and Touch*. London: RNIB.

- making sure the home environment is bright and well lit
- keeping the environment the same; so don't move the furniture around without telling your child.

Binocular vision, tracking and focusing

If you have any concerns about your child's eyesight arrange for her to see an optometrist to have her eyes checked, or her GP, who may refer her to the hospital.

Hand–eye coordination

You can help your child's hand–eye coordination with any games which help fine motor skills such as craft activities, construction toys, drawing, throwing and catching balls. Ideas for games are listed in Chapter 5, Physical Development.

Visual perception

Many children with special needs have problems with some aspects of visual perception.

Visual discrimination

See Chapter 3, Cognitive Development, for games to help.

Visual memory

See Chapter 3, Cognitive Development, for games to help.

Visual closure

Try games in which a picture or object is gradually revealed, encouraging your child to make visual inferences, such as:

- jigsaws
- dot-to-dot pictures

- colouring activities

- writing and drawing

- construction games including Lego, marble run, train sets and bricks.

Visual form constancy

Encourage your child to recognise an object however it is presented:

- Get her to look at things from different angles, to tell you what something is when viewed in an unusual way.

- Compare sizes of objects such as saucepans or Russian dolls.

- Play with magnetic shapes. Turn them around and see if your child can recognise the shape when the orientation is changed.

- Take photographs of objects viewed from different angles. You could use a bird's eye view from above. Make a game of recognising the objects.

Visual figure ground

Encourage your child to pick out details from a busy background, for example:

- Get her to choose specific clothes from a drawer full of different clothes.

- Encourage her to tidy up – putting away clothes or cutlery.

- Get her to do sorting activities such as her toys, animals or dolls. For other sorting activities see Chapter 3, Cognitive Development.

- Ask her to lay the table.

- Do jigsaw puzzles and get her to pick out the right piece from the mass in the box or leave the last few pieces on top of the half-completed puzzle and get her to find them.

- Look at books like *Where's Wally* – finding tiny details in busy pictures. Start simply and build up the complexity of the pictures in the books you use.

- Spot details when out and about.

- Play spot-the-difference games or word searches.
- Get her to play with Lego.
- Play board games together.

HEARING
General advice for helping children who have a hearing impairment

- Make sure you have your child's attention before speaking to her.
- Get close to her and on the same level and make sure your face is in the light.
- Use lots of natural gestures when you talk and use lots of facial expressions.
- Get rid of all background noise – turn off radios and TVs.
- Do not shout as it distorts mouth patterns making it more difficult for her to understand.
- Remember to give her lots of time to respond.
- Use simple sentences, speak clearly and a little more slowly than normal.
- Encourage the use of all other senses and adopt a multi-sensory approach.
- Give her clues about what will happen next by using gesture, pictures and routines.
- If she has a significant hearing loss talk to professionals about the best long-term approach for her.

Encouraging listening

- Reduce the amount of background noise in the house to encourage your child to tune into sounds rather than tune them all out.

- Go on listening walks, around:

  - the house to hear the noises of creaking floorboards, clocks ticking, fridges humming

  - the garden to hear birds or the wind rustling leaves

  - the town to hear the noise of traffic, the sound of pedestrian crossings, sirens and the fountain in the park.

- Make deliberate mistakes when singing nursery rhymes or reading books to encourage her to listen carefully.

- During a story pause for her to fill in the relevant sound effect.

- Ask for silence and discover what you can hear – the boiler or cars outside.

- Play with noisy toys – animals that make noises, books with car horns or squeaks.

- Play the Quiet game – when everyone has to be silent for as long as possible and the last one still quiet is the winner.

- Play What's the Time Mr Wolf? She has to listen for 'dinner-time'.

- Play traffic-lights games – when you shout 'green' she can run, 'yellow' walk slowly and 'red' stop still.

Musical games

Musical activities are a good way to encourage listening, concentration, timing and anticipation:

- Listen to music of all varieties such as classical, pop, folk, jazz or world music. Encourage her to move or dance to the music.

- Encourage her to play musical instruments – drums, xylophones, castanets, cymbals, kazoos, mouth organs and so on.

- If you can play an instrument do so, and get her to listen and, if possible, have a go herself. Play loud and soft, fast and slow and different rhythms for her to listen to.

- Sing nursery rhymes and songs and encourage your child to join in singing, clapping or moving in time to the rhythm.

- Sing action songs such as Wind the bobbin up, Wheels on the Bus, Miss Polly had a Dolly, I'm a Little Teapot, Head, Shoulders, Knees and Toes, Hokey cokey, Underneath the Spreading Chestnut Tree, Peter Rabbit had a Fly upon his Nose, Dingle Dangle Scarecrow or Five Little Monkeys Jumping on the Bed.

- Play games such as Musical Chairs, Bumps, Mats and Statues where she has to listen carefully for the music to stop.

- Use a tambourine – shake it to get her to move around the room, bang it for her to stop.

- Consider sending her to music classes. Music and movement classes are widely available for young children. As she gets older, she may be able to progress on to a musical instrument – the recorder is one of the easiest and least expensive.

Dance to music

TASTE

Try to offer your child as wide a range of tastes and textures as you can, even if she has a particular preference. One good way to do this is to get her to help you cook.

We all have strong preferences for food and that is fine. If you are concerned, however, that your child has food fads which make it difficult for her to have a balanced diet then seek advice because it can be a very complex issue.

TOUCH

To encourage your child to explore and develop her sense of touch, to use her hands and to obtain the therapeutic benefits of sensory play, try the following ideas:

- Make a lucky dip. Have a large box and put in objects that she can recognise from the feel alone. Start with two very different things – a metal spoon and a silk scarf – then add a greater variety of objects which are more similar in feel.

- Many art and craft activities involve playing with different textures, particularly finger painting, collage and modelling with play dough, plasticene or clay. See Chapter 5, Physical Development, for more ideas.

- Messy play – use sand, lentils, uncooked rice, shaving foam, cornflour, soap flakes, cooked spaghetti or mud pies.

- Water play – put in colours or bubble bath to make it more interesting.

- Cooking activities – particularly those which allow your child to use her hands to mix and knead pastry or bread.

- Gardening – particularly using hands to fill pots with compost, planting out seedlings and so on. See Chapter 5, Physical Development, for more ideas.

Massage

Babies are shown to do better when touched and held and there is evidence that some self-stimulatory behaviour may be due to the lack of opportunity to touch and be touched. Most of us can vouch for the benefits of a massage so it may be something that you could try with your child to encourage relaxation, well-being and togetherness.

Try a foot, hand or forearm massage with her. Choose a good time, when she is calm or relaxed or you would normally be sitting quietly together. Tell her what you are going to do. Start with something short. Use a firm confident touch, not a light, tickly one.

Use a massage oil like grapeseed oil or sweet almond oil (beware of nut allergy). Oils must be cold-pressed so get them from health food shops rather than using cooking oils. You could use talcum powder or aqueous cream if you want something non-oily. For an aromatherapy massage add just one or two drops of essential oils to the massage oil. You must only use one or two drops because they can irritate the skin. Make sure you buy good quality oils from a health food shop or specialist retailer and it is important that you have a dropper top on your bottles to control the quantities used.

There are many classes, books and courses available to teach proper methods of massage.[2]

SMELL

We probably undervalue the sense of smell, which can be very evocative and therapeutic. It is worth finding ways of introducing a variety of smell to your child.

- Use perfumes, herbs and spices when you can.

- Plant aromatic shrubs, flowers and herbs (such as rosemary, curry plant, mint, lavender and thyme) in your garden for her to touch and smell.

---

2   Longhorn, F. (1993) *Planning a Multi-Sensory Massage Programme for Very Special People.* Wootton, Beds: Catalyst Education Resources Ltd; Maxwell-Hudson, C. (1988) *The Complete Book of Massage.* London: Dorling Kindersley; and Sanderson, H., Harrison, J. and Price, S. (1991) *Aromatherapy and Massage for People with Learning Difficulties.* Birmingham: Hands On Publishing.

- Put food essences like vanilla or almond in water for water play.

- Look at books that incorporate smells, for example, scratch-and-sniff books and *Smelly Old History* (Oxford University Press).

David loves picking handfuls of herbs like mint for cooking and choosing lotions and potions for his bath!

Aromatherapy

Try using aromatherapy oils, but avoid the following which can induce epileptic fits: boldo, calamus, hyssop, mugwort, pennyroyal, rue, fennel, sage, tansy, thuja, wintergreen, wormseed, wormwood and rosemary.

The following oils are relaxing and uplifting: bergamot, lavender, roman camomile, geranium and sandalwood. They can be used alone or in combination.

- Dab some aromatherapy oils onto cotton wool to smell.

- Vaporise some oils on a burner, a vaporising ring on a light bulb, in an air spray or by putting a few drops on a damp handkerchief and placing it on a radiator.

- Mix a couple of drops of essential oils with a carrier oil or a little bit of full-fat milk and add it to your child's bath or into water for water play. You should not put oils straight into the bath as they will not disperse and may cause skin irritation.

To aid your child's sleep you could place a few drops of lavender or camomile oil on a handkerchief tied to the end of her bed.

You can obtain essential oils and further information from health food shops and specialist suppliers, and there are many good books available.[3]

3   Tisserand, R. (1988) *Aromatherapy for Everyone.* Harmondworth: Penguin; Worwood, V.A. (1990) *The Fragrant Pharmacy – A Home Care Guide to Aromatherapy and Essential Oils.* London: Macmillian; or Price, S. (1983) *Practical Aromatherapy.* London: HarperCollins.

SENSORY AWARENESS

Body awareness

Some children cannot tell where parts of their body are without looking at them. Always draw your child's attention to how her body feels in different positions. Try the following games for promoting body awareness:

- Rough-and-tumble games – rolling around, wrestling.
- Forward rolls, cartwheels, rolls around a bar, rolypolys down a hill (rolling like a log).
- Twister.
- Draw a picture of a person and label the different parts. You could draw round your child if you have a large enough piece of paper and then label it.
- Play Simon Says. It is good for learning parts of the body: 'Point to your elbow'.
- Name parts of the body as you tickle them or wash them.

  We play a game in the morning when we lie in bed called Talk About Daddy, and it involves saying 'Daddy has beautiful eyes, Daddy has beautiful ear lobes' etc.

- Sing songs like Hokey Cokey, Head, Shoulders, Knees and Toes, If You're Happy and You Know it, Here we Go Round the Mulberry Bush. You can make up verses to focus on different parts of the body, for example: 'If you're happy and you know it, slap your thighs'.
- Trampolining, riding and swimming all involve your child's body moving into different positions.

Learning left and right

- Play the Hokey Cokey and Simon Says and focus on practising left and right.
- Talk about whether your child is left- or right-handed. If she is left-handed, then she would naturally use her left hand to pick up a pen.

- Use any helpful routines such as where she sits in the car, the house is on the left, to talk about left and right.

Crossing the mid-line

Try to think of ways to make your child cross the mid-line to reach things she needs. For example, if she is doing a puzzle put the pieces on the opposite side to her dominant hand or if you are playing a card game have the card stack in a position so that she has to cross the mid-line. Hand her things on the opposite side to the one she uses habitually.

- Encourage her to draw large pictures on paper pinned to the wall so that she has to cross the mid-line to cover the paper.

Spatial awareness

For a good understanding of the relationship between objects encourage your child to do the following:

- lay a table for tea
- place objects in/on/under/in front of/behind/next to/to the right/left of another object
- play dressing up
- play jigsaw puzzles, noughts and crosses, Connect 4 and battleships
- use construction toys, for example Lego, bricks, railway sets and marble runs
- do craft activities such as drawing, collage, mosaics and Fuzzy Felt
- make patterns on pegboards.

To develop an understanding of the relationship between herself and other objects take every opportunity to talk to your child about what she is doing in terms of her relationship with objects and people around her (e.g. 'Look, you are behind the tree', or 'We are up high in the bus'). Encourage her to do the following activities:

- jump off and onto things
- play Leapfrog, Stick-in-the-mud, Hopscotch, Hide-and-Seek and dodging games – see Chapter 5, Physical Development, page 132
- crawl under a rope, through a tunnel or into a confined space
- play with crates and cardboard boxes and in dens and tents
- play with hoops; for example, getting her to step into a hoop and pull it up over her body and vice versa. Or play Musical Hoops, which is like Musical Bumps except that when the music stops she must stand in a hoop
- climb stairs, ladders, trees or onto logs
- play Simon Says
- play in playgrounds or at soft play centres on slides, swings, climbing frames, roundabouts and tunnels
- do an obstacle course that you have set up in your garden, the park or at a soft play centre which involves different activities. You could make her go round the tree, up the climbing frame, slip down the slide, crawl through the hoop, walk along the bench and put the ball in the bag
- Swim, trampoline or ride a horse, all of which place children in an unusual position to which they have to get accustomed.

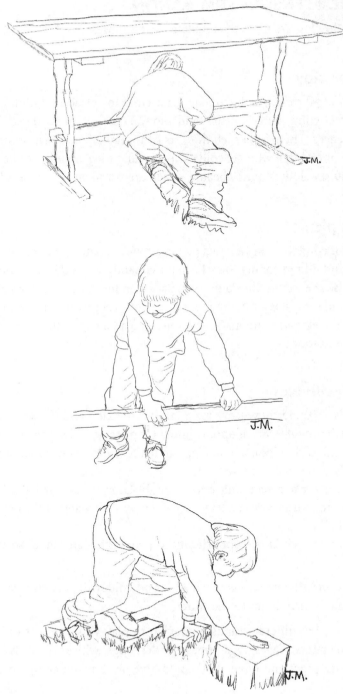

Obstacle course

IDEAS FOR SENSORY STIMULATION

The following are ideas to stimulate all the senses.

Outdoor play

Go out in all weathers. Encourage your child to splash in puddles and mud, feel wind, rain, fog, hail and snow. These are fantastic sensory experiences. There is no such thing as bad weather, only inappropriate dress. For children who get cold easily because they are not mobile you can buy ski clothes quite cheaply which are warm and waterproof.

Make a picnic

Get your child to make her own picnic. Provide a lunch box. Put out the bread and fillings for her to make her own sandwich and let her choose what else she wants. She could even pack it in her own rucksack with a drink and carry it with her to the picnic spot, whether it is at the end of the garden or out in the park. If it rains spread a rug in the house and have an indoor picnic.

Playing with water

Water is a wonderful sensory material. It is relaxing and therapeutic to handle. It provides lots of opportunities for playing and experimenting. It is wonderful to look at and feel, can make lovely sounds and, if you add oils, can smell good too.

You can use a paddling pool, trough, large bucket or baby bath outside, and inside you can let your child play with water in the bath or the sink.

Give your child the opportunity to play with water in all sorts of ways:

- To provide variety you can add food colouring, essences and smells or bubbles to the water.

- Give her different kinds of utensils to play with, such as old colanders, sieves, jugs, tubes, bottles, cups, whisks, funnels, pots, pipes and tubes. You could give her kitchen equipment to play with – saucepans and ladles, bowls and whisks. Alternatively you could supply bath-time toys.

- Experiment with floating and sinking light and heavy objects: sponges, plastic bottles, balls, balloons, stones and weights.

- Give her toy fish, boats or dinosaurs for pretend play.

- Get her to wash a doll or the dolls' clothes or to do the washing up with toy crockery and cutlery.

- Fill a paddling pool for her to splash, jump and kick in. She could throw balls into the pool to hit a target or just to make a splash.

- Make paper boats or boats made from bits of driftwood and twigs. Float them on the paddling pool.

- Play Pooh Sticks.

One of the best toys our son has ever been given was a sprinkling flower which was attached to the end of a hose and moved randomly spraying everything. Children love running in and out of the water spraying themselves and others.

- Ask her to water the garden with a hosepipe or watering can.

- Have water fights using water pistols or old washing-up liquid bottles.

- Get her to help wash the car, her bicycle or the windows.

- Pretend to paint the house, the shed or bicycle with an old paintbrush and a bucket of water. You could add some food colouring.

Playing with bubbles
Bubbles recipe

¼ cup washing-up liquid
1 cup water
glycerine (optional)

Mix the above ingredients together.

Children love blowing bubbles. They can pop them with one finger, clap them, catch them on the wand, count them or simply watch them.

Playing with sand

Sand is a wonderful substance to play with. When it is wet you can use it to build constructions and when it is dry you can pour it like a liquid. There is no right or wrong way of playing with it.

You could put sand in a large bowl, an old baby bath or on a plastic mat inside. It can be bought from toyshops or, more cheaply, from builder's merchants where it is called play, washed or silver sand.

Encourage your child to play with sand in any way she wants. Here are some suggestions:

- Give her a variety of pots, jugs, bottles, sieves, funnels and other utensils for pouring and experimenting with dry sand.

- Build sandcastles and fill moulds.

- Create roads and building sites, zoos, farms, villages and towns by introducing toy vehicles, blocks, wooden houses and animals.

- Make patterns, draw and write in sand.

- Hide objects in the sand and have a session of searching for treasure.

Playing with sand

Creating a sensory garden

As well as making your garden visually interesting and having children's toys and equipment such as paddling pools, climbing frames and sand pits, you could make it a multi-sensory garden. First think about issues like access – getting around the garden, any steps, the need for raised beds and so on. Then look for lots of ways to introduce sensory stimulation, for example:

Sight

- Use plants with masses of bright, colourful flowers such as daffodils, tulips, dahlias, zinnias, alliums, rudbeckia; annuals such as marigolds, cornflowers, sunflowers and nasturtiums. Grow them in large blocks for maximum impact.

- Overhanging trees are stimulating as the wind moves the leaves – weeping willow is a lovely tree to run in and out of.

- Attract wildlife into your garden by putting up bird feeders, bird baths or bee homes, and plant buddleia and lavender to attract butterflies and insects.

- Put up a mobile of old CDs which catch the sunlight.

Sound

- Put up wind chimes or mobiles made of plastic flowerpots, shells or found materials.

Wind chimes

- Have a child-safe water feature, such as a bubble fountain, which gives the sound of running water. You can get solar-powered pumps.

- Plant trees, ornamental grasses and bamboos through which the wind can whistle. The seed heads of oriental poppies (papaver orientale) rattle when shaken.

Smell

- Plant aromatic herbs to brush against and smell; for example, mint, marjoram, sage, lemon balm, chives, rosemary, lavender, thyme, basil, fennel and curry plant.

- Include plants such as old-fashioned scented roses, honeysuckle, viburnum, winter flowering honeysuckle, daphne, pinks, mock orange, sweet peas, sweet William and stocks.

- Plant a scented lawn with pennyroyal, camomile or creeping thyme.

Touch

- Use bubble fountains and safe water features such as rills and pumps so children can play with the water.

- Grow plants and trees with tactile leaves, branches and stems, for example lamb's ears, hare's foot clover, hare's tail grass and quaking grass.

- Have a patch for making mud pies.

Taste

- Grow your own fruit and vegetables!

For gardening ideas for children see Chapter 5, Physical Development. There are many inspirational books on gardening with ideas that could be adapted, or for more information on sensory gardens contact Thrive, which is listed in Chapter 12, Resources.

CHAPTER 7

Social Development

WHAT ARE SOCIAL SKILLS?

Children are born with a social instinct which enables them to communicate and form relationships with their parents, family and other people. This social instinct also generates learning in other areas, notably linguistic and cognitive, and is closely connected with emotional development. Children learn to make friendships and associate, negotiate, empathise and cooperate with other people.

CHRONOLOGICAL DEVELOPMENT
Early development

Babies are sociable from the day they are born. A baby learns that he is a physical being, separate from his mother, and where his body begins and ends. Children learn that they can manipulate people to get what they need and therefore see the point of social interaction. They learn that if they cry they might get food, if they smile they get a smile back. They use people to learn to communicate and to find out about the world. They begin to copy adults in what they do.

Love and acceptance

Children need love and security, and to be accepted for what they are by parents who are responsive to their needs. This gives them a sense of worth which allows them to feel loved and accepted even when they do something wrong.

If children feel safe and valued at home and have good relationships with their family they learn that relationships are secure, enjoyable and not arbitrary. This gives them the confidence to go out of the family and develop trusting relationships with other people. They will have the confidence to take risks and make mistakes without fear of failure. Children who do not feel secure may have more trouble developing relationships later.

Sharing and turn-taking

Children learn the early social skills of sharing and turn-taking. Turn-taking is important in communication but is also critical to social development as it is the starting point for early social interaction. Initially, parents prompt children to take turns, but as children get older they can internalise the rules of turn-taking and use them without support.

Children also learn to share. In doing this they recognise that other people have needs as well as themselves and they cannot have their own way all the time. Over time they appreciate the benefits of sharing and turn-taking when they see that they too gain when others share with them.

Widening social circle

In a child's early years his main relationships are within his family. But as he gets older he develops relationships with other adults – teachers and support staff – as he attends different and new environments such as school. This wider circle of adults has an influence on the child through the way they respond to him and by acting as role models.

Testing the boundaries

Children start learning about social rules by finding out what is acceptable behaviour. Parents set children limits for acceptable behaviour and children challenge them to find out where those limits are set. They push at those boundaries to see how far they can go. Once they have found the boundaries they can feel secure and safe and learn to operate within them. The more consistently the boundaries are set, the easier it is for children to work out what is acceptable behaviour. A child who does not have clear boundaries will take longer to learn how to behave.

Theory of mind

Young children think that everyone thinks as they do and knows what they know. But at about the age of four children begin to appreciate that others may have a different viewpoint and perspective from their own and to form an idea of what that might be.

A child also has to learn that other people can have false beliefs, i.e. that people can hold ideas which are not necessarily true. More information on this is in Chapter 3, Cognitive Development.

Understanding the feelings of others

Young children are egocentric in that their attention is focused on their own needs and desires and they believe the whole world understands their point of view. There has been a debate over the age at which children can 'decentre' and think of another person's point of view. It seems clear that from quite an early age children are able to show an awareness of others' views[1] at least sometimes – by comforting a child who has fallen over, for example. However, clearly as children mature they become more aware of the different needs and perspectives of others.

As children learn to understand and appreciate views other than their own they develop an empathy for other people and a greater understanding of the world.

1   Donaldson, M. (1987) *Children's Minds*. London: Fontana.

Early peer relationships

As well as with adults, young children start having relationships with their peers. Initially these are so fleeting that they are not socially influential, but as children get older they take on increasing importance. Peer relationships require different skills. Children have to make themselves understood, cooperate, learn to give and take, approach others, control aggression and show affection. These relationships demand and develop increasing communication, cognitive and social skills.

Teachers, adult leaders, school, friends and the media affect children by exposing them to different situations, behaviours, manners and approaches. They can have negative and positive effects.

Relationships with peers and acceptance by them becomes increasingly important to children and they are influenced by prevailing attitudes and interests. There is a whole culture which passes from child to child with elaborate rules, regulations and even initiation ceremonies. There are rules which children must obey. It can be supportive but may also be cruel with fighting, hair-pulling, 'sending to Coventry', taunting and teasing taking place.

Early peer relationships

Learning social rules and social skills

Children learn to behave in a way that is acceptable to the society in which they live. Each society dictates the rules by which its members need to live – for instance, we believe it is wrong to harm people and steal things. These rules will vary from one society to another, but we all need to abide by them in order to be accepted in our society.

Children also have to learn that how they interact with people will vary according to the situation and the respective roles of the people involved (for example, they behave very differently playing with their friends to when they talk to their head teacher).

We ask our children to develop a range of social skills which include good manners, being polite, saying 'please' and 'thank you', showing consideration for others, sharing, taking turns, being positive in play and relationships and using appropriate language. We also expect children to have self-help skills so that they can stay clean and use the toilet independently.

Friendships

Early friendships are short-lived and based on shared interests – maybe they both like playing with dolls or trains. As children get older, they develop friendships which are based more on shared views and personality than just play. In middle childhood best friends change regularly, but by late childhood there is more loyalty and commitment and friendships tend to increase in intensity rather than number.

There is a wide variation in the number and nature of friendships different children have. Some will have a few close friends whom they will stick by, while others are very gregarious and have a big circle of friends and acquaintances.

Friendships become more mature as children's abilities develop, particularly their communication and cognitive abilities. Friendships are an increasingly important part of children's lives as they get older, and a very valuable one because children learn so much from friends about the feelings of other people, about the world and about themselves. They learn to negotiate, weigh up arguments, consider differing views and make judgements. They will stimulate and excite and introduce new ideas and experiences.

Friendships provide emotional support and, as children get into later childhood, they turn to their friends rather than their parents to talk things over and discuss difficulties.

Children often form loose groups who go round together, maybe at school or in the neighbourhood. It is a step towards independence as they are able to do things away from their family, but not on their own.

Moral development

Young children do not have a sense of right and wrong. They learn to follow the rules imposed by adults because of the patterns of reward they dish out. We reward good behaviour – a child helping to tidy up – and we tell children off for bad behaviour – a child hitting someone. Children follow rules rigidly because they don't want to be punished.

Children gradually take on board the standards of behaviour that their society expects and internalise them so that they can exercise self-control and behave in a morally responsible way. They get to know within themselves that it is wrong to steal. Even without an external presence they will be guided by their conscience and not steal. Piaget argues that this change occurs when children learn to take into consideration the viewpoints of others. Children then look at the intention, not just the consequence; and can consider complex situations more flexibly. More mature children will see that a child who breaks two cups accidentally is less 'bad' than a child who breaks one cup deliberately.

Even if children know the difference between right and wrong, it does not mean they will always choose the side of right; other motivations may be too great. This is just as true for adults.

Children also have to see that rules are defined by particular social groups and that these will vary from group to group. What is acceptable at home may not be acceptable in other people's houses or vice versa. Children have to find a way of accommodating this.

To understand whether rules are fair requires advanced cognitive thinking. The ability to think in abstract terms about such issues as fairness may be just beginning to emerge in late childhood and early adolescence.

Conformity

Young children, being egocentric, are not especially influenced by peers because they are more interested in themselves and less aware of others. As they develop a greater awareness of others it becomes more and more important for them to conform, because they need social approval and do not want to stick out from their peer group.

The extent to which children (and adults) want to conform depends on their personality, their self-esteem and their social sensitivity. Someone with high self-esteem, who does not care much what other people think, may be non-conformist; whereas someone with low self-esteem, who is sensitive to the views of others, may be keener to conform.

Negotiating

In mature relationships children need to be able to negotiate not manipulate. When people negotiate they need to consider the views of each side fairly, give their opinion, consider all of these and agree a compromise jointly. This process of talking about issues, feelings or situations develops cognitive ability because children consider issues from a number of angles and make a considered response. It also leads to moral development because children are having to address moral issues – is it fair, is it true, is it right?

To negotiate successfully children have to understand their own feelings. 'Do I feel happy or comfortable doing this?' They have to be able to recognise their feelings and have the self-esteem to say, 'No I am not happy with this'.

PARALLEL DEVELOPMENT
Personality/temperament

When children are born they have a certain temperament, a style of behaviour which is natural – emotionality (fearful, anxious, enthusiastic), activity (impulsive, slow), sociability and variations in concentration. A baby's temperament is then subject to other influences, including the experiences he has and his social relationships; and these shape his personality.

Gender identification

Children gain an idea of whether they are boys or girls at about the age of two but it does not become completely fixed until they are about six.

From an early age there are clear differences in the way that boys and girls behave and play. For example, boys play in a more aggressive and physical way whereas girls are often more advanced in their language skills at an early age. Most researchers agree that although there may be some biological factors at play it is socialisation which is most significant in determining gender differences.[2] It may partly be due to children identifying with a same-sex parent. It may also be because we give our children gender-stereotyped models as parents, at school and on television. Consciously or unconsciously we reward behaviour which we think is gender-appropriate. We reward boys for being competitive and girls for being nurturing and considerate. Also, as children mature, they have a concept of themselves as boys and girls and so will take notice of gender-appropriate models and will disregard other information. 'Dolls are for girls – I am not playing with them.'[3]

> Nick had an orange lunch box with teddies on it which he took to school when he first started. It was a bit girly but I did not want to make him conform to stereotypes and it was the only one we had. After a few weeks he came home one day and announced it was a girl's lunch box and refused to use it again. One of his friends had said something at school.

Types of play

The following types of play have been identified by Mildred Parten who argued that there is a progression in children from solitary play through to cooperative play.[4] However, according to the situation and

2   Birch, A. (1997) *Developmental Psychology*. London: Macmillan.

3   Martin, C.L. and Halverson, C.F.Jr (1987) 'The roles of cognition in sex role acquisition.' In D.B. Carter (ed.) *Current Conceptions of Sex Roles and Sex Typing: Theory and Research*. New York: Praeger.

4   Parten, M.B. (1932) 'Social participation among preschool children.' *Journal of Abnormal and Social Psychology 27*, 243–269.

how they feel, children will still play in different ways at different times. Even when they are able to play cooperatively there will be times when they may wish to play alone or play alongside someone in a companionable way. The way children play will also depend on whether they are at home, in school, with older or younger children or with adults.[5]

Solitary play

Children play alone, perhaps for relaxation or to practise new skills. We all need time alone, away from other people and as children get older they go off to their own space to play for longer periods.

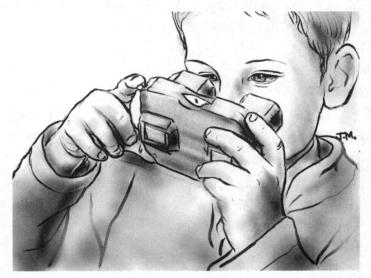

Solitary play

Observing play

Children sometimes stand by and watch others do something without joining in.

5   Cohen, D. (1987) *The Development of Play*. London: Croom Helm.

Parallel play

Children may play alongside others on a similar task or activity but with no interaction between them; for example, playing in a sand pit together.

Associative play

This is when children play with the same toys on the same activity but each child has his own agenda. It often ends in tears when they find themselves in opposition.

Cooperative play

Children learn to negotiate a way of sharing an activity with each other. They can share goals, ideas and toys, take turns and resolve differences by negotiation.

Self-identity

Children develop a concept of self over a period of time. It has been suggested that a child's self-concept is made up of three things:

- an awareness of his body
- an ability to use language to describe himself as 'I' or 'me' as appropriate
- an understanding of his experiences, his abilities and his desires.[6]

A baby learns about his physical self and as a young child develops a mental image of himself based largely on physical attributes such as the colour of his hair or eyes. As he matures he can think of himself more in terms of his interests and personality ('I like green, I like trains') and his emotional response to life ('I don't like going to new places').

6   Gardner, H. (1982) *Developmental Psychology*. Boston: Little Brown and Co.

Self-esteem

Self-esteem is the element of our self-concept in which we value ourselves against others and against our own standards. Children develop their self-image initially from how their family react to them, how they are treated and what is said to them. Parents who have a real knowledge of their children and are loving, accepting, supportive and encouraging will help their children to grow up with high self-esteem.

A positive self-image and good self-esteem enable children to go out and make friends. If a child has poor self-esteem he will feel that he is not worth knowing and his ability to make relationships and his general development will be inhibited.

Children's self-esteem may also be modified in the light of their relationships with other children – how peers react to them and whether they are easily accepted or rejected. They may start comparing themselves with their friends as to how intelligent, attractive, athletic or funny they are and research suggests that they are able to be quite objective.

ACADEMIC THEORIES OF SOCIAL DEVELOPMENT

There is still much discussion about how and why children develop as they do. Here is a brief summary of academic theories.

Psychodynamic approach

Freud saw the development of the personality as a series of stages. He introduced the idea of *identification*, arguing that children adopt the characteristics of an older person, usually a parent, without direct teaching, because they identify particularly with them. By identifying with parents, children take on their values and attitudes and want to live up to their expectations. The need for approval and fear of rejection by the people they love is a strong motivation.

The learning theory approach

Learning theorists believed that environmental factors, rather than personality, affect the way children behave. Pavlov[7] argued that association affects the behaviour of dogs, while later theorists, including Thorndike and Skinner,[8] argued that it is because we 'reward' certain behaviours and therefore 'reinforce' them that children's behaviour is shaped. This work underlies many behaviour management and modification programmes.

Later, Bandura argued that children learn their social behaviour, whether simple actions or complex behaviours, from observing and imitating others.[9] Social learning theorists also argued that identification was a powerful tool for children to learn styles of behaviour and how to become like someone they know and respect.

Cognitive–developmental approach

Piaget's approach took into consideration children's cognitive development and how it affects social and emotional development. Children's understanding of the social world and their ability to develop relationships and a moral conscience depend on their cognitive development. In particular, they depend on an ability to see another's point of view and to think in a more complex and flexible way.

Vygotsky and Bruner also argued that it is through social interaction that children learn. See Chapter 3, Cognitive Development, for further information on their ideas.

7   Pavlov, I.P and Anrep, G.V. (1927) *Conditioned Reflexes.* London: Oxford University Press.

8   Skinner, B.F. (1938) *The Behavior of Organisms.* New York: Appleton-Century-Crofts.

9   Bandura, A., Ross, D. and Ross, S.A. (1963) 'Imitation of film-mediated aggressive models.' *Journal of Abnormal Social Psychology 66*, 3–11.

GAMES AND ACTIVITIES

CHRONOLOGICAL DEVELOPMENT
Love and acceptance

The basis of a good early relationship must be a strong attachment on the part of the child to his parents. Parents need to provide their child with a firm understanding that he is loved and accepted for what he is regardless of his problems and difficulties. They need to demonstrate to him that, whatever happens, whatever he does, however he behaves, their love continues unabated. For parents of a child with special needs that acceptance may well be more difficult to achieve because they have to come to terms with their own sense of disappointment, failure or anxiety.

If you are finding your relationship with your child difficult

Find things you and your child both enjoy doing together so you can have genuinely positive experiences, such as going for a walk, to the cinema, swimming or to the park.

If your child is naughty make sure that you criticise the behaviour and not the child. Say 'Look. You have drawn on the wall, that is a naughty thing to do', rather than 'You have drawn on the wall, you naughty boy'. It may sound pedantic but it is depressing for anyone to be told that they are stupid, naughty or bad.

Try to ignore bad things and focus on the good. See Chapter 9, Additional Practical Advice, on behaviour management techniques.

Appreciate successes and positive things that happen.

Give yourself some time off, whether it is a few hours or a holiday. It may take the pressure off.

Share your experiences with people who are in a similar situation. It often helps to talk and it can feel particularly liberating to talk to people who know how you feel and maybe feel exactly the same way as you.

Identify if there is anything else going on in your life which may be impacting on your relationship with your child. Is there any situation which is causing you stress? Try to tackle that without letting it affect your relationship.

Sharing and turn-taking

Turn-taking is absolutely fundamental to an ability to interact with people. If you try to get your child to play turn-taking games you may have to be very firm to begin with, insisting that he and anyone else involved obeys the rules scrupulously. That way he is likely to see the point more quickly. You will have to oversee the turn-taking until he has internalised the rules and takes turns naturally and unconsciously with others.

Try any activity which he enjoys and turn it into a two-person turn-taking activity, for example:

- bubbles – your blow, my blow
- feeding the ducks – your turn, my turn
- emptying the shopping trolley – your turn, my turn
- marbles – take turns rolling marbles down a ramp or through a marble run.

Try turn-taking board games but start off with simple games that your child really enjoys. Play with just the two of you, so he won't have to wait for very long for his turn, and make sure the game does not last too long. You could try Snap, Dominoes, Snakes and Ladders, Lotto, Pelmanism or Beggar my Neighbour.

At home encourage your children to take turns with treats – sitting in the front seat of the car, having the first bath or doing the washing up.

Take turns on play equipment – slides, swings, trampoline or an obstacle course in the garden.

Sharing out sweets

Share food for the family such as a cake, biscuits, packets of crisps or fruit. Rather than buy individual packets for each person have one large packet and share. Get your child to help share out the food.

Share out food in a teddy bears' or dolls' picnic.

Exaggerate the turn-taking in conversations by responding positively to him and then waiting very quietly for his next communication.

Play games such as rolling or throwing a ball to each other, or take turns playing Hide-and-Seek and Chase.

Widening the social circle

Encourage your child to make relationships with other people. Start with people within the family – grandparents, uncles and aunts – then friends, carers, teachers and club leaders.

Find safe and appropriate places for your child to meet new people of all ages, make friends and encounter new situations. He should be able to do this through family, play activities and friendships at school and locally. However, it may be that thought needs to be given as to how he enters these environments; i.e. is this the right kind of club or is the play area safe? It may be that he will need to access provision specifically for children with special needs, e.g. a special needs playgroup or a family through respite care. But it is important that all children start moving outside the family to experience new ideas, people and situations.

Children need to learn to be independent and part of that is making relationships with other adults and peers so that they are not totally dependent on their parents.

> Kate was being a bit of a nuisance in the playground at school, rushing up to people and asking to see their tummies and their keys. A lot of it was her way of coping in an unfamiliar situation and of getting attention from me as I chased after her. In the end I stopped and, though keeping my eye on her, I let her get on with asking to see tummies and looking at everyone's sets of keys. She has to forge her own way with people when I cannot be there to interpret her to the world and, equally, other parents have to find a way of dealing with her too, not just through me.

Testing the boundaries

Techniques for behaviour management are covered in Chapter 9, Additional Practical Advice.

Theory of mind

See Chapter 3, Cognitive Development, for games.

Understanding the feelings of others

It is crucial that children develop an understanding and an interest in how other people are feeling if they are to make successful relationships. Children with special needs can find it difficult to develop this awareness. This will seriously impede their ability to make relationships so it is important to help them in this.

> When I am sick Simon thinks it is hysterically funny and laughs as I vomit. He also gets incredibly angry if I am sick and he is not around to watch me because he enjoys it so much.

A child has to understand his own emotions before he can begin to appreciate other people's. See Chapter 8, Emotional Development, for ideas on developing this skill.

Talk about how you feel at times: 'I'm feeling cross today because the plumber did not turn up and I waited in all day' or 'I'm sad because I heard that Aunty Dot is poorly'. Talk about how others feel: 'Look, that man is cross because the car nearly hit him'.

Talk about the emotions in stories as you read them.

Talk about the emotions your child's actions generate in other people; for example, if he hits someone, brings you a drink, snatches a toy and so on.

Early peer relationships

Some children are very adult-orientated but it is important for their future independence that they develop relationships with their peers. The usual order in which children make relationships is: with their principal carer (usually the mother), the other parent, their close family, other adults, older children, same age children and finally younger children. Try the following ideas:

- Give a sibling or visiting child a quasi-adult role, for instance, handing out the pocket money, biscuits or sandwiches: something in which your child will be interested and in which he will be keen to be involved.

- Get your child to share out a cake or a pudding for a group of children.

- Give him a job which involves communicating with his siblings and/or visiting children. You could get him to take round some biscuits and say 'Do you want a biscuit?', or you could ask him to ask what someone would like to drink or to tell children to go and wash their hands.

- Set up a game he particularly likes; for example, a marble run which he can play alongside others.

We bought a big trampoline for exercise but it turned out to be brilliant for social interaction. Ryan loved jumping with his brothers. He learnt to make eye contact, to became aware of their movements and accommodate them, to copy what they did and even asked them to tickle him. It was lovely to see.

- Play a board game such as Snakes and Ladders with your child and another child.

Playing games with others

- Play games involving other children; for example, I went to the Supermarket, the Quiet Game (when everyone tries to stay quiet for as long as possible), What's the Time Mr Wolf? and Follow my Leader.

- Play games which are highly motivating and require each child to have a role in a joint operation – rather like a production line. An example might be playing in the sand pit where one child fills the scoop, another child empties it.

- Throw and catch balls.

- Play on playground equipment, particularly see-saws and boat swings.

- Play Hide-and-Seek, Chase and Tug-of-war.

- Have three-legged races or wheelbarrow races.

- Get him to show another child how to do something the other can't do.

Joining a club

Children are encouraged to join all sorts of club activities from a young age. Joining a club is the obvious way to enable children with special needs to participate in different activities and to meet other children and make friends.

However, before you do this it is worth thinking carefully about the following issues:

- What are your child's needs, strengths and interests? What would motivate and stimulate him? What would help him with his skills or his emotions? What strengths does he have that could be nurtured and encouraged?

- What is your objective for your child – making friends, social interaction, learning a new skill, exercise, respite for you, an opportunity for relaxation or the chance for him to express feelings or be creative?

- What skills and abilities are involved in the activity itself and in being a member of the group? Is your child at about the right level for them? Some activities require a number of skills – to work in a group, to be independent, to operate as part of a team, to cope with success and failure, to express themselves or to learn new skills. Can your child cope with all the elements? Can he cope alone or would he need support? If so, who will provide it?

- Think about the structure of the activity. Is it largely free play, is it self-directed, is it very structured? Would that be appropriate? Some children can cope with a structured environment, others may need the opportunity to do their own thing.

- How competitive is the activity? Some clubs become very serious very quickly, with people being picked for teams or competing for badges and medals. Others may be more an opportunity to practise and develop skills.

- Make sure the club is age appropriate as well as at the right development level for your child.

- What is the environment like? Is it safe for your child and others? Are there any distractions?

- What are the people like who run the activities? Would they understand your child's problems and be able to deal with them positively? What about the other children? Do they know your child? How would they respond to him?

- Would it help if someone like a sibling or a friend went along too? (You might have to balance this against the fact that your other child might not want his style cramped.) Perhaps there is a club which a sibling has already attended and therefore is familiar.

- How is it going to fit in with other commitments and the needs of other children?

Team sports such as football and rugby can be highly competitive but also very motivating. It requires considerable maturity to work as a team and cope with the joint responsibility of winning and losing. Individual sports – swimming, gymnastics, tennis, badminton, trampolining and martial arts – at least do not have such a team element; but it varies from club to club how competitive these are. There are lots of dance activities, ballet, tap and music and movement classes, which are relaxed and fun. Art and craft activities can be good for children with special needs because they are creative and the

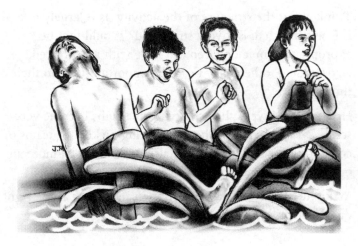

Swimming

emphasis is more on the process than the end result. There are all sorts of music activities, from music and movement, to music therapy, to learning an instrument either in a group or individually.

Beavers, cubs, rainbows, brownies and other children's youth clubs offer a more sociable set-up with a variety of activities which change each week. They offer the opportunity to try different things, which might be good for some children but hard for others who need more predictability.

Trampolining might be good for someone who likes routine and structure because it is organised in an orderly way with people taking turns and having specific moves to practise.

Then there are the clubs specifically for children with special needs. Local Mencap branches run clubs, as do other organisations. You may find clubs for specific activities like dancing, gymnastics, sailing or swimming for children with special needs. Provision will vary very much from area to area and it is worth checking with local organisations to find out what is going on. They may not offer the opportunity for your child to mix with 'normal' children but they should provide a safe and secure environment, with experienced instructors, for your child to enjoy himself and meet others like him within his own age group.

Swimming club

There is a trade-off between activities which are highly motivating and those which are relatively easily organised. Your child may be highly motivated by football but that might be very difficult to organise successfully because it requires a high level of physical and social skills. On the other hand, there may be an art class run by someone with experience of special needs. This is a solitary and non-competitive activity which your child would enjoy even though it would not be his first choice.

Do your research first by asking around amongst other parents to find out what is available. Local authorities, social services, Action for Leisure (see Chapter 12, Resources, for contact details) and notice boards in the community and at libraries have listings of local clubs.

When you have identified what you would like your child to do, visit the club. Talk honestly to the club leader about your child, his needs and your aims. Make sure that you are happy with the leader because the success of it may come down to the leader's personality and willingness to make it work. Give the club any literature you may have which explains your child's condition. Tell them about any health implications, behaviours and mannerisms he may have which might affect them, for example: 'He may not necessarily look at you but he is listening; he does not like physical contact and he has a high pain threshold so he has to be watched in case he is getting into trouble'. Perhaps talk to them about possible reactions the other children may have and give suggestions for responses.

In some cases you may feel there is no need to emphasise or even mention at all your child's special needs because this might be the one opportunity for him to feel completely 'normal'. Just make sure that there is no risk of anything happening that might endanger him physically or expose him to a situation he could not handle.

> I sent Rob, who has dyspraxia, to the local art gallery for regular art classes. I didn't say anything to the organiser because it was his one chance not to be singled out as different. The work he produces may not compare favourably with that of his peers but since it does not affect anyone else it does not matter. On the other hand, when he went to the local pool for swimming lessons, the instructor noticed quite quickly that he was finding things more difficult than others and suggested a series of

private lessons, then reverting back to group lessons. With football, however, I was very upfront because the difference in skills was so marked. However, he was so keen to do it that we went ahead.

Social rules and social skills

Behaving in a socially acceptable way is a very important skill for children with special needs. It would be nice to think that we lived in a culture where people were accepted for what they are and allowances were made for disabilities. However, the reverse is probably true as higher standards of behaviour are often expected of children with special needs than their peers. Because a child with special needs may not have the same social sensitivity as other children, he does not necessarily respond to the looks of disdain when he picks his nose or sucks his thumb in public and sometimes may actually enjoy the reaction. These skills, therefore, often have to be taught by using the behaviour management techniques of rewarding good behaviour and ignoring bad (described in Chapter 9, Additional Practical Advice).

However, remember that rules vary from family to family and culture to culture. While all parents want their children to be accepted and acceptable, in the end you have to decide where you draw the line. Recognise that other people draw it differently because they have different priorities, experiences and situations. Everyone has fixations on different things – eating nicely, not interrupting, saying 'please' and 'thank you' – and it is much easier to spot where your child fails than where he succeeds.

Concentrate on one or two areas that you think are most important, and do not try to tackle too much at once. Some social niceties are confusing and unhelpful if introduced too early. A child with very limited language should be concentrating on words which are highly motivating rather than learning to say 'please' and 'thank you'.

Sophie was taught 'please' by a carer and consequently lost the word 'yes' and gained 'pee' (her version of 'please') for a few years. It was polite but not very meaningful. 'Is this your coat, Sophie?' 'Pee.'

Christopher had an obsession with babies and would go round trying to kiss them. Some parents were horrified by the sight of this six-year-old racing up to their baby or toddler and would scream at us 'Get your child away'. When we went to France on holiday people thought it was charming and perfectly natural to show interest in young children. Though we were tempted to move to France we instead tried to encourage Christopher to go up to people and ask 'What's the baby's name?' which people found more acceptable.

If you are thinking about social rules in general try the following:

- Look at books together and talk about how people are behaving. The following books are about how to and how not to behave: *Bad Good Manners Book* by B. Cole (1997), published by Picture Puffin; *Dinner Ready: A Pig's Book of Table Manners* by J. Gedye (1989), published by Macdonald, or the *Values* series (e.g. *I Don't Care* learning about respect) by Wayland Publishers.

- Talk through what is going to happen in new situations. If you are going to do something new – say, go to a wedding, dentist or cinema – prepare your child by talking through what is going to happen and what he should do. It helps to give it meaning if you can find books or a video showing the situation. Alternatively, try role play to practise what is going to happen.

Having consideration for others

One social rule is to show consideration for others and if your child is still very much concerned with himself then this may be tricky.

- Be a good role model for your child. If you want him to be kind and considerate, then it is a good idea to lead by example. You cannot expect a child to grow up to be a concerned altruistic person if those are not the attributes rewarded at home.

- Talk about what you are doing and why. Be explicit about your consideration for others. We will let Mummy sit in the front of the car otherwise she will be sick. We will let Jordan choose the game to play because he is our guest.

- Use pretend play to examine what it is like to be someone else: a mother, teacher, someone who is sick.

- Use books to talk about situations in terms of how it feels to be hit, kicked, ignored or teased.

- When groups of children of different ages play together they can often naturally model how older children take care of younger ones.

Self-help skills

It is important that children have good self-help skills, which enable them to be independent and therefore 'socially acceptable'. Spend time on helping your child with the following practical life skills. It is often easier to stop a habit occurring than to change it once it is established, so respond promptly but be careful not to reward the behaviour by over-reacting.

Using the toilet independently

See Chapter 9, Additional Practical Advice, for information on this.

Feeding

It is important socially that children learn to eat 'nicely'. See Chapter 5, Physical Development, for ideas.

Dressing and undressing

See Chapter 5, Physical Development, for ideas.

Staying clean

Issues such as dribbling and having a clean face after meals are important as children get older because it is not considered acceptable for an 11-year-old to have a runny nose, for example. Other children particularly can find it very off-putting so it can be a barrier to social interaction.

- Draw your child's attention to how his face feels. Does it feel dry or wet? You want to encourage him to recognise the signs of a grubby face or dribble on his chin and take action.

- Encourage him to dab his chin dry or wipe his nose.

- Ensure he always has a tissue in his pocket and knows how to ask for one.

Respecting personal space

Some children get very close to the people to whom they are talking, causing discomfort among them because it is closer than the distance we find acceptable. If your child does this remind him to take a step back.

Show him where it is acceptable to touch people – on the arm, for example, rather than on other parts of the body such as the face or chest.

Stopping unpleasant habits

Many young children fiddle with their genitals, pick their noses or indulge in other unpleasant habits in public but drop them fairly quickly. However, some children with special needs continue these habits to an age when it is not socially acceptable. If your child does any of these:

- Be calm and cool, and do not reward his behaviour by showing shock and horror. This may be the reaction he wants.

- Try distraction – give him something to do which means he cannot continue with the habit in question.

- Tell him 'no' and give him a time and place when it is acceptable. 'No, we see your willy in the bath, not in public.'

- Whatever you suggest he does instead, try to ensure that it will always be acceptable and that three years further on you have not got to 'unteach' it again.

Other important elements in social skills are language skills (see Chapter 4, Language Development), managing emotions, particularly aggression (see Chapter 8, Emotional Development), and moral development (see below).

Social Stories

Carol Gray has devised a method of teaching social skills to children on the autistic spectrum which she calls 'Social Stories'.[10] These are particularly successful with children who have some cognitive understanding.

Choose one behaviour that you want to introduce or change; for example, stopping 'throwing objects'. Make a small book using simple pictures and words to illustrate how and when your child should throw things. Make the book relevant to him by using the appropriate names, situations and illustrations.

Show for whom the book is, what it is about, what the right behaviour is, what the behaviour you want to stop is (if relevant) and finish on a positive note.

The following is the Social Story that was used with Christopher to stop him kissing inappropriately at school.

Christopher's Story – Kissing

We kiss people to show them that we love them.
Christopher kisses his Mummy, Daddy, Nick and Billy.
Christopher might kiss other people in his family or his friends.
Christopher can kiss his teddy, because it is soft and cuddly and he loves it.
We don't kiss paper or pencils or other things in school.
I will try not to kiss paper and other things. I am a good boy.

In addition, you can use social stories to tackle all sorts of everyday situations which might challenge your child; for example, hair-washing, going to the toilet or going to the petrol station.

10   Gray, C. and Leigh White, A. (eds) (2002) *My Social Stories Book*. London: Jessica Kingsley Publishers.

Friendships

You cannot impose friendships but some children need help to mix with their peers because they are very dependent on adults.

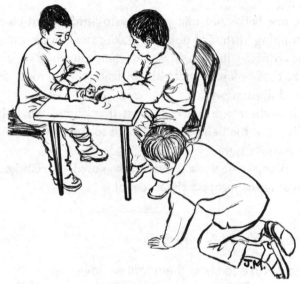

Some children need help to play with their peers

Early friendships are fostered by parents, probably for practical reasons, because they control who visits the house. As children get older they need to be given the freedom to choose their own friends and for parents to trust their judgement. If you are concerned about your child's friends, particularly if you feel he is vulnerable, arrange for them to come to your own house so at least you have some awareness of what is going on.

Set up play opportunities by inviting children round or going out with other children and their families. Start with children who are familiar to your child such as relatives, family friends or classmates.

Introduce your child to slightly older children who may be more accommodating, aware and responsible. You could try to find a befriender, someone who could play with your child.

Open-ended free play may be the most challenging for children ('off you go and play') so it is best to start with something structured – give them something specific to do, for instance painting or completing a puzzle together. Also, start with something familiar to your child so that the social angle is the only new and demanding element.

Set up parallel play situations, particularly with games he enjoys such as bubbles, playing with a garage or in the sand.

Help your child to make friends by getting him to play alongside other children copying their play, rather than going up and saying 'Can I play with you?' in which case the answer will often be 'no'.

You could ask your school to start a 'buddy scheme' in which a child is chosen to work with, look out for and help your child at difficult moments like play-time, lunch or PE. Children are 'buddies' for a few weeks, maybe on a rotating basis, and will make an effort to play with and include your child. From this natural friendships may well develop. Sometimes it can go wrong when children smother or baby the child with special needs. A similar approach to 'buddies' is the 'circle of friends' idea where a group of children are charged with including the child with special needs in their activities.

> My daughter's junior school was worried about her socialising with other children at play-time so they decided to focus on clapping and skipping games. They provided the equipment and taught games and rhymes. A skipping team from London even came to give an amazing and inspirational demonstration for the children. It was a great success for Victoria, who worked hard at learning to skip at home. The bossy girls took her under their wing and helped her to join in, so she was actively involved in the playground, and made friends. It was also good for her physically because skipping is great exercise. A bonus was that the boys even joined in because they used nylon, non-girly ropes. It stopped a lot of poor behaviour because there was something to do in the playground.

Peer relationships

The very nature of these relationships means that children have to negotiate them alone and all you can do as a parent is watch them from afar, which can be very hard. Try to be supportive of your child, show that you love him whatever is happening and provide a safe haven for him. Remember it is a topsy-turvy and fast-changing world. One day he moans because no-one will play with him and the next day you discover he has told someone else 'I don't want to be your friend any more'. All you can do is talk about how people should be treated, encourage him to think about his own feelings and those of other people and to make connections – 'how did he feel when someone said that to him last week?' If he is having a tough time give him strategies for dealing with it; for example, by encouraging him to have lots of friends, or by telling him to walk away from difficult situations and find someone else to play with or play on his own.

Bullying

Sometimes, things may get out of hand and your child may be the victim of bullying. Children with special needs can often be the target of bullying because anyone who is different from others may be singled out.[11] Your child might tell you what is happening or you may have to look out for signs such as an unwillingness to go to school, unhappiness or ripped clothes.

If it is happening at school then approach the head immediately. Most schools have a policy on bullying. The government and organisations like Kidscape (see Chapter 12, Resources, for contact details) offer information and resource material. The school will need to talk to him and the bully and identify what action to take. This might include:

- giving the bully some kind of behaviour modification programme

- getting all children to confront the issue of bullying: how it feels to be bullied, how to react, what to do as a bystander

- raising awareness of special needs so that children are more knowledgeable and considerate

- introducing a buddy scheme or a circle of friends (see above) to ensure that your child has playmates and someone looking out for him.

11   These ideas come from *Preventing Bullying: A Parent's Guide*, a pamphlet published by Kidscape, which includes many others, and from *Tips to Help Protect Your Child from Bullying*, a pamphlet published by the National Autistic Society. See Chapter 12, Resources, for contact details of these two organisations.

Look at the bullying incidents and identify what happens and when, to see if there is anything that could be done to improve the situation. It could be that lack of equipment at play-time may mean that children are bored and turn to bullying. Some more equipment, activities and ideas for play might be the answer.

If your child is being bullied you will need to:

- Give him lots of love and reassurance and the opportunity to talk about what is happening and how he feels.

- Teach him an appropriate response; for example, to shout 'no' and walk away. Practise this using role play. Think up good responses to taunts.

- Make sure he is as socially acceptable as possible in his habits, clothing and interests.

- Encourage self-esteem and confidence by giving him lots of opportunities to feel positive about himself by doing things he enjoys and is good at.

- Work on improving social skills and make sure he has opportunities for making friends away from school through clubs or with others in the locality.

- Make sure he has an opportunity to express his feelings of unhappiness or anger creatively and physically, perhaps through racing around, playing music, painting or swimming.

Moral development

The most important thing is to make sure you are consistent in the boundaries you set and the way you control behaviour by rewarding good behaviour and ignoring bad. In this way children will learn more quickly what they are allowed to do.

Model good behaviour yourself. Demonstrate the attributes you wish your child to emulate.

Talk about other people's feelings. Try to develop a sense of empathy.

When he is able to understand, start to talk about the moral dimension of situations he faces. Explain what is happening and point out the effects of his potential behaviour on others so that he can regulate his behaviour. When you tell him off, don't just say 'Don't hit Sam' but talk about how it feels to be hit, how we don't like being hit and why, therefore, we should not hit others.

Try to draw parallels between events. 'Do you remember when Freddie broke your toy? You did not like it, so you must not break other people's toys.'

Conformity

How far you will want your child to conform will depend on your own situation, personality and viewpoint. There is a whole debate to be had about how far children with special needs should conform and how far the world should accept them as they are. Conformity makes life easier but, on the other hand, most of us have issues about which we feel so strongly that we are prepared to forge our own path. On some issues we want our children to fit in and be like everyone else. So make sure that your child does not stand out in a way that will make him the butt of teasing (see the section above on Learning social rules and skills). However, on other issues we want them to take a stand and be confident to be different. After all, you may want your child to be able to say no to bullying, drugs, cigarettes or underage drinking at some future date.

> I have a particular fixation with society's excessive use of the motor car to the detriment of the environment and our health, and one day when the school decided to hire a coach to drive the children 300 metres to the local church for a service I rebelled and decided to walk my children there and back instead. On the day I felt rather ridiculous as the four of us toiled up and down the road being overtaken by the coach full of waving children. However, friends did point out that it is important for children to see that you should look at the issues and make a decision without necessarily bowing to peer pressure.

Negotiating

An ability to negotiate only starts to emerge in late childhood and comes from lots of practice at talking to others, doing joint activities and considering other people's points of views. You could establish a chart to show whose turn it is to have first bath. This removes all need for argument, gives your child control and could then be the basis of negotiating: 'Can I swap today?'

PARALLEL DEVELOPMENT
Personality/temperament

Children's personalities are all different and they should be respected and allowed to develop.

Gender identification

Do not stereotype your child but allow him to develop in the way he wishes.

Types of play
Solitary play

Be aware that all children need to play alone at times. Some parents have found that schools worry because their child spends some play-times alone. It may just be that he needs some time away from people and social pressures rather than these being any particular 'problem'.

Some children are very dependent on others and find it difficult to play alone. If your child is like this, focus on a game that he enjoys and could conceivably play on his own. For example, choose dolls, train sets, cars, drawing, painting or looking at books. Try one of the following approaches:

- Use a timer to get him to play alone for a very limited time – say, one minute – and then very gradually increase the time spent by 30 seconds or so per day. Reward him at the end with praise or whatever reward system works for him.

- Alternatively, you could play with him, making it fun. Then gradually over time remove the help and support you are offering by just talking, not participating; then moving further away; then doing another activity in the same room, maybe reading the paper and just intervening with words as and when necessary. Then try moving to the next room, popping your head through the door as and when, until he is able to continue on his own happily.

Parallel play

If your child is finding it difficult to play with other children, it is probably best to encourage him to play with an adult first.

- Play alongside him – so if he is playing with cars play alongside, copying what he is doing.

- Take him to playgrounds or swimming, or to soft play areas where children play around each other. He may start to become aware of others and interested in what they are doing.

- Encourage him to do some kind of creative play, such as drawing, painting or making models, alongside another child – a sibling or classmate.

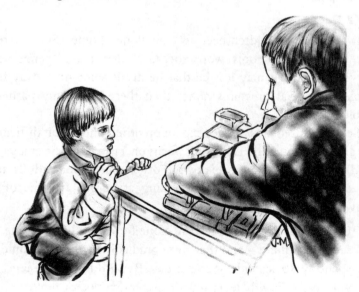

Parallel play

Cooperative play

See the section on Friendships above for ideas on encouraging social play.

Self-identity

Make sure your child has a clear awareness of who he is by playing games which focus on parts of the body, such as tickling games and naming games – 'Where is your elbow?'– and Simon Says. Sing action songs like Head, Shoulders, Knees and Toes, Tommy Thumb and If You're Happy and You Know it .

Make up a scrapbook and stick in tickets, stickers, postcards, photographs and programmes to build up a picture of all the experiences he has had which you can then talk about.

Make up a photograph album for him.

At the end of each day talk about what has happened to him and how he felt about the events of the day to develop a sense of his personal history. He could write a diary, or dictate his thoughts to you.

Talk to him about what he likes and does not like and how he feels.

Self-esteem

See Chapter 8, Emotional Development, for ideas on developing this.

CHAPTER 8

Emotional Development

WHAT IS EMOTIONAL DEVELOPMENT?

Initially a child gains awareness of herself as a separate individual who can influence and affect her environment and the people around her. From her experiences and the attitudes of those around her come a sense of self and self-esteem which affects her own attitude to life. She develops an awareness of her own emotions and those of people around her and an ability to deal with them and channel them into socially acceptable forms. Social and emotional development are very closely connected.

CHRONOLOGY OF DEVELOPMENT
Early development

Children first learn that they are physically separate from their mother, where their body is and how to control it. They recognise their name and themselves in a mirror or in photographs. They go through a phase of being dependent on their principal carer and get anxious when left, but are able to cope better as they gain greater confidence and a sense of security.

Love

Children need a firm base of love, encouragement and acceptance, which they normally get from their parents. This gives them a sense of worth and acceptance for what they are which allows them to feel loved and valued even when they do something wrong. Children need parents who are responsive to their needs, consistent, loving and non-judgemental.

Love

When children feel secure they have the confidence to go out into unfamiliar situations, experiment, try new activities and meet new people.

Attachments

In their early years, children need to establish firm attachments to a small number of people who are caring, responsive to their needs and consistent in their care. This enables them to develop trust in adults, which will be the basis for future positive relationships.[1]

Self-awareness

Children develop a concept of their own identity ('I am a girl and I am called Martha'). Initially, this concept is limited to physical attributes, skills and favourite things.

Sense of security

Parents set the boundaries for what is acceptable behaviour. Children test those boundaries by trying things out and seeing the response they get. If they find those boundaries are firm and consistent they will not feel the need to constantly test the boundaries, but will become secure in the knowledge of what is expected of them. They also feel that their parents are in control of the family and of the wider world.

However, just because they have firm boundaries does not mean that they cannot have freedom within the boundaries: freedom to make choices, to be flexible, to explore and experiment within the boundaries.

If the boundaries are always shifting children will not know what is expected of them and will feel insecure. They will also see that they can control their parents. Furthermore, they will realise that in that case their parents cannot control the family, let alone the world beyond; in which case the world becomes a frightening place.

Fears

Most children will have some fears at some point, including occasional nightmares. Some are a result of experience (being bitten by a dog) or parental warnings (fire), others are symbolic (ghosts or monsters).

---

1   See Holmes, J. (1993) *John Bowlby And Attachment Theory*. London: Routledge.

Some symbolic fears may indicate an underlying problem or fear of parental punishment.

Understanding and expressing emotions

We don't know how children learn about emotions. Possibly we all have an innate facility for recognising emotion and for sharing a sense of connectedness with others. Children may learn by copying others, so they laugh when you laugh, cry when you cry etc.[2]

Understanding the feelings of others

Children learn to recognise emotions in other people, such as anger, happiness or sadness, and then to respond appropriately. They learn to comfort someone who has hurt herself or is upset. This ability to empathise with others is also a vital part of social development.

Children at first think other people's emotions are the same as their own, so when they are happy they think everyone else is happy too. They have to learn that other people have different emotions to them.

Powerful feelings

Children have very powerful feelings at times, of love, happiness, fear, anger, frustration, etc. and they need to be allowed to experience them. Often we try to stop ourselves and our children from having these feelings by denying the emotion or distracting the child. We say 'Don't get so cross, come and do this puzzle'. Children should not be denied the feelings that they have. Negative feelings that children have been forced to suppress will only emerge in other more difficult ways.[3] Children have to recognise and accept their feelings before they can find a way of dealing with them.

2   Jordan, R. and Powell, S. (1995) *Understanding and Teaching Children with Autism.* Chichester: John Wiley and Sons.

3   Roberts, R. (2002) *Self Esteem and Early Learning.* London: Paul Chapman Publishing.

There is a close connection between feelings and behaviours and it is the parents' job to help children find a way of expressing those feelings in a way that is consistent with them but acceptable. Children will feel anger at times and may express their aggression but in a way that does not hurt anyone, perhaps by channelling it into other activities.

Self-esteem

Once children start having an awareness of others they will also realise that other people may have views on them and this will affect their view of themselves: their self-esteem ('I am good at colouring, my hair is pretty'). How a child values and judges herself comes from how she feels about herself and how others make her feel. In the early years a child's self-esteem will be largely derived from the treatment she gets at home. If parents are attentive, accepting and full of praise and encouragement, and give consistent and positive messages about their child and the things she does, she will grow up with positive self-esteem. If she is told all the time she is naughty or stupid she will inevitably develop poor self-esteem.

When children move outside the family to playgroup and school they start mixing with other children whose reactions also have an impact on self-esteem. This impact is likely to be positive if it is a good reaction and they make friends easily, and negative if it is not.

In our society, adults and peers rate competence and independence highly. Children who do not show these abilities may feel as if they are failures and children who are defined as failures are at greater risk of not realising their potential. It is important, therefore, to avoid judging children but to be genuinely respectful and value them for what they are.[4]

Children from quite an early age can see how they are doing compared to others and there is evidence that they can be quite

---

4   Donaldson, M. (1987) *Children's Minds*. London: Fontana.

objective in their assessment of their abilities. When children say that they are not good at reading they are often admitting to a reality.[5]

An ideal self

In middle childhood, children begin to think of what kind of person they would like to be. There is evidence that it is a positive thing to have a moderate gap between how children perceive themselves and how they would like to be ideally, as it gives them something to aim for.

Controlling emotions – public and private self

In later childhood children develop a conscious awareness of having a public persona and private thoughts and feelings that they do not want to share. They start to learn to hide their own feelings. They learn that other people can also hide their true feelings and say things that are different to what they think. If there is too great a disparity it can become a problem later in adolescence.

Independence

Children gradually gain independence from their parents, their family and their teachers in a variety of ways over a very long period of time. We live in a very technically advanced country and this has the effect of keeping children much more dependent on adults for longer. Children are kept at home because it is perceived as too dangerous to let them play in their community, on the streets or in the fields, or to walk to school alone, as was possible in the past.

It is really important for children's development, self-esteem and happiness that parents find ways of giving children as much independence as they can handle.

When children are given independence parents have to make sure that the element of risk is kept to a safe level. Children have to be able to

5   McMichael, P. (1977) 'Self-esteem, behaviour and early reading skills in infant school children.' In J.F. Reid and H. Donaldson (eds) *Reading: Problems and Practices.* London: Ward Lock Educational.

admit to any mistakes – not moral failings – so that they can learn from them without fear of being rejected. We all make mistakes and they are the most effective way of learning.

A life without mistakes is a life without challenge. But it is vital that children can own up to mistakes, learn from them and not feel that they will be told off, rejected and blamed.[6] Otherwise they will not want to take further responsibility.

GAMES AND ACTIVITIES

Sense of security

A sense of security comes from having consistent boundaries, so children know where they are and what is expected of them. Agree your ground rules with your partner so that you are both interpreting them consistently. Have relaxed attitudes to the same things and clear, strong boundaries where you think it matters. You can only fight so many battles at any one time, so choose the issues which are really important to you.

Fears

Children have phases of being fearful about things, some of which are rational and some of which are not. Do not dismiss children's fears as being trivial. It is important to acknowledge those fears and to find the cause of them.

Understanding and expressing emotions

Children with special needs can often find it difficult to express how they feel about themselves and others. You could help by doing the following:

6   Roberts, R. (2002) *Self Esteem and Early Learning*. London: Paul Chapman Publishing.

- Give your child the language to express how she feels by talking about your own feelings – surprise, happiness, sorrow or anger – and what has caused those feelings. 'I am happy today because it is my birthday.' 'I am annoyed about breaking that bowl.'

- Explain what is happening around you in terms of how people are feeling. 'Oh look, the little girl has lost her balloon. She is crying because she is unhappy.'

- Talk about the feelings of people in books and on TV. Talk about what has happened and why they feel as they do, how they appear and how they express those feelings.

- Role play situations in which you express emotions.

- Play a game where you both have to make a happy face, a sad face, a surprised face, etc.

Understanding the feelings of others

See Chapter 7, Social Development, for ideas on this.

Powerful feelings

If your child is feeling overwhelmed by feelings of unhappiness or anger, hold her to give her a sense of physical security until she has worked through those feelings.

Do not deny her powerful emotions or stop her expressing them. Instead acknowledge those feelings, show her that you understand how she feels and talk about them.

Do not underestimate her feelings; though the issue may seem trivial to you, it might be very important to her. Popping a balloon may be the equivalent for her of you smashing a family heirloom.

Talk to her about her feelings. Give her the vocabulary to express how she is feeling. If she is screaming because her friend has eaten her piece of cake, tell her 'You are feeling angry because Kate has eaten your cake'. She may feel jealous because she has not been invited to the party, disappointed because she is ill and cannot go to gym club, or happy because it is her birthday.

Share her feelings rather than ignore them. After all, if something happens to adults talking it over with people is one way for them of accepting it. Sympathetic acceptance also makes a child feel better because she will take with her the idea that people care even if nobody is around to comfort her every time.[7]

Powerful feelings

Express feelings of your own: 'I am fed up today because the washing machine has broken down again' or 'I am sad today because I heard that Aunty Diana is poorly'. Model how you deal with powerful feelings, by talking a problem over with friends and family, by asking for a hug, by sitting quietly alone, by jumping up and down with joy.

Give your child choices as to how she could deal with her emotions safely and acceptably. 'I know you are feeling angry, you can go to your room until you feel calmer, you can talk to me or you can go outside and play in the sand. What do you want to do?'

Offer her a reward if she can find a way of working through her feelings appropriately.

Use role play and imaginative play to work through situations in which such feelings arise.

7   Miller, L. (1992) *Understanding Your Four Year Old*. London: Rosendale Press.

Make sure you, your partner and other carers are being consistent in your approach to her and, if you have different views on how to respond to powerful emotions, find some middle ground that you can all agree on.

If your child seems to have a lot of emotional outbursts, look at what is happening in the lead-up to them and what happens as a consequence. You may be able to see a common cause or a set of circumstances and, if so, identify what could be done to help. Use the ABC of behaviour management described in Chapter 9, Additional Practical Advice.

Managing emotions

Give your child lots of opportunity for energetic physical exercise to get rid of any pent-up feelings of aggression and frustration – a punch-bag, soft play, running, chasing, trampolining, swimming (lots of splashing) or rough-and-tumble games.

Give her opportunities to express her feelings through creative play – playing musical instruments, dancing, painting or modelling with materials like play dough and plasticene.

If she has to express herself physically when feeling strong emotions, then give her a safe and socially acceptable way of doing it. You could give her a kosh ball, stress ball or bean-bag to squeeze, or tell her to stamp her feet or clap her hands.

Self-esteem

Many children with special needs do not have poor self-esteem because they do not have enough awareness of other people to be affected by their views. They remain egocentric. However, for some other children with special needs, it is a concern.

Within a child's notion of self-esteem the following four elements have been identified:[8]

8   Coopersmith, S. (1981) *The Antecedents of Self-Esteem*. San Francisco: Freeman.

- significance – feeling loved and valued
- competence – feeling able to do some things well
- virtue – feeling morally good
- power – feeling able to control herself and exert some control over others and her environment.

These elements may be helpful when you are thinking about the self-esteem of a child with special needs as her own specific disability may make it very difficult for her to feel success in certain areas. A child with challenging behaviour may find it difficult to feel 'morally good', whereas a child with physical disabilities may feel she is not very competent.

Significance

Accept your child for what she is.

Praise your child's achievements. Judge the right level of praise so that it is appropriate to the activity and to her. Generally, children thrive on praise and encouragement and some children will need masses of praise with words, signs and body language all being used to reinforce the message. However, some children have such low self-esteem that they will not accept praise. Such children need to be praised in a way that they can accept. For example, the praise might have to be very specific and limited and not overdone. If she has done a picture you might not be able to declare 'Oh what a lovely painting', but you might be able to say 'This section here is quite good'.

Equally, don't make praise worthless by overdoing it or by praising actions which have involved no effort. Give praise where it is due. Recognise genuine effort and achievement. If you praise indiscriminately your praise becomes worthless. Knowing what is praiseworthy comes from knowing your child well and having realistic goals (see Chapter 2, What Everyone Needs to Know).

Show your appreciation of any work she does whether it is drawing, painting, model-making or writing by having an 'exhibition' space. This could be a wall, the fridge or a pin board where work can be displayed.

Take time to talk to your child and discuss things to give her confidence in her own views. Ask for her opinions and treat them seriously.

Competence

Play games or do activities where there is no right or wrong, such as playing with water or sand, painting, modelling or swimming.

Encourage her to take part in activities which make her feel good, particularly physical activities like swimming, going for a walk or a bike ride. Physical activity gives a sense of purpose and feelings of self-fulfilment and well-being.

Feeling loved

When doing different activities set realistic goals (see Chapter 2, What Everyone Needs to Know). It is important to gauge the level of difficulty of any activity carefully so that it is appropriate to the child. Children need to be able to see that they have made an effort, overcome some difficulties and succeeded. It is no good if the activity is too easy because that is not interesting or motivating. Equally it is no good if it is too difficult; she will just give up in despair and feel even more useless.[9]

9   Donaldson, M. (1987) *Children's Minds*. London: Fontana.

Make her as independent as possible – see the section on Independence below for further ideas.

I can do this

Virtue

In order for children to feel secure and confident that they are acceptable and are behaving appropriately, they need to have firm boundaries. If it is OK to climb on the furniture one day but not the next, children won't know where they are, whether they are being good or bad. They need to have firm boundaries laid out for them at home which are consistently upheld. Then they will know that provided they stick within those boundaries they are doing OK. See Chapter 9, Additional Practical Advice, for more ideas.

It is important for self-esteem that any criticism is directed at the behaviour and not at the child. Rather than saying 'You naughty boy' say 'It is naughty to throw your food all over my best dress'.

Power

Offer choices at an appropriate level because it gives children the chance to exercise some control over their lives. The choices have to be genuine and at an appropriate level – not 'Shall I take this job offer?' but 'Which puzzle do you want to do?', 'Which game do you want to play?', 'What would you like for pudding?' or 'What colour would you like your room painted?'

Make sure you can fulfil the chosen option. It is no good offering a choice and then backtracking when you realise a child has chosen the 'wrong thing'.

Also make sure your child has the necessary understanding to make the choice and to communicate it to you. Use photographs, pictures or symbols if you cannot use signs or spoken language.

Allow her to make the 'wrong choice' (in your opinion) because that is how she will learn; for example, spending birthday money on a cheap toy that will break.

Additional points

When a child reflects on herself and her abilities, she has a general self-image in her mind as well as specific areas such as academic ability, sportiness or appearance. Certain skills will be more important to a child than others, and they will have more bearing on her overall feeling of self-worth. If, for example, maths is not something that is important to your child she will be able to accept that she is not good at maths without it affecting her general level of self-esteem. However, if it *is* important to her, poor performance at maths will have an effect on her self-esteem. If you wish to improve her general self-esteem, it is important to focus on the areas which are critical to her, whatever they may be.[10]

If you are concerned about your child's level of self-esteem, see what is happening outside the home, at school or in the community, to

10   Harter, S. (1987) 'The determinants and mediational role of global self-worth in children.' In N. Eisenberg (ed.) *Contemporary Topics in Developmental Psychology*. New York: Wiley.

make sure the positive messages given at home are not being undermined elsewhere.

Deal with failure positively by modelling how you cope with failure. For example, you don't have to be good at everything; you can still enjoy drawing even if you are not a great artist; losing a game or a race is not the end of the world.

Sometimes having a close relationship with another adult whom she feels is more 'objective' may be a good way to improve her self-esteem.

Your child's awareness of her own special needs

It varies hugely when, if ever, children with special needs realise that they have a disability. How you explain the nature of the disability, the reasons for it and the consequences, let alone how they learn to accept it, will also depend so much on individual circumstances. You could try the following ideas:

- Be honest but sensitive.

  Eliot was born without his lower arm and he asked us whether it would grow back. We had to say 'no'.

- Talk to your child about her disability: what it means and how it affects her. Give her positive ways of thinking about and dealing with it. 'It is more difficult to learn things, but you will do it, we are all helping you and you are really good at swimming, aren't you.'

  My daughter asks me why she is different and I tell her that no-one is the same – some have poor eyesight, ears that stick out or bad eczema. Children always find the weak spot, it is a question of how you deal with it.

  Maddy says she does not mind being different, she is 'special'. She says she is not ordinary but 'extraordinary'.

- Read books with positive images of children with disabilities.
- Introduce her to other children who have similar needs through local organisations or nationally if she has a rare

disability. It is important that she knows that there are other people like her.

Amy has Down's Syndrome and goes to her local school and so rarely meets anyone with Down's Syndrome but really enjoys it when she does.

Harry has been known to say to people 'You can't say that to me, I've got Down's Syndrome'.

Independence

Gaining independence is part of growing up. Children are gradually given more freedom and independence from their parents, perhaps to wash and dress themselves, make friendships and play out alone. It is a difficult process for all parents to manage because they worry about giving up control and letting go.

Full independence is obviously a long way off for any young child, but you may know already that your child with special needs is not likely to achieve it. However, the further along the path towards independence she can get, the better it will be for her. It opens up new experiences and is good for self-esteem. You will also benefit.

It can sometimes be hard to let go because she seems so dependent and vulnerable, because you don't trust other people to care for her as well as you do or, perhaps, because you don't trust your own child. Try to be objective and if necessary seek the perspective of other people on her potential for independence.

I have to find ways of allowing Lauren to do things by herself and become independent otherwise she will be marked out as different and it will be a barrier to her being accepted by friends and peers.

Independence is included in this chapter but it is almost a summation or a product of a range of skills – language, physical, cognitive and social as well as emotional. It is how a child uses all those skills to look after herself.

Approach giving independence gradually, move step by step and give her independence she can handle. Make sure that all of you can cope with anything that might go wrong.

Start by giving your child independence within the home:

- Give her choices.

- Develop her self-help skills: toileting, eating and dressing. See Chapter 5, Physical Development, and Chapter 9, Additional Practical Advice.

- Create the right environment at home so that she can be as independent as possible. Think of things from her point of view. Can she reach the toys, can she get a cup for a drink, can she reach her clothes, can she turn on the light?

- When you are encouraging a child to be independent things may slow down in the short term. You will have to teach her how to do things and let her practise, so give yourself lots of time. In the end it will pay off so don't think 'Oh, it is quicker to do it myself'.

- Establish routines because they give children a framework in which they can be independent. They know what is going to happen and can predict the routine and perform it with less and less help. Use routines in the house at meal-times, bath-time and so on.

Then move on to the garden, making it secure and safe so that she can have freedom within it.

Then you can try moving out of the house, to familiar environments such as the homes of family and close friends and her local community.

- Encourage her to form relationships with others outside the immediate family – grandparents, aunts and uncles, friends and neighbours. She will have to learn to convey her needs and desires to others. This will help her language and social skills and provide stimulation and excitement.

- Ask good friends if she can come over to play for short periods on her own.

- Find ways of letting her have experiences outside her immediate family and school such as going to friends' houses, attending appropriate clubs or going to respite care.

- Take advantage of safe situations to give her the opportunity of experiencing some freedom and excitement; for example, playing in a park with you some way off, or playing out with older friends.

- Routines outside the house also help develop independence. If you go to the same shops regularly the shopkeepers will be familiar with your child and she with them. So, for example, if you buy your bread at the same baker's each day, you may be able to send her in alone to buy the bread while you wait outside. You would know that the shop staff would be helpful, and there would be no great problem if somehow she did not make herself understood. If, on the other hand, you go to a variety of shops all the time it will take longer to have that level of independence because the chances of something unexpected happening would be greater.

Independence

Assessment of danger

Part of becoming independent is being able to make a sensible assessment of danger and risk. The following introduce the idea of risk to your child:

- Encourage her to consider cause and effect; for example, the water is hot, it will burn me.

- Allow her to take small, controlled risks and very gradually build up her awareness.

- Model how you deal with new or risky situations such as crossing the road, handling sharp knives or picking up hot pans.

CHAPTER 9

Additional Practical Advice

BEHAVIOUR

BEHAVIOUR ISSUES

Deciding what is appropriate behaviour is quite hard at the best of times. With a child with special needs it can be difficult to establish the right balance between making allowances for your child and being excessively strict to make him conform to society's expectations.

There are a number of issues at play:

- We are concerned about what other people think and probably respond differently in public, when we want children to be quiet and obedient, to at home, when we like our children to be lively, talkative and inquisitive. Public expectation can be hard, particularly if your child looks perfectly 'normal' but has difficult behaviours.

- Children are usually better behaved for others than they are at home where they feel accepted and can truly be themselves, relax and let off steam. This is perfectly natural and normal. The relationship between a parent and child is unique. So it is not very helpful when people say to you 'Oh well, he doesn't do that with me' as if it is clearly all your fault.

- As a society we have become much less accepting of odd behaviours and eccentricities and forget that children are different from each other and that they all have strengths and weaknesses. We seem to expect all children to be academic, attentive, agile, communicative and emotionally literate, and when they fall short of our expectations we think there must be something wrong which can be labelled and treated. It might be easier if we were all more accommodating and accepting of all children.

- In many ways, we have made matters much worse for children because they are so limited in their play, freedom and early experiences by our busy lifestyles and fears for their safety. They need space and time, freedom to explore, experiment and mature. Many children have lost the opportunity to play in groups with other children as their parents did when young – messing around, older ones looking out for younger ones, getting into a bit of mischief, learning about danger, experimenting with friendships and working out who they are.

- What is acceptable behaviour for a child will vary according to his specific problems and it is a matter of judgement that only you can make.

I find it very hard when George gets comments from strangers for his poor behaviour when I can see that, for him, he is actually doing incredibly well in a new or difficult situation.

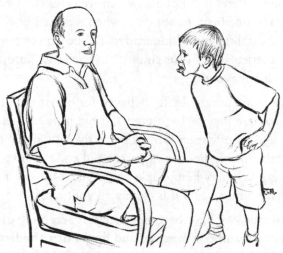

Ignoring bad behaviour

- You often have to empower other adults to tell your child off if he is behaving badly or inappropriately. Adults can be frightened of telling off a child with special needs because they do not know how he will react or what standards are expected. You have to tell people explicitly what your child might do, what you consider acceptable behaviour and what to do if he misbehaves. For example, you might have to tell someone that if he messes around with his food just to withdraw it.

I found out that Alice took advantage of the dinner ladies at school because they never said 'no' to her. I had to tell them it was okay to say 'no' and to be firm.

GENERAL RULES FOR RESPONDING TO YOUR CHILD'S BEHAVIOUR
Give attention for good behaviour and ignore bad behaviour

The golden rule for dealing with your child's behaviour is to *give attention for good behaviour.* When your child is being good, perhaps behaving nicely, playing properly or making an effort, praise him, give him some attention or a reward so that he is more likely to repeat the behaviour. The theory is that children's behaviour is reinforced by how we react to it – if something good comes out of it they are more likely to do it again.

Whenever I find I am losing it with Matthew I make sure I increase the amount of praise I give him for good behaviour. The carrot works better than the stick every time.

At the same time *bad behaviour should be ignored* as far as is possible because by doing so you are denying him any reward. If your child says a rude word and you don't react then he probably won't bother repeating it. On the other hand, if he is naughty and gets a big telling-off that might be enough of a reward for him. It might seem strange but he is getting your undivided attention.

Children with special needs often want attention and they may not be able to see the difference between good and bad behaviour, so it is vital that parents only respond to good behaviour.

It is also worth remembering that we may be very good at noticing amazing things such as new words or climbing to the top of a slide for the first time, but we often fail to notice when they are just doing what they are told, even though this is good behaviour and should be rewarded.

> Often when I find my children's behaviour is becoming difficult I realise I have let up on the praise and it just requires a conscious effort to get back on track by focusing on all the positive things they are doing – 'You ate your tea well', 'That is a lovely picture', 'Shall we play football in the garden later today?' and totally ignoring the wind-ups, the whinging and the silly language.

The carrot is always much better than the stick. It is easy to think you are not being strict enough and that you should come down hard on a child who is misbehaving. This generally does not work because all you are doing is giving him attention for bad behaviour and therefore an incentive to continue.

Be consistent

Being consistent is critical. If boundaries are established and interpreted consistently, children will know what is expected of them and what is not acceptable behaviour. This gives them a sense of security and confidence in their behaviour. If parents are not consistent children will not know from one day to the next what they are allowed to do and what reaction they will get, and they will feel unsure and insecure. Their behaviour will be poor because they will not have a clear idea of what is expected of them.

In the real world of your own home it is hard to be consistent all of the time – things happen unexpectedly and you can't be prepared for every eventuality. However, the more consistent you are the easier it will be for your child to get the message. So although it is tempting to think that it is easy to dismiss professionals for advocating consistency in an unrealistic way, it is worth scrutinising how you are responding to behaviour to make sure you are being as consistent as you can.

CHANGING BAD BEHAVIOUR
Say 'no' quietly but firmly and give an alternative or distract him

If your child is doing something you don't want, respond quietly but firmly; for example, say 'No banging' or 'No hitting'. Say what it is that your child is doing wrong because he may not understand what he is doing that is unacceptable. Make sure you have your child's attention before you speak to him.

It is often not enough to say 'no' on its own because children need to be given something positive that they can do. Rather than say 'Don't jump on the bed' say 'No, don't jump on the bed, go and play with the car' or 'No, don't jump on the bed, go and jump on the trampoline'. If you say 'no' you must mean it and win the issue. It is better to give in straightaway and to allow the behaviour than to say 'no' and then give in because you cannot stand any more of your child's whines and moans.

Sometimes, however, with behaviour which is deliberately intended to get your attention even a 'no' is too much of a reward and it is best to be selectively deaf and look the other way.

> Deepak went through a phase of spitting and the only way to combat it was to ignore it completely. It worked eventually but there was one awful moment when he spat on his grandmother's shiny new black patent shoes and I had to ask her to ignore it!

Respond immediately

If you are going to react to behaviour, respond immediately so your child knows exactly what he is doing that is wrong. There is no point mentioning it two hours later because he will probably not have a clue what you are talking about.

REWARDS

Sometimes praise is not enough and if you want your child consciously to change his behaviour then you might want to set up a reward system for it. You select the behaviour you want to change, for example, getting dressed and coming down promptly in the morning. When your child is successful you give an immediate reward – a sweet, a sticker or some money.

It is critical that the reward you select is motivating to your child so, if possible, let him select the reward – you may be surprised what he chooses. Think about what motivates him, not you. You often have to keep reinventing rewards to keep them interesting so that your child maintains his motivation. You must be careful to drop the reward once the good behaviour is established.

Food and sweets are an obvious choice but for health and diet reasons it is better to think of an alternative. Examples are bubbles, stickers, colouring pencils, money, tickles, time watching TV or playing on the computer, reading a book together, going for a walk, cooking, time alone with a parent, a cycle ride or a train or bus ride. Absolutely anything can be used as a reward as long as it is meaningful and works for your child. It will be even more motivating if your child only receives it as a reward and never or rarely at any other time.

> Stacey loved the Tweenies so her star chart was actually a Tweenie puzzle in pieces – instead of a star she got a bit of the puzzle which she eventually completed.

Star charts

You could set up a star chart, identifying a specific behaviour you want to change. An example could be staying at the table during meal-times. Your child would then get a sticker or a star each time he succeeded. This would go on a chart and when he had collected enough he could trade them for a stated reward. Star charts are great for concentrating everyone's minds on what the problem is – your child knows categorically what is expected of him and you as a parent know which behaviour you are focusing on, which means you are more likely to be consistent.

> Lucy's star chart was initially to gather five stars and then she could go and buy some bubble bath (a huge treat after years of bad eczema had banned bubbles). The buying of bubble bath then turned into a reward of having bubbles in her bath in the evening, provided she had eaten her tea without hitting herself.

Make the chart interesting by decorating it with pictures or stickers or by turning it into a race track.

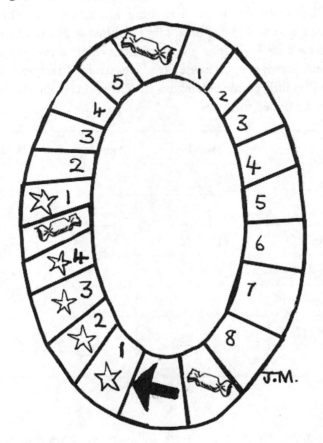

A star chart

Ensure that you start with success, so help your child get that all-important first sticker — you may have to modify the criteria to ensure success.

As the behaviour becomes more established, make the rewards rarer until they can be phased out. When your child starts maybe he needs two stars to get his reward of 10p, next time make it three stars for 10p and then four stars, etc. Eventually you will want to drop the rewards altogether and just rely on praise to keep the behaviour going.

Other ideas

Do a star chart for yourself: children often love role reversal.

For older children, rather than using stickers on a star chart, you could use a system of giving tokens for identified good behaviours. You could draw a smiley face or give a sticker or points every time your child tidies his toys or gets himself ready for school. In schools children often collect little plastic teddies in a jar. The stickers, points or teddies can then be traded for treats.

Jobs	Monday	Tuesday	Wednesday
Make bed	1		
Clear table			
Cleen teeth	1		
Pack school bag	1		
Lay the table			
Hang coat up			
Total	3		

1 point = 10p

I find star charts either work within a few days and we then conveniently forget about them or they don't work at all and we try a different approach.

BEHAVIOURAL PROBLEMS
Look at what the behaviour means

If you are getting persistent problems look very carefully at the behaviour within its context to see if in fact your child is gaining anything or if there is some other meaning to the 'bad behaviour'. All behaviour is a form of communication and it may be a very useful one for children with limited communication skills. So see what he is trying to communicate. It can help to look at behaviour in terms of the ABC of behaviour:

- A – Antecedents – what was happening in the run-up to the incident.

- B – Behaviour – what the behaviour was.

- C – Consequences – what the child gets as a consequence of the behaviour.

- C – Communicative intent – what the child is trying to communicate.

Sometimes it is worth drawing up a chart and jotting down anything that happens so you can then look back and see what it means. You could find that you are unintentionally rewarding your child for his behaviour and that you need to change your response to him in some way. It could be that he is using his behaviour to communicate. Bad behaviour can mean so many things. He may be saying 'I cannot do something because it is too difficult'. He may be angry about the way he is being treated or bored because he has been made to do the same thing too often. He may be uncomfortable, ill, over-excited, over-stimulated, over-tired or simply may just not know what to do and want some attention.

Here is an example of using the ABC of behaviour method: one day Freddy came home from school and was really angry and threw a precious ornament against the wall smashing it to pieces.

- Antecedents – Freddy came home from school with his sisters. He had hurt his knee in the playground and wanted to tell someone about it, but everyone was busy with normal family life – his mother was getting tea ready.

- Behaviour – he got annoyed and angry, picked up the ornament and threw it against the wall.

- Consequences – his mum came in and shouted at him, making him more angry and upset.

- Communicative intent – he wanted to talk to his mum about what had happened at school, but everyone was getting on with other things and no-one was picking up on his need for a hug and a chat, so he threw the ornament to get attention.

Common causes of behavioural problems

With the ABC method you can sometimes get to the root of the problem, which enables you to take avoiding action in future.

Behaviour is also a method of communication. For many children who have poor language skills, the only way they can express that they do not like something, want attention or are feeling angry or upset, is through bad behaviour. Working on improving communication skills is vital even if it is going to take a long time.

Sensory overload

Be aware of sensory issues. Some children hate loud bangs, crowded places, fluorescent lights, claustrophobic atmospheres or physical contact, and can react in what may seem like an extreme way. Extreme weather such as wind, thunder and lightning affect some children. Even changes in floor surfaces – tarmac to grass or cobbles – can upset children.

> We took Joe to an aquarium once which we thought he would enjoy because it was colourful and stimulating. However, he kept hitting people and running off down fire escapes and we could not get him back. We quickly realised it was not a case of bad behaviour but of total sensory overload. He had no other way of communicating that the environment was making him feel terrible. We just took him out and are now more careful about where we take him.

Tiredness

When children get tired they get fretful and irritable, and do not know what to do with themselves. It is best to ignore the behaviour and give them strategies for finding a quiet activity they can do on their own.

The environment

Sometimes it is a matter of changing the environment so that the behaviour is stopped; for example, removing a fuse from electric equipment so it does not work, putting a lock on a door high up so your child cannot open it or removing precious objects from his reach.

> Tom kept sweeping stuff off the table as he came into the classroom. When I looked at the situation I suggested that the

learning support assistant walked in on the table side so he would no longer be able to. It worked.

Boredom/stimulation

It can be very difficult to get the right balance between stimulation/over-stimulation or relaxation/boredom. Be sensitive to your child's needs. Children who have limited play and concentration can be easily bored as they do not have the range of activities open to them, and if they are learning basic skills they can end up repeating the same activities endlessly. Equally, too many toys can cause sensory overload.

MODIFYING INAPPROPRIATE BEHAVIOUR

Some children learn a behaviour which becomes a problem because they then use it indiscriminately or inappropriately; perhaps they kiss everybody and anybody or take their clothes off whenever they want to. Older brothers and sisters can often introduce new language (like swear words) or behaviour to a child who then copies it and may use it at any opportunity. Sometimes children quickly grow out of these behaviours but if your child doesn't, try the following ideas:

- Try to tackle these behaviours before they become too much of a habit, when they will be more difficult to break.

- Stay very calm and serious about inappropriate behaviours – a lot of squealing when a child pulls his trousers down in public will do nothing to discourage it.

- Suggest an alternative, acceptable action to replace the behaviour. The child who kisses people indiscriminately could be told to say or sign 'hello' or to shake hands if he needs physical contact. A child who tells everyone he loves them could be taught to say 'like' instead, and the child who hits when he is happy could be encouraged to clap.

- Sometimes it is a matter of encouraging your child to do things at the appropriate time. A child who liked showing people his penis could be told to 'Put it away, you wash it in the bath'.

Stay calm

- Sometimes you may need to reduce the behaviour gradually over time. Bouncing on all the furniture could be limited to one sofa only and then to the trampoline in the garden.

- Use social stories. For details see Chapter 7, Social Development.

- If you can, talk to your child about his behaviour, why it is inappropriate and how he should behave.

SANCTIONS

The use of sanctions with children with special needs is a very difficult area. You have to be very cautious as to whether it is appropriate to use them and, if you do, how you do. Sanctions that are punitive and negative do not help a child because they tell him what he should not do rather than what he should do. Children need to be told explicitly how they should behave.

First you have to recognise that there are situations where it is actually you, as the parent, who needs to be removed from a situation. This is because you have reached the end of your tether rather than because your child has done anything 'bad'. In this case, if your child cannot understand that he needs to give you some space, you have to find a way of distracting him. Find him an activity such as watching television or having a biscuit which will take him away from you and give you a break. All parents have moments like this so you need a strategy to give yourself 'time out' when you are overloaded.

If your child's behaviour is unacceptable, it is best to use the positive management techniques of firm boundaries and distraction described above. In situations where his behaviour is deteriorating give him something to do which is acceptable. The trouble with sanctions is that his behaviour may well be a method of communication, not 'bad behaviour' as such; and if he does not have the level of understanding necessary to realise what is going on he will feel, at the very least, confused and hurt by any sanctions imposed. Imagine a child misbehaving because a change in his environment has disturbed him. He is sent out of the room which makes him feel even worse, rather than receiving the reassurance and comfort that might make him calm down. It can also be argued that punishment does not work with any child because it suppresses rather than removes behaviour and it tells children what they should not do rather than what they should do.

However, there are times when it may be appropriate to use an immediate sanction so that a child can see his behaviour in terms of cause and effect. For example, if he eats disgustingly, the consequence of his behaviour will be that his food is removed. The sanction must be immediate, you must be prepared to see it through and your child must be clear what acceptable behaviour is expected of him.

One sanction that you might be able to use is 'time out'. This is when you take your child out of the situation, perhaps because he has been aggressive, to sit at the bottom of the stairs or some place where he gets no attention. If you use this sanction, make it positive by telling your child what he has to do to be reinstated, for example 'You can come back when you can play nicely with your sister' or 'eat properly'. However, you must be sure that he has sufficient understanding for it to be an appropriate sanction, that it will not just escalate the behaviour and that he is not even more of a risk to himself or his environment out of sight.

I would urge caution with the use of sanctions or punishments because whenever my children are behaving appallingly I can see that it is usually caused by total exhaustion, sensory overload or some unhappiness, which they cannot express. Also, the awfulness of children's behaviour is almost always a

symptom of how I feel at the time. I have had some terrible
moments when I have smashed bowls, thrown toys out of the
window, even showered the children with the washing – tea
towels, knickers etc. raining down on them – but it has always
been because I have been at the end of my tether, because I am
tired, premenstrual, bored or cheesed off, not because they
have done anything spectacularly awful.

SELF-HARM

Some children with special needs harm themselves by head-banging or
hitting or biting themselves. It is very distressing to watch and every
effort should be made to prevent it from happening. Look at the
situations in which your child self-harms and see if you can isolate the
cause or causes. Use the ABC method described above. You may be able
to see a pattern – frustration, boredom, self-stimulation, anger, fear –
and therefore be able to eliminate the root cause or mitigate against it.

Luke hits himself when things take an unexpected turn so it helps
to try to prepare him for the unexpected.

Improvements in a child's ability to communicate will help enormously
to relieve many of the powerful emotions he suffers. If you cannot
prevent self-harm, try the following strategies:

- Respond coolly, without getting upset and angry.
- Give him an alternative, acceptable action, such as stamping
  his feet, crushing a stress ball, biting a rubber toy or using a
  punch-bag.
- Change the environment to make the behaviour more difficult.
- Find a protective device, such as wrist pads strapped onto his
  wrists or a helmet, as a short-term measure.
- Talk about his feelings of anger or frustration and try to find a
  safe outlet for his emotions.
- Make sure he has lots of physical exercise.

OBSESSIONS

Many children have mild obsessions with football, cars or pop groups, but some children have extreme obsessions which may last for a long time. Research suggests that you cannot stop a child's obsessive nature and that if you try to do so he will only become more unhappy and more obsessive because he does not know when his next 'fix' will come.

If an obsession is not dangerous or anti-social, give your child the opportunity to indulge it provided it is in an appropriate and acceptable place. Children's obsessions change over time anyway. They can be irritating, but remember they could be a lot worse.

> Natalie loves loading the washing machine and turning it on. I have just got into the habit of always letting her do it and she is happy to accept that she can only do it when there is washing to be done.

- Try gradually to reduce the time spent on self-stimulatory behaviour or repetitive conversations about supermarkets, cars and so on.

- Use obsessions positively as an opportunity to encourage your child to learn more. An obsession with toy cars could be used to encourage him to count them or develop imaginative or cooperative play with other children.

- Warn your child if anything is going to happen which may affect his obsessions so that he has a chance to prepare himself.

- If the behaviour is dangerous or anti-social, you have to stop it and find an alternative; for example, a child who likes biting on electrical flexes could be given an appropriate plastic to bite on.

- Obsessive behaviour should diminish as his understanding, communication and play skills develop. By helping him improve in these areas you will be lessening his need to be obsessive.

AVOIDANCE

Children can use bad behaviour to distract adult attention and avoid doing something. Look at the task and make sure it is not inappropriate – perhaps too hard or too boring. If it is unnecessary put it away; if it can be modified to make it more interesting or easier, do so. However, there are some things which have to be done.

Avoidance

STRATEGIES TO IMPROVE BEHAVIOUR
Devote time specifically to your child

Make sure you spend time playing with your child without distraction or interruption. Let him choose what he wants you to do together and respect that choice. Even a short period in which you devote yourself wholeheartedly to your child can pay off, because subsequently he will be more accepting of the other calls on your time.

Concentrate on language skills

Concentrate on improving your child's communication skills because, as these improve, he will be more able to use language rather than behaviour to express what he wants and how he feels. Improving communication skills is a long and slow business but it is vital because they will be another more effective way to convey how he feels. It is also very important that you respond immediately to your child's attempts to communicate rather than ignoring him initially so that he then has to resort to bad behaviour. Encourage your child to use language rather than behaviour by perhaps saying 'Don't hit me, tell me what you want'.

A place to switch off

Children need a time and a place to switch off and do whatever they need to do to relax. We all need time to recharge our batteries without doing something improving and without demands being made. It is important that children know when they need to get away from everyone to avoid flashpoints. Make sure your child has a place he can retreat to if he is beginning to feel overloaded, where he can play quietly in whatever way he likes – maybe with dolls, maybe lining up toys or rocking to music until he feels able to participate again. Encourage him to recognise when he needs to go there to cool off and respect his right to be left in peace.

A place to switch off

Give him warning

Plan things ahead with your child so you can tell him what to expect and how to behave. Use books and photos if relevant.

Use an egg-timer or oven-timer to set a time-limit for an activity.

Try not to be confrontational

Try to be flexible and non-confrontational with your child, especially as he may not necessarily be naughty, just trying to express his feelings.

When I ask David to do something I take the approach 'you don't need to do it now, but you have to come back and do it later' and negotiate a solution.

Managing powerful emotions

Children at this age need help to deal with many powerful emotions. Do not deny the emotions they are feeling. See Chapter 8, Emotional Development, p.249 for suggestions of strategies.

Give your child choices

Children need choices in their lives because this enables them to feel they have some control over what is happening. It is easy to see how children might become very passive or very angry or both in turns if they are constantly being told what they are going to do and when and where.

Make sure your child has lots of opportunities for making choices at an appropriate level – choice of food at meal-times, games, or how to spend birthday money. It is important that he is given the freedom to make the wrong choice and that he is given the opportunity to learn to live with the consequences. See Chapter 8, Emotional Development, for more on choices.

Talk to your child

If your child is able to do so, discuss issues with him and develop strategies together to tackle problem situations.

If you are having a period of poor behaviour and you are trying to work out the cause, say, of bed wetting or reluctance to go to school, it is probably not best to talk about it when he is really upset. Find a time when he is relaxed and willing to talk, maybe at meal-times, bath-time or walking home from school.[1]

Model good behaviour yourself

Make sure that you are being a good role model yourself in the way you resolve arguments through negotiation and express happiness, anger and frustration.

SLEEP

If you are happy with your child's sleep routine, whatever it might be, then continue as you are and disregard other people's experiences and attitudes. If, on the other hand, you are having problems – your child is not sleeping or having disturbed nights – then you are perfectly entitled to do something about it. We all need a good night's sleep – children and adults alike – and we all function much better for having slept well. Children need to learn how to have a good night's sleep – it is an important life skill.

Sleep is a hard behaviour to change. At night you are tired and problems seem worse: it takes a lot of courage and determination to change your child's sleep routine when your whole body is telling you to forget it and take the easy short-term solution.

However, it is quite possible to change sleep routines, if you remember that once you start you must not give up. Whatever approach you take you must make sure that you follow it through. If you don't want your child to come into your bed and you decide to return him to his own room if he wakes up, you have to keep on doing that however many times it is required. As soon as you give in and let your child come into your bed he will get the message that it is worth persisting because he will eventually succeed. You want to give him the opposite message:

1   Roberts, R. (2002) *Self Esteem and Early Learning.* London: Paul Chapman.

that it does not matter how many times he tries, he will still sleep in his own bed.

A good night's sleep

It may take some time, but then again it may not. It took one family I met three nights to get their son to go to sleep on his own, it took another family 18 months.

When you decide to tackle sleep problems pick a good time when there is little else going on in your life, perhaps in the summer when the nights are warmer and when you are at home (not when you are on holiday or have people staying). Equally, don't give yourself endless excuses for putting it off.

Make sure that all those who are looking after your child follow the same procedure – respite carers, family and friends who have your child overnight.

If possible share the burden so you can get some sleep.

THE THEORY OF SLEEP TRAINING

The theory of sleep training is quite simple: children need to learn to go to sleep on their own. You should be able to leave your child awake in his room and let him go to sleep by himself. Then, if he wakes up in the night (as he will inevitably), he will be able to resettle himself and go back to sleep alone without having to involve you.

If your child has problems with going to sleep or with waking in the night you should examine his sleeping routine and see if he is able to go to sleep by himself. It may be that he has developed some routine in going to sleep like having you there or watching TV. When he wakes at night he cannot resettle himself without his particular routine.

THE PRACTICE OF SLEEP TRAINING
Bed-time routine

Establish a good bed-time routine, maybe having a bath, reading a book and then going to bed. Make it calm and orderly – don't start playing rough-and-tumble games to excite him. Don't make it over-long and elaborate but relaxing, soothing and comforting.

When it is time to go, say goodnight and leave in a confident way.

> I found with Ben that the cuddles would last for ages and that sometimes I fell asleep in bed. In the end I set an egg-timer and when it went off that was my cue to leave. Ben was able to accept it.

Make sure that there are no practical problems – that your child is not too hot or too cold, that he has eaten and drunk sufficiently. Think about any sensory issues – the feel of sheets and the weight of bedclothes – some children like to feel weighed down with heavy blankets, others find that oppressive and need a very light duvet.

Some children like it to be absolutely dark, others like a light to be left on somewhere, for example the landing light or a bedside lamp. You can buy very low wattage lights which can be plugged into wall sockets and give a gentle glow.

Settling down

If your child will not settle on his own then you have two options:

- *The direct approach* – once you have said goodnight to your child, leave him. If he gets up take him straight back to bed saying 'time for bed'. Make sure you don't have any conversation, no more kisses, no eye contact, just be very cool and businesslike. You have to keep returning him to his bed for as long as it takes, whether it is three times, five times or twenty times, until he finally gives up and goes to sleep. Having seen what is expected of him, the next night should not be so bad and the next even easier, until eventually he settles down of his own accord.

- *The gradual approach* – stay with your child while he falls asleep but each night move slightly further away – from his bed to the chair next to his bed, to sitting on the floor, to the threshold, to the landing and then finally out of sight.

Choose whichever method suits you both, as well as your situation and temperament, but whichever you do make sure that you stick with it.

To make it slightly easier you could start off by settling your child quite late so that he is naturally tired and more likely to comply. Gradually bring the time forward to a more acceptable time.

Waking in the night

Children who wake in the night are often those who cannot go to sleep by themselves. If you have solved the problem of settling then you may have solved this too. All children wake in the night because of bad dreams, needing the toilet or coughs and colds and other illnesses. Your child should be able to settle himself again after a quick reassurance from you. If not then think about the rewards he is getting from you – a cuddle, a drink, a visit to your bed or a chat. You need to stop these rewards and you can do this in one of two ways:

- Immediately – just stop all rewards and take your child back to bed, giving no eye contact, conversation or cuddles.
- Gradually – slowly reduce the rewards until they are non-existent. If you used to give a drink – give less, from milk reduce to water then nothing. If it was a cuddle, reduce the time until it is just a kiss, a stroke and then nothing.

Getting into the parental bed

One of the best things about being a parent is when your child comes into bed for a cuddle in the morning (provided it is not *too* early). If you like that too then it is fine; however, if you want to establish good sleep routines then it is better not to let your child sleep in your bed even for a short time.

If your child gets into bed with you in the middle of the night then you should take him back to his own bed with a minimum of fuss and eye contact and keep repeating it for as long as it takes for him to give up and go back to sleep. Some children can be so quiet that they get into bed without you realising it. Try to devise something to alert you like a bell on a closed door, so that you wake up and can respond immediately.

Staying up later

As children get older they inevitably need less sleep. This can be quite difficult to adjust to if you have been used to having your evenings to yourself. Children, as they get older, can usually be expected to stay in their rooms reading or listening to music until they are ready to sleep. Children with special needs may not be able to entertain themselves in this way.

> Meena used to be brilliant at going to bed at seven o'clock, then all of a sudden she was staying up until nearly ten most days and rather than sit in her room reading as I imagined a normal child would, she would follow us round the house saying 'What Mummy doing?' 'Going bananas. Go to bed!'

Accept that children will want to stay up later as they get older. Find a compromise:

- Find quiet activities that your child can enjoy in his room; for example, listening to relaxing music, drawing, doing puzzles and games or looking at books.

- Put him to bed late and then gradually bring the time forwards by five minutes each day until it is a more reasonable time.

- Make sure your child is well exercised and therefore physically tired by making sure you do some exercise every day – taking skateboards and scooters to the school playground after school, going for a longer walk on the way home, playing in the garden or going for a swim.

- Make his bedroom a nice place to be with toys and games but also relaxing, warm, cosy and conducive to sleep.

- Explain that he can stay up and play but that you will not play with him after a certain time, perhaps nine o'clock.

We keep out of the way, shutting ourselves in one room – talking or reading the paper with all lights off around the house until he has settled. If anything exciting is happening – people coming around or one of us going out – we just accept that he will be up until the excitement is over. There is no point at all getting irritated by it because we cannot win.

Waking up too early

If your child wakes too early and immediately wants to be on the go, it can be equally hard.

- You could try using an alarm clock, a radio alarm or timed light, which, when it comes on, is the signal that it is OK to get up. Say your child wakes up at 5.30 a.m., you could start with the alarm coming on at 5.30 a.m. then, very gradually, move it forwards until it is ringing at an acceptable time.

- Make sure your child has the sort of toys, games and books in his room that he might play with on his own.

- You could have a stair gate or stable door across the child's bedroom so he stays in his room but is not enclosed.

- In the summer, when it is light so early in the morning that children wake up earlier, you could try an extra blind or blackout curtains to darken his room.

Other points

If your child is ill, your priority is to make him feel comfortable; so forget good sleeping practice until he is fully recovered.

If you are following the above approach without success, it may be because you have not identified the reward your child is getting. Think very carefully about what is happening when he wakes up.

If he wakes up in the night and is not tired enough to go back to sleep give him strategies for dealing with it. Adults cope by reading quietly or making a drink, so suggest the same to him.

Some families find themselves developing extraordinary sleeping routines to get their children to bed. If you find yourself in this situation, it is probably best to get professional advice. Ask your health visitor for advice or a referral to a specialist sleep clinic.

If you have fears and anxieties about your child, because of his needs and the experiences you have had, they will loom greater at night and they may interfere with your ability to leave your child alone in his room. You may need help to address those issues before you can successfully tackle sleep training.

TOILET TRAINING

Toilet training is one of the most emotive areas of child development. On the one hand it is an important life skill that enables children to become independent; on the other, there is no point tackling it if you or your child are not ready. Try to ignore social pressure, think of the needs of your child and never let it become an issue.

A child is ready to be toilet trained when he is doing a proper wee or poo in his nappy, not just constant dribbles; which shows that he has sufficient muscle control to consciously hold and release his wee and poo.

When you decide to introduce your child to toilet training think of the following issues:

- There will be a lot of clearing up to do in the initial stages and it is vital not to show any anger or irritation, so make sure you are in the mood to handle it.

- Try at a time of relative peace and calm, not when your child is changing schools or you are expecting a new baby.

- It is much easier to practise at home when you don't have to worry about other people's expensive sofas and carpets. The summer is a good opportunity because children wear fewer clothes which can be washed and dried more easily, and you can spend time outside.

Before you start:

- Make sure you have lots of extra pants because you will get through *loads*.

- Get the right equipment for your child – maybe a potty, an insert into the toilet seat for small bottoms or special equipment which is available through your occupational therapist.

- Decide on a word, sign or symbol to mean toilet. It might be the word, or Makaton sign or symbol, or you may make up something yourself. If your child does not yet use the word himself, use it every time you go to the toilet to reinforce it. Make sure everyone who works with your child uses the same expression.

THE THEORY

The theory is very simple: try to get your child to do something in the toilet and then praise him like mad so he learns what is expected of him. Ignore all failures completely.

Be as relaxed as you can. It is important not to get cross, upset or frustrated at clearing up the mess because this can be counter-productive and make children upset and uncooperative.

Once you have started you must persist, however long it takes. If you feel you have misjudged it and your child is not ready then give up and try again in six month's time.

THE PRACTICE

Show your child what to do by taking him to the toilet and showing him your wee and poo. School can also be a good model because there are often 'class trips' to the toilet at break-time and it gives the children an idea of what to do.

At some point you have to take the plunge and take his nappies off. Put him on the toilet when you think there is a good chance of him performing. Keep putting him on the toilet every half an hour or so. If you are successful praise him excessively 'Well done, lovely wee in the toilet' and ignore all accidents.

Use any clues your child gives you that he might be about to perform and put him on the toilet; for example, if he disappears into the corner, starts wriggling or becomes manic. You really want him to succeed so you can praise him to the skies.

Initially you will control when your child goes on the toilet but after a while he will make it clear if he does not want to do anything and eventually he will be able to say or sign that he needs the toilet. He may be too late, but praise him anyway for trying. It will take time for him to learn to read his body's signals.

Getting your child to wipe his bottom and wash his hands

Some children are reluctant to wipe their bottoms. There are all sorts of reasons for this so look at:

- balance issues – can he physically twist round?

- sensory issues – look at using different wipes and paper

- use a reward system to encourage him if it is a matter of laziness

Using the toilet independently

- use social stories and visual clues such as photographs and pictures to show him what to do, if he does not understand the idea.

Points to remember

Sometimes a child is reluctant to sit on the toilet, so you could try entertaining him by reading books while he's on the toilet or blowing bubbles. Boys may like trying to 'fire' at a ping-pong ball in the toilet. You do not want him to sit on the toilet for hours, but you need him to have a go.

Some children do not like the sensation of letting go into the toilet pan. Try using a disposable bowl under the toilet seat like a commode.

Some children like the security of their nappy. Start by getting your child to poo or wee in his nappy but when he is sitting on the toilet. Later, you could cut a hole in the nappy so he still has the security of the nappy around him, before finally encouraging him to use the toilet conventionally.

Make the toilet a comfortable place. Your child needs to feel secure so make sure he can sit on the toilet comfortably with his feet supported so that he is not in any danger of falling off or in!

Modern disposable nappies are so good that children may feel little incentive to get rid of them. You could use cloth nappies and see if they are more of a motivation.

Some children have no social sensitivities and therefore have no qualms about poo. They can find it rewarding to soil their pants or play with it and relish the mess it makes. Make sure in this case that you are not rewarding your child in any way by getting angry or making a fuss with all the clearing up.

Be patient. It may take days, weeks or months to train your child to use the toilet and you may find that you have accidents and lapses for a long time to come. Changes of routine, different environments and emotional upsets can affect toileting. Also, children who are not so sensitive to social niceties may lose interest after a while, so you have to make sure you keep up the praise and, if necessary, rewards.

If your child starts wetting or soiling himself after being dry for a long time, you may have to look at it as a behavioural issue and see what the underlying cause is.

Dry at night

As with toilet training there is a huge range in the age at which children are dry at night. If you notice that your child consistently has a dry nappy in the morning then it is worth removing his nappies to see what happens. Remember that it is unusual for children to wet their bed deliberately. Try the following ideas to establish a good routine or if things start to go wrong:

- The key can often be drinking more. Drinking lots will strengthen the bladder and make it function better. Encourage him to drink lots during the day, in particular earlier rather than later. Some drinks like blackcurrant can aggravate the bladder so are best avoided. You could try a star chart or reward system for drinking six drinks a day.

The key may be drinking more

- It can be difficult for some children to drink at school because there may be no water available during the school day. At lunchtime children are often in a hurry, being hurried along or may have been put off the school jug of water because the glasses are dirty or someone once spat in it. Talk to teachers and arrange that the dinner ladies encourage your child to drink up, arrange for him to take a bottle of water or squash into class or pay for school milk.

- Because children don't wet beds deliberately, don't set up a reward system for dry beds, although you should acknowledge them. Always ignore wet beds.

- Ensure that he goes to the toilet immediately before bed and talk to him about how he needs to get up in the night if he needs the toilet.

- Make sure there is enough light so he can get out of bed and go to the toilet independently or you can hear him if he calls.

- Use a mattress protector, and have a supply of clean sheets discreetly ready so you are not hunting around in the airing cupboard in the middle of the night.

- If appropriate leave a potty at the end of his bed so he can find it easily in the night.

- You can wake your child for a wee just before you go to bed but you must make sure he is properly awake – get him up and make him walk to the toilet. If he does not want to do a wee that is fine, you can't force him. Do not place him on the toilet asleep or half-asleep because you are only encouraging him to wee in his sleep. Over time you could gradually wake him earlier and earlier until it is not necessary at all.

- If your child wets the bed just before it is time to get up, get up half an hour earlier so he can go to the toilet and then gradually move the time back again.

- If your child is able to, talk about the problem and what he would like to do about it.

- If it becomes a problem, seek professional advice through your health visitor.

CHAPTER 10

Education

When your child is at the right school you can feel confident that she is in an environment in which she is happy, making good progress in learning new skills and experiencing opportunities for personal, social and educational development. If you have good methods of communication teachers can also be a wonderful source of information, advice and encouragement to you as a parent. It can be great to feel that you are working in tune with your child's school to enable her to move forward.

CHOOSING A SCHOOL FOR YOUR CHILD

Choosing the right school for your child is one of the hardest decisions a parent has to make.

Think about your child's needs

The first thing to do is to consider your child's individual needs – cognitive, language, physical, sensory, social and emotional. Think what they are likely to be in the next year or two. Don't look too far ahead: it is impossible to know what the future holds. You can deal with future issues if and when they arise.

Decide on priorities – it may be that she has a specific problem which needs to be addressed as a matter of priority, such as language development, or that she needs a safe and nurturing environment.

Seek objective advice and views from professionals and talk to other parents about their experiences.

Write down the important issues as this information can be used as a checklist when talking to schools.

While she is at primary school age, you probably want to keep her options as open as possible; but by the time you are deciding on a secondary school you will need to consider longer-term issues including her level of independence and where you expect her to be post-16.

The choice of provision

Most parents have a choice for their child's education. You can choose between a mainstream school where she will be educated in a class with her 'normal' peers, a special school for children who have special needs and, sometimes, a resourced unit where children with special needs are taught in their own class but within a mainstream school. Some special schools cover a broad range of needs, others are for a specific disability or group of needs. Some special schools are state schools run by the local education authority (LEA) and others are run privately or by voluntary organisations.

Some parents have also set up more flexible arrangements where a child is educated some days in the local school and some days in a special school. Some special schools have arrangements with nearby mainstream schools allowing some integration for certain lessons or activities. Think about what would really be best and see if it could be arranged if it does not exist already.

Morning stretches

The advantages of educating your child in a mainstream school are:

- She will learn alongside her 'normal' peers, who should be good role models and provide normal behaviour, social skills and language to emulate.

- She will have the opportunity to make friends with children who live nearby.

- She is likely to be in her local school and will grow up to be part of and well known in her community. Fellow pupils will know her as will their families and friends.

- You will be more likely to take her to school yourself because it will probably be nearby. Therefore you may have a better idea of what is happening in school. It will be easier to see her in the school environment.

- You can have regular contact with other parents who will probably live locally.

The advantages of educating your child in a special school are:

- The staff at a special school should have more training, experience and patience in teaching children with special needs.

- Classes are generally much smaller and so she is likely to get more individual attention.

- The environment of a special school is more likely to be nurturing and supportive. She will probably not be so exposed to opportunities for bullying and teasing. She will not stick out as different and odd.

- The curriculum is more likely to be modified to suit her needs.

- She may have more access to different facilities and opportunities which may be motivating or therapeutic, such as horse-riding therapy, sensory rooms and swimming sessions.

- She may also have greater access to professionals such as occupational therapists, physiotherapists and speech therapists.

Special needs teacher

The advantages of educating your child in a resourced unit are:

- She will have specialist teaching in a small class where children are all at a similar level.

- She will have access to extra help, therapists and appropriate programmes.

- She can integrate with mainstream activities and classes as appropriate.

- She will have 'normal' role models to follow.

- She will be educated alongside other children with special needs so they do not feel 'different' or isolated, and with whom she may find it easier to build friendships.

However, remember that these are broad generalisations and they may not necessarily work in this way for your child. Just because a child with special needs goes to a mainstream school does not mean she will necessarily make friends locally; she may feel isolated and different. Equally, a teacher at a special school may not know a lot about her particular condition.

What is available?

When the time comes to look for a school for your child, there are several things to consider:

- Start early – the procedures take a long time especially if you end up in dispute with your LEA. Start looking at schools at least a year before your child is due to start school or before she is due to transfer to a new school.

- Ask for a list of schools from your LEA.

- Have an open mind, visit as many different types of schools as possible and do not rule anything out until you have seen it. It is helpful to know what provision is available and how different schools operate. Even making a decision that a school is not right for your child will inform your own choice and can give weight to your argument.

- Go back as often as you need, particularly to the ones you visited in the beginning because you may see them in a different light or have different questions after your experience at other schools.

- Ask professionals for their views but make up your own mind. They have their own prejudices and their answers may be affected by their knowledge of financial restraints or the places available. Your own views need not be affected by such considerations, merely by what is best for your child.

- Listen to what other parents say about a school but always make your own judgement. Each child is different, so even if a school is not suitable for another child it does not mean it is not appropriate for yours. Also remember that other people have their own expectations and priorities for a school, and they may not be the same as yours.

Visiting schools

Take your list of priorities and questions with you. Look at different aspects of the school:

- Find out about the teachers, learning support assistants (LSAs), support staff, therapists and specialist teachers. Try to talk to different staff members, however briefly.

- Consider the ethos and atmosphere. When you go round the school look at the behaviour and demeanour of the children, how they are treated by staff and how the staff treat each other. Is it a happy environment? Is it a noisy and lively place or quiet and calm?

- Find out how committed the school is to meeting children's needs, even if that is contrary to 'policy'. Is there any flexibility in the way the school is managed and run to make it easier to meet the needs of a child who is not typical?

- Look at a school from your child's perspective. What would be her experience and view? What pressures or pleasures would it bring and how would it affect her?

- What are the facilities like? Is the fabric of the building in good condition? Is there a good range of equipment and facilities?

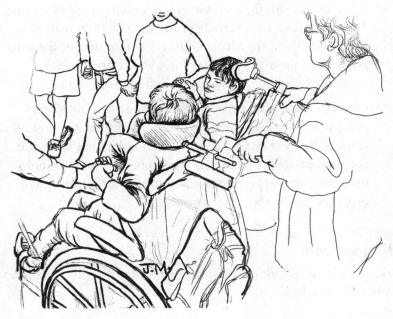

Visiting schools

- Visit the school on your own or with a friend. If you are seriously considering the school you could take your child along later to see how she responds to the environment and how the staff interact with her. You could ask to sit in on a class – if they refuse to let you that might also tell you something about the school.

- Find out what opportunities are available to the children: sensory room, swimming sessions, music therapy, riding, trips out, community contacts, contacts with other schools, residential trips etc. and how the school would manage your child's special needs.

Questions specifically for mainstream schools

- Find out if any other pupils, past or present, have had similar special needs to your child and how it worked.

- Ask the head what value he or she gives to special needs children within the school. The response will give a good indication of the ethos of the school and the attitude of the head.

- Use any flexibility in the system. For instance, an extra year in a pre-school setting might give a child the chance to mature and catch up sufficiently to try a mainstream education.

Making a decision

When you have visited all the relevant schools in your area, you will probably have found at least one that you consider suitable. Sometimes a decision is very clear-cut but often the perfect school does not exist and it is a matter of weighing up the issues and deciding which is the better option for your child at the time.

> Alex's educational psychologist did not support the idea of a mainstream school but when we moved house to a town ten miles away our new educational psychologist was all in favour! It just shows there is no 'correct decision'.

Write down the pros and cons of the schools you visit.

Be wary of choosing a school on the basis of a few personalities because heads and teachers do change jobs.

Recognise your prejudices and preferences and be aware of them when you decide which school is most appropriate for your child. We all bring our views to bear, e.g. 'my child's needs are so severe she needs to go to a special school' or 'children with special needs have a right to be part of their community'. By declaring them it is easier to be clear in your own mind whether it is the right decision for your child.

Sometimes it helps to discuss things with someone independent. You could use the Parent Partnership Service at your LEA. This provides information and support and aims to help parents make informed decisions.

If your child's special needs are such that they cannot be met locally then contact your LEA and relevant voluntary organisations for information on schools nationally. *The Gabbitas Guide to Schools with Special Needs*, published by Kogan Page, lists all special schools. If you choose a school which is not run by your LEA you will have to make a very convincing case to them that your child's needs cannot be met in local schools and only in your chosen school. The LEA has a duty to accept your decision provided it is suitable, not damaging to other children at the school and an efficient use of resources. If the LEA does not agree with your decision, then you will have to enter into discussions and may have to take the issue to tribunal to be settled independently.

Having made the decision

Once you have made a decision you should approach the school directly to fit in with their entry procedures and/or ensure that the information is fed into the statutory assessment procedure outlined below.

Give your choice of school a chance to work by ironing out initial difficulties and recognising that everyone's education will have peaks and troughs. Children change as they grow, schools change and the demands of the education system grow, so keep it all under review.

GETTING THE BEST OUT OF YOUR CHILD'S EDUCATION
Ensure that the school has all necessary information

It is important that when your child starts at a new school, it goes as smoothly as possible. Make sure the school has good information before she starts.

- Be honest and open about her special needs. Give a report about anything that might be relevant to the school, perhaps the need to manage change or for access improvements.

- Send any useful information or reports from her current school or nursery or from any professionals involved in working with her.

- Make sure the school makes contact with her previous school or playgroup.

- If she is going to have an LSA working with her it is worth suggesting that two people share the role to prevent excessive reliance on one member of staff.

- If she is vulnerable to changes in routines, explain how staff going on courses, teachers going on sick leave or changes of classrooms will have to be properly managed.

- Put teachers in touch with any professionals or organisations which can provide support. The LEA employs specialist teacher advisers (for hearing impaired, visually impaired and physically disabled) to provide information, ideas and equipment to schools to help children with their learning and independence. Organisations such as the Down's Educational Trust, Makaton or local autistic societies can give expertise and information and offer relevant courses.

I arranged for a speaker from Down's Ed to come to my daughter's school to talk to all staff about Down's Syndrome – not just teachers but the LSAs, admin staff and dinner ladies.

Ensure your child is prepared for her new school

You want your child to settle in quickly, so:

- Most schools offer 'taster' days where children meet staff and are shown the site. Ensure she attends or, if this is not possible, arrange an individual visit so that the new school and teacher are familiar.

- Try to ensure that she knows some of the other pupils by enrolling her in the local playgroup or by setting up a social activity with other children who already attend or are moving to the school.

- Talk about the new school with her; maybe have photographs for her to look at.

Establish a good relationship with your child's school

Whatever the school, it is vital to establish good relations with your child's school and all its staff. It should be a two-way dialogue because everyone – teacher, parent and pupil – will benefit from sharing information, practice and goals.

Parents have a different perspective on their child from teachers. Parents are their child's best friend and ally and have wider and longer-term concerns than teachers. There should be a joint agenda, with teachers supporting parents as much as the other way round.

You have to build up trust with the school. You have to feel confident that they know your child, are working with her in a positive and encouraging way, that they would talk to you honestly about any problems that might arise and that they would respond appropriately to any concerns that you might have. You can only develop that trust by working hard at communicating effectively with the school early on. You need to give information and ask for information in return. Once you have developed that trust you can probably relax a little. Spend time getting to know all the staff at school and building up a relationship and understanding with them. It is not just teachers but LSAs, teaching assistants and dinner ladies who will be very important to your child too.

If you can, go into school to help. Most schools welcome the support parents can bring. You could offer to help in class once a week or so. Some teachers do not like parents helping in their child's class so you might have to help in a different class, give administrative support or help on school trips or with fundraising. If you get to know staff and they get to know you it will help build up a good relationship. Also, it helps you to have an understanding of how schools operate, what and how children learn, the atmosphere and ethos of a school and how your child fits in and is treated.

> It can be difficult to help at school if your child has a one-to-one LSA because he will be confused as to who to turn to. I helped in the class above my son and found it very useful because it gave me information on what they were doing. It supported my view that he could not cope in the class above and should be kept down a year.

Establish good communication with the class teacher

All parents say that their children never tell them what happens at school. The conversations go something like this: 'Did you have a good day at school?' 'Can't remember' or 'What did you do at school?' 'Don't know', usually accompanied by a scowl. However, you can usually pick up information from things they let slip as you are chatting. When they ask how to read a word, which number follows 299 or why someone hits them at school, you can get an idea of what they are up to. It can be different with many special needs children because progress is slow, communication delayed or they do not tend to transfer information from one setting to another so you don't get much feedback. You need to ask the teachers to provide that information instead.

Equally, the teachers need the same kind of information from you otherwise they too are operating in a vacuum. You need to tell them what she did at the weekend or if anything significant happened; for example, she went swimming, had a haircut or her father's gone away on business. That should help the staff understand her behaviour if there is a problem or give them a point of communication or an idea for an activity which would be relevant and interesting.

Many schools use a 'home book' or 'home–school book' which is a daily diary in which parents and teachers can write to provide and ask for information, make requests for materials, communicate about homework and so on. It is good to use these to establish a dialogue.

If your child is in a mainstream school she may not need a home book as such but a diary, in which to record homework and other specific messages that she may forget to tell her parents; for example, a request to bring in a photo of herself as a baby.

Children can also take photos and objects between home and school so that they can talk about what they are doing in the other setting.

Writing

Deal with problems as they arise

If you have a problem or a concern make an appointment to see the teacher. Try to nip any problem in the bud rather than leaving it too long. It can be difficult as a parent to feel confident that an issue is of sufficient magnitude. Some teachers can be very defensive or give an impression of being far too busy and far too competent to welcome a parent's intervention. If you express concerns about what is going on you can be made to feel that you are a pushy and interfering parent. In the end, though, the subject of the matter is your child, you do know her best and your responsibility is to her, because no-one else is going to look out for her in the way you do. So if you have a concern, ask.

It is probably best to air any concerns with the teacher in person rather than in the home book because, unless you are very good with words, it can look rather stark and confrontational in black and white. Informal meetings are best if you want to resolve issues amicably.

Ensure that your child gets the education she needs

Make sure you say what you want your child to learn at school. All children follow the National Curriculum, but it may be that specific areas are more important to your child, such as language, play or social skills. Children can be given exemptions from certain subjects so that they can concentrate on other more important ones. Schools may claim that a child has 'accessed the National Curriculum' because she has sat through a history lesson; but you have to ask yourself whether exposure is the same as learning and whether the time would be better spent doing something else. Parents do have the right to make requests and teachers usually value their perspective. Use the annual review of the statement (see page 308 for information on statutory assessments) or parents' evenings to suggest objectives for the year.

Make sure professionals such as physiotherapists and speech therapists are liaising with both you, as parents, and the school so that everyone is kept informed of recommended activities. Do what you can to get all the services to work together – education, health and social services.

Make sure you are sharing achievements otherwise there is a danger that skills are not generalised in different settings.

> Ellie swam a length of the swimming pool but had never done so with us so we had no idea she was capable of it until school told us and I went to watch. On the other hand, at home she was using much more language than at school.

Reading

Support your child's learning at home

Do what you can at home to support what teachers are doing in class. Often the home is a more natural and meaningful environment for learning. You will need information about what your child is doing at school. Teachers should be happy to give you:

- A timetable for the week so you will know for example that PE is on Wednesdays and RE on Fridays.

- Termly themes. Each class sets themes for each subject, such as materials, fairy tales, water, etc. If you know what she is doing you can reinforce it at home by, for example, reading the same stories or singing the same songs.

- Information on what she is doing in literacy and numeracy and how you can best support her – perhaps by encouraging her to practise writing certain letters, reading sight vocabulary or doing simple addition sums. Ask if you can go in to talk to the teacher about the strategies used in school so that you are all using the same method; for example, whether they print or use cursive writing and what methods they use to teach maths.

Establish a good relationship with the learning support assistant

If your child is in mainstream education then she may have an LSA for part of the time she is in school. In a busy class of 30 children, he, or more likely she, will be responsible for supporting your child and carrying out any therapy programmes required. Some LSAs are highly trained and experienced; however, many are not. Make sure that the LSA has the information she needs about your child, her condition and her needs. Build a good relationship and a means of communication with the LSA.

It is usually recommended that a child has more than one LSA because if the relationship is too cosy the child can become dependent on the LSA. The LSA may then become a focus for inappropriate behaviour and also a barrier to her playing with her peers. A good LSA will act as a support to her, offering help only when necessary so that she can gradually increase her social skills and understanding of classroom language and activities, and become more independent.

Learning support assistant

I had an arrangement with Kirsty's school that I went in to see the staff once a week or fortnight rather than get daily bulletins. However, if something significant had happened during the day, the teacher would always come out to see me in the playground at the end of school.

Support your child's friendships at school

You may have to be more pro-active in encouraging your child to make friends if she finds this difficult or if she is at a school some way from home.

If it is not clear who her friends are, ask her teacher if she has any particular friends at school or if there is someone she thinks might be appropriate. If you can, invite them round to play for a short period; or it might be easier to arrange a joint activity with another family such as a picnic in the park. See how it develops. Sometimes it is easier to ask several children round to play as it may be less daunting for them.

If your child is in mainstream school and is not making friends find out if anything is going on that needs attention. Some parents find their children are so stressed by the educational demands of the classroom that they spend play-times alone to recover. Other children become so dependent on their LSA that she becomes a barrier to them playing with other children. Sometimes special needs children in mainstream schools are in fact educated for much of the time separately and so do not really have much chance to interact. Address these issues with the school and see Chapter 7, Social Development, for ideas to help.

If your child attends a school some distance away then it may not be feasible for her to see schoolfriends very often. In this case, you may need to make more effort for her to meet local children through neighbours and community activities and by enrolling her in children's clubs.

The other day Hannah and her friends were performing a dance routine for me. Her friends would give Hannah a nod at the moment she had to 'come in' enabling her to participate fully. It was lovely to see.

HOW SCHOOLS PROVIDE ADDITIONAL SUPPORT FOR CHILDREN WITH SPECIAL NEEDS

Many children have special needs at some point in their educational career and these are normally catered for by teachers providing appropriate materials and 'differentiating the curriculum'.

If your child is at school and you think she has special needs which have not been identified or have not been addressed then you should discuss your concerns with the class teacher, the special education needs coordinator (SENCO) or the head. If the school agrees that there are problems which cannot be addressed within the normal class structure then extra support is provided. This happens in the following way until your child receives a level of support which enables her to make satisfactory progress.

'School Action'

If your child has been identified as having special educational needs the school will provide additional help appropriate to her; for example, extra support in class, group work, additional lessons or extra equipment.

The class teacher may write an individual education plan (IEP) for your child identifying what help she needs, what the targets are and how they will be measured and monitored. The school must inform you of this and should consult you about your views.

'School Action Plus'

If the above action is not enough then the school moves onto 'School Action Plus'. This allows the school to bring in outside expertise, for example from an educational psychologist or speech therapist, who will assess your child and provide a programme of work or advice to staff.

If this is still not helping her make sufficient progress then the next stage is the Statutory Assessment of Special Educational Needs.

Statutory Assessment of Special Educational Needs

If your child is not yet at school but has significant special needs which will seriously affect her ability to participate and progress at school, then she may need to be assessed. This is so that when she starts school at the age of four or five her special needs are identified and properly addressed by her teachers, school and LEA. The parent or an educational professional requests a Statutory Assessment of Special Educational Needs (SEN).

The statutory assessment or statementing process is long and complex. Below is a brief summary of how it works but for further free information you can get *Special Educational Needs (SEN): A Guide for Parents and Carers* and *Special Educational Needs Code of Practice* from the Department for Education and Skills at:

DfES Publications Centre
PO Box 5050
Sudbury
Suffolk CO10 6ZQ
Tel: 0845 6022260

A statutory assessment is carried out by the LEA for children with more serious and complex problems to identify what the needs are, how they should be met and which is the most appropriate school.

As a parent you have two main responsibilities:

- to give as much information as you can about your child

- having considered all the schools which might be appropriate, to choose the one you think would be best for your child.

The procedure

You or your child's school can apply to the LEA for a statutory assessment.

There is an initial form to complete in which you have to give a brief description of your child, her educational progress and the professionals involved. The LEA has six weeks in which to decide whether there are sufficient grounds to proceed with a statutory assessment.

If the LEA decides to proceed it will gather reports from all the professionals involved with your child; for example, educational psychologists, speech therapists, paediatricians and social workers. As parents you will be asked to report on her progress and give your views on her educational needs. You can also send in any assessments you have arranged privately.

The LEA will then consider all the reports and may decide to draw up a draft statement of special educational needs, which will include a description of her special educational needs, the help she should get, the educational objectives and the non-educational needs and provision. However, it will not state the school she should attend.

The LEA will send you a copy of the draft and all the reports and you will be given two weeks to consider them and seek any clarifications and amendments. At this stage you can express a preference for a school for your child. The LEA must agree with your preference for her school as long as it is suitable, not damaging to the other children at the school and that it is an efficient use of resources.

Once you have reached an agreement, the LEA will issue the final statement which will name the school she will attend. It will come into force immediately and the LEA has a duty to fulfil the requirements of the statement. If you move to another area the statement moves with your child and the duty falls on your new LEA.

The whole process should take about 26 weeks.

The LEA can decide that there are insufficient grounds for a statutory assessment or for a statement and it should let you know why. If you disagree with the decisions made you can take your case informally to the local disagreement resolution service and/or to the Special Educational Needs Tribunal.

Annual review

The statement is reviewed at least annually to ensure that it is still appropriate. The head teacher appoints a date, and teachers, professionals and parents are asked to send in a report on the child's progress. A meeting is held to review the reports and establish targets for the coming year. It is an important opportunity for parents to give their views and to state what their hopes are for the future. The LEA revises the statement in the light of the annual review meeting.

If your child is due to change schools the review, which is held in the academic year prior to the change, considers her needs and makes a recommendation for the next school placement to the LEA.

Support during the statementing process

The LEA has to provide a named officer within the LEA who will be your point of contact and provide information to you.

Parent Partnership officers, as mentioned above, provide support and advice to parents during the statutory assessment. They are independent and neutral; their duty is to help parents make informed decisions about their child's education. Contact your LEA for your local service.

Voluntary organisations, such as Mencap, the Advisory Centre for Education and Network 81, can provide information and advice which is relevant to your child's particular needs. The *Special Education Handbook* published by the Advisory Centre for Education gives information on statementing and the appeal process. See Chapter 12, Resources, for contact details.

> I had such a long battle with the LEA about schooling that the office's number appeared on my BT 'Friends and Family' list of most often called numbers!

CHAPTER 11

Financial and Practical Support

FINANCIAL SUPPORT

Having a child with special needs can lead to extra costs for the parents, so listed below are some of the sources of financial support.

Social security benefits

There are various social security benefits you can claim for your child and for the main carer.

Your local Citizens Advice Bureau can give advice by phone or in person. Look in your phone book for the contact details. Many voluntary organisations (e.g. Royal National Institute for the Blind and the National Deaf Children's Society) also give helpful advice on what is available and how to apply.

Disability Living Allowance

Disability Living Allowance (DLA) is a tax-free allowance for adults or children who need help with personal care, with getting around or both. There are two components:

- Care (for extra and additional care) available from birth, paid at three rates:
    - high – for people/children who need help both day and night

311

- middle – for people/children who need help during the day or night

- low – for people/children who need some help during the day.

- Mobility (for help getting around) available from age three, paid at two rates:

  - higher – for people/children unable or virtually unable to walk, available from age three

  - lower – for people/children who need someone to provide them with guidance and supervision for most of the time they are outdoors in unfamiliar surroundings, available from age five.

To qualify, you have to be able to demonstrate in the information you provide that your child requires more help than a child of the same age who is not disabled. When you fill in the forms give as much information as you can and be as specific as you can so you can demonstrate to the administrator who reads your form what your child is really like.

A decision maker at the Department of Social Security will decide whether you qualify and for which category. You can ask for a review if you are not happy with the decision. You must write and request it within one month and enclose any additional information. If you are still not satisfied you can go to appeal within one month of the date of the decision.

Ask your social worker, the Citizens Advice Bureau or a local voluntary group, e.g. Mencap, for help completing the questionnaire.

Carer's Allowance

The Carer's Allowance (CA) is paid to those who care full-time for a child who gets the DLA at the middle or higher rate. You must be caring for your child for a minimum of 35 hours per week and be earning no more than £75 (2003 figures) per week after deduction of taxable allowances. The allowance is taxable. The application form is very straightforward.

If you receive the CA you automatically get credited with National Insurance contributions so that your pension is protected.

Income Support

If you are on a low income and have savings of less than £8000 (£12,000 for if you are over 60), you can claim Income Support. To claim Income Support, contact your local social security office, listed in the phone book as Jobcentre Plus or Social Security; or you can ring the Benefit Enquiry Line.

Child Benefit

Child Benefit is a tax-free benefit paid to the mother. If you do not already receive this benefit contact the Benefit Enquiry Line.

For information and application forms for the DLA, the CA, Income Support and Child Benefit call the Benefit Enquiry Line on 0800 882200.

Housing Benefit

If you are on a low income, have savings of less than £6000 and pay rent you can claim Housing Benefit from your local council. Contact your local council – district, borough or unitary authority – for forms. If you receive Income Support or Jobseeker's Allowance you will get these forms in your claim pack.

Council Tax Benefit

If you are on a low income, have savings of less than £6000 and pay council tax you can claim Council Tax Benefit. You can get forms from your local council – district or borough council or unitary authority. If you receive Income Support or Jobseeker's Allowance you will get these forms in your claim pack.

Council Tax Band Reduction Scheme for People with Disabilities

Each house is allocated a band according to its value for the purpose of calculating council tax. If the house has been altered for a disabled person – for example, doors widened to allow wheelchair access – then you can apply to your local council to have the council tax band reduced.

Home Responsibilities Protection

Home Responsibilities Protection (HRP) is a scheme which helps to protect your basic state retirement pension. If you do not work, or your earnings are low and you are caring for someone, you may be able to get HRP. HRP reduces the number of years you need to have received credits to your National Insurance record because you were unable to work.

If you get Income Support you will probably get HRP automatically. If you get the CA you will get National Insurance credits and probably not need HRP.

For more information ask for leaflet *PM9 State Pensions for Carers and Parents: Your Guide* from your social security office or by calling the pension information line 0845 7 31 32 33. Or visit the website at www.pensionsguide.gov.uk.

Tax credits

Child tax credit

Child tax credit is for people who are responsible for at least one child. It does not matter whether you or your partner works. The amount of tax credits will depend on various elements, including the number of children you have and whether or not they have a disability. The amount of tax credits you receive will also depend on your annual income. You are likely to get some tax credit if your income (joint income if you are a couple) is less than £58,000 per annum. The money is paid to the main carer directly.

Working tax credit

Working tax credit is paid to low income, working people with or without children who work 16 hours or more a week. Assistance can be given with childcare costs. Working tax credits are included in your pay and the childcare component is paid direct to the main carer.

For more information and application forms call the Tax Credits Information Line on 0800 500222.

Additional financial support

Family Fund Trust
PO Box 50
York YO1 9ZX
Tel: 01904 621115
Textphone: 01904 658085
Website: www.familyfundtrust.org.uk

The purpose of the Family Fund Trust is to ease the stress on families caring for a severely disabled child under 16 by providing grants and information on the care of children. The trust is an independent organisation funded by the government. Grants are given for such needs as washing machines, holidays, leisure activities, driving lessons, bedding, clothing and other items related to the care of the child. Assistance can only be given to those families whose gross income is less than £21,000 and who have savings of £8000 or less (2002 figures). Further information and application forms are available from the address above.

Family Welfare Association
501–505 Kingsland Road
London E8 4AU
Tel: 020 7254 6251
Email: fwa.headoffice@fwa.org.uk

The Family Welfare Association offers a wide range of services to support some of the poorest families in the country (befriending services, respite care, family centres etc.). It also provides one-off grants to anyone living in the UK who is in need of financial assistance at a time of crisis in their lives. Money can be given for a range of needs such as clothing, fuel bills and household items. Grants are usually between £100 and £200. Applications are made through a health visitor, social worker or Citizens Advice Bureau.

TRANSPORT
Blue badges – disabled parking

You can apply for a blue badge to allow you to park in disabled parking spaces or on yellow lines if you are out with your disabled child. To qualify, your child has to receive the higher rate for the mobility component of the DLA or be registered as blind. To apply, contact your local social services.

Cars

Motability
Goodman House
Station Road
Harlow
Essex CM20 2ET
Tel: 01279 632666
Website: www.motability.co.uk

Motability is a national charity which helps disabled people become more mobile. It enables disabled people to use the higher rate of the mobility component of the DLA to lease or buy a car.

EQUIPMENT
Free nappies

If your child is over three and still using nappies you can apply for free nappies from your health authority. Contact your health visitor.

Pushchairs and wheelchairs

If your child is over two years and six months old and still needs a pushchair you may be able to have one on loan. Contact your health visitor, GP, social worker or occupational therapist.

Alterations to your home – Disabled Facilities Grant

You may need to make modifications to your home because of your child's needs or to enable him to be more independent, such as widening doors or providing a downstairs toilet. Disabled Facilities Grants are available through your city, borough or district council but they are means tested. If you think you need to make modifications contact your occupational therapist or social worker to assess your child. Your situation will be referred to the local council, which will also make an assessment and decide on its level of contribution.

RESPITE CARE

You may need some time off from caring for your child to give you a break and a chance to do things which are normally impossible or to enable you to spend more time with your other children. Your child will also benefit from meeting new people and having different experiences. Provision of respite care varies according to people's needs. Breaks could be for just a few hours, a whole day, an overnight stay, a weekend or a week.

Social services have a variety of schemes to give parents of children with special needs some respite care. Sometimes a carer will come to your home to look after your child, enabling you to go out. There are schemes to enable children to stay regularly for the day or overnight with another family. In addition, there are some residential respite care homes for children with disabilities.

Respite carers have all been checked by social services and trained to look after disabled children, and they usually receive a fee for their work. Social services provide any necessary equipment but parents are usually expected to take their child to the respite carer. Some social services departments charge for the service.

Contact your local social services to find out about schemes known as 'Family Link' and 'Take-a-Break', and family help schemes and family support services.

Holiday play schemes

Many social services departments and voluntary organisations (notably Mencap and the NCH) run play schemes for children with special needs during the summer holidays. These provide both enjoyable and educational experiences for children and respite for parents. Sometimes parent support groups and schools run similar schemes. Children can also attend local play schemes with the support of a worker. Contact social services or enquire through local organisations, schools and recreation centres to find out what is available.

CHAPTER 12

Resources

BIBLIOGRAPHY
ADHD

Flick, G.L. (1998) *ADD/ADHD Behaviour Change Resource Kit: Ready to Use Strategies and Activities for Helping Children with ADD*. New York: Centre for Applied Research in Education.

Green, C. and Chee, K.Y. (1995) *Understanding ADHD: A Parent's Guide to ADHD*. London: Vermilion.

Jones, C.B. (1991) *Sourcebook for Children with ADD*. San Antonio, TX: Communication Skill Builders.

Pentecost, D. (2000) *Parenting the ADD Child: Can't Do? Won't Do?* London: Jessica Kingsley Publishers.

Autism/Asperger Syndrome

Attwood, T. (1993) *Why Does Chris Do That?* London: National Autistic Society.

Attwood, T. (1998) *Asperger Syndrome: A Guide for Parents and Professionals*. London: Jessica Kingsley Publishers.

Aud Sonders, S. (2002) *Giggle Time – Establishing the Social Connection: A Programme to Develop the Communication Skills of Children with Autism*. London: Jessica Kingsley Publishers.

Beyer, J. and Gammeltoft, L. (1999) *Autism and Play*. London: Jessica Kingsley Publishers.

Dickinson, P. and Hannah, L. (1998) *It Can Get Better*. London: National Autistic Society.

Flowers, T. (1985) *Reaching the Child with Autism through Art*. Arlington, TX: Future Horizons.

Gray, C. (1993) *Original Social Story Book*. Arlington, TX: Future Horizons.

Gray, C. and Leigh White, A. (eds) (2002) *My Social Stories Book*. London: Jessica Kingsley Publishers.

Hannah, L. (2001) *Teaching Young Children with Autistic Spectrum Disorders: A Practical Guide for Parents and Staff in Mainstream Schools and Nurseries*. London: National Autistic Society.

Harris, S.L. (1994) *Siblings of Children with Autism: A Guide for Families*. Bethesda, MD: Woodbine House.

Hesmondhalgh, M. and Breakey, C. (2001) *Access and Inclusion for Children with Autistic Spectrum Disorders*. London: Jessica Kingsley Publishers.

Howlin, P., Baron-Cohen, S. and Hadwin, J.A. (1998) *Teaching Children with Autism to Mind Read: A Practical Guide*. Chichester: John Wiley.

Ives, M. and Munro, N. (2001) *Caring for a Child with Autism: A Practical Guide for Parents*. London: Jessica Kingsley Publishers and the National Autistic Society.

Jordan, R. and Powell, S. (1995) *Understanding and Teaching Children with Autism*. Chichester: John Wiley.

Moor, J. (2002) *Playing, Laughing and Learning with Children on the Autistic Spectrum*. London: Jessica Kingsley Publishers.

Potter, C. and Whitaker, C. *Enabling Communication in Children with Autism*. London: Jessica Kingsley Publishers.

Powers, M.D. (1989) *Children with Autism: A Parents' Guide*. Bethesda, MD: Woodbine House.

Richman, S. (2000) *Raising a Child with Autism: A Guide to Applied Behaviour Analysis for Parents*. London: Jessica Kingsley Publishers.

Schopler, E. (ed.) (1995) *Parent Survival Manual: A Guide To Crisis Resolution in Autism and Related Development Disorders*. New York: Plenum Press.

For children

Amenta, C.A. (1992) *Russell is Extra Special: A Book about Autism for Children*. New York: Magination Press.

Beach, F. (2001) *Everybody is Different*. London: National Autistic Society.

Gorrod, L. (1997) *My Brother is Different*. London: National Autistic Society.

Hall, K. *Asperger Syndrome, the Universe and Everything*. London: Jessica Kingsley Publishers.

Hoopman, K. (2000) *Blue Bottle Mystery*. London: Jessica Kingsley Publishers.

Hoopman, K. (2001) *Of Mice and Aliens*. London: Jessica Kingsley Publishers.

Matthews, J. and Williams, J. (2000) *The Self-Help Guide for Special Kids and their Families*. London: Jessica Kingsley Publishers.

Sainsbury, C. (2000) *Martian in the Playground*. Bristol: Lucky Duck Publications Ltd.

Behaviour management

Dodd, S. (1994) *Managing Problem Behaviours: A Practical Guide for Parents and Teachers of Young Children with Special Needs.* Sydney, Australia: Maclennan and Petty.

Phelan, T.W. (1995) *1–2–3 Magic: Effective Discipline for Children 2–12.* Glen Ellyn, IL: Child Management Inc.

Cerebral palsy

Boos, M.L., Duffy, L., Pearson, D.T., Walter, R.S. and Whinston, J.L. (1995) *Cerebral Palsy: A Complete Guide for Caregiving.* Baltimore, MD: Johns Hopkins University Press.

Cogher, L., Savage, E. and Smith, M.F. (eds.) (1992) *Cerebral Palsy – The Child and Young Person.* London: Chapman and Hall.

Finnie, N.R. (1997) *Handling the Young Child with Cerebral Palsy at Home.* London: Butterworth Heinemann.

Geralis, E. (ed.) (1991) *Children With Cerebral Palsy: A Parent's Guide.* Bethesda, MD: Woodbine House.

Griffiths, M. and Clegg, M. (1988) *Cerebral Palsy – Problems and Practice.* London: Souvenir Press.

Miller, F. and Bachrach, S.J. (1995) *Cerebral Palsy – A Complete Guide to Caregiving.* Baltimore, MD: Johns Hopkins University Press.

Stranton, M. (1992) *Cerebral Palsy. A Practical Handbook for Families and Carers.* London: Vermilion.

Child development

Barnes, P. (1995) *Personal, Social and Emotional Development of Children.* Buckingham: Open University Press.

Bruce, T. (1996) *Helping Young Children to Play.* London: Hodder and Stoughton.

Bruner, J.S., Jolly, A. and Sylva, K. (1976) *Play: Its Role in Development and Evolution.* Harmondsworth: Penguin.

Grieve, R. and Hughes, M. (eds.) (1990) *Understanding Children.* Oxford: Blackwell.

Lansdown, R. and Walker, M. (1991) *Your Child's Development from Birth to Adolescence.* London: Frances Lincoln Ltd.

Lee, C. (1990) *Growth and Development of Children.* London: Longman.

Sylva, K. and Lunt, I. (1982) *Child Development: A First Course.* Oxford: Blackwell.

Wood, D. (1998) *How Children Think and Learn* (second edition). Oxford: Blackwell.

Down's Syndrome

Baird, G. and Buckley, S. (1994) *Meeting the Educational Needs of Children with Down's Syndrome.* Portsmouth: University of Portsmouth.

Bruni, M. (1998) *Fine Motor Skills in Children with Down Syndrome: A Guide for Parents and Professionals.* Bethesda, MD: Woodbine House.

Buckley, S., Emslie, M. and Haslegrave, G. (1993) *The Development of Language and Reading Skills in Children with Down's Syndrome.* Portsmouth: University of Portsmouth.

Cicchetti, D. and Beeghly, M. (1990) *Children with Down's Syndrome: A Developmental Perspective.* Cambridge: Cambridge University Press.

Cunningham, C. (1990) *Down's Syndrome: An Introduction for Parents.* London: Souvenir Press.

Goodey, C.F. (ed.) (1991) *Living in the Real World – Families Speak Out about Down's Syndrome.* London: Twenty-one Press.

Kumin, L. (1994) *Communication Skills in Children with Down's Syndrome, A Guide for Parents.* Rockville, MD: Woodbine House.

Mepsted, J. (1996) *Developing the Child with Down's Syndrome.* Plymouth: Northcote House.

Merriman, A. (1999) *A Minor Adjustment.* London: Pan.

Miller, J.F., Leeldy, M. and Leavitt, L.A. (1999) *Improving Communication of People with Downs Syndrome.* Baltimore, MD: Paul H. Brookes.

Newton, R. (1992) *Down's Syndrome.* London: Little, Brown and Company.

Pueschel, S.M. (1990) *A Parent's Guide to Down's Syndrome.* Baltimore, MD: Paul H. Brookes.

Winders, P.C. (1997) *Gross Motor Skills in Children with Down Syndrome.* Bethesda, MD: Woodbine House.

For children

Cairo, S., Cairo, J. and Cairo, T. (1985) *Our Brother has Down's Syndrome. An Introduction for Children.* Toronto: Annick Press.

Stuve-Boden, S. (1998) *We'll Paint the Octopus Red.* Bethesda, MD: Woodbine House.

Thompson, M. (1992) *My Brother Matthew.* Bethesda, MD: Woodbine House.

Dyspraxia

Boon, M. (2001) *Helping Children with Dyspraxia.* London: Jessica Kingsley Publishers.

Cocks, N. (1996) *Watch Me I Can Do It: Helping Children Overcome Clumsy and Uncoordinated Motor Skills.* New York: Simon and Schuster.

Kirby, A. (1999) *Dyspraxia, the Hidden Handicap.* London: Souvenir Press.

Kirby, A. and Drew, S. (2000) *Guide to Dyspraxia and Developmental Coordination Disorders.* London: David Fulton.

Macintyre, C. (2001) *Dyspraxia 5–11: A Practical Guide.* London: David Fulton.

Portwood, M. (1996) *Developmental Dyspraxia.* London: David Fulton.

Education

Gabbitas (updated annually) *Gabbitas Guide to Schools for Special Needs.* London: Kogan Page.

Wright, J. and Rueban, D. (2000) *Taking Action: Your Child's Right to Special Education.* Birmingham: The Questions Publishing House.

Hearing impaired

Courtman Davies, M. (1979) *Your Deaf Child's Speech and Language.* London: Bodley Head.

Gregory, S. (1995) *Deaf Children and their Families.* Cambridge: Cambridge University Press.

Gregory, S., Knight, P. and McCracken, W. (1988) *Issues in Deaf Education.* London: David Fulton.

Fletcher, L. (1987) *Language for Ben.* London: Souvenir Press.

Lynas, W. (1990) *A Current Review of Approaches to Communication in the Education of Deaf Children.* Manchester: The Ewing Foundation (available from The Ewing Foundation, c/o Centre for Audiology, Education of the Deaf and Speech Pathology, University of Manchester, Oxford Road, Manchester M13 9PL).

McCracken, W. and Sutherland, H. (1991) *Deafability not Disability: Guide for Parents of Hearing Impaired Children.* Clevedon: Multilingual Matters.

Nolan, M. and Tucker, I. (1988) *The Hearing Impaired Child and Family.* London: Souvenir Press.

Smith, C. (1992) *Signs Make Sense.* London: Souvenir Press.

For children

Archer, E. (2000) *Making It! Zoo Keeper.* London: Franklin Watts.

Church, D. (2003) *Friends going Swimming.* London: Franklin Watts.

Colledge, A. (1999) *Northern Lights.* Chippenham: Piper's Ash.

Condon, J. (2002) *When It's Hard to Hear.* London: Franklin Watts.

Woolley, M. (1998) *Think about Being Deaf.* London: Belitha Press.

Language

Armstrong, A. (1999) *Language Steps.* Ponteland, Northumberland: STASS Publications.

Bliss, L.S. (1993) *Pragmatic Language Intervention: Interactive Activities.* Eau Caire, WI: Thinking Publications.

Cooper, J., Moodley, M. and Reynell, J. (1978) *Helping Language Development.* London: Arnold.

Garvey, C. (1984) *Children's Talk: The Developing Child.* London: Fontana.

Kersner, M. and Wright, J.A. (eds) (1996) *How to Manage Communication Disorders.* London: David Fulton.

Manolson, A. (1995) *It Takes Two to Talk.* Bisbee, AZ: Imaginart Press.

Quill, K.A. (1995) *Teaching Children with Autism Strategies to Enhance Communication and Socialization.* Baltimore, MD: Paul H. Brookes.

Quill, K.A. (2000) *Do-watch-listen-say: Social and Communication Intervention with Children with Autism.* Baltimore, MD: Paul H. Brookes.

Schwartz, S. and Heller Miller, J.E. (1988) *The Language of Toys: Teaching Communication Skills to Special Needs Children.* Betheseda, MD: Woodbine House.

Shaw, C. (1993) *Talking and Your Child.* London: Hodder and Stoughton.

Sussman, F. (1999) *More Than Words.* Austin, TX: Pro-ed.

de Villiers, P.A. and de Villiers, J.G. (1979) *Early Language: The Developing Child.* London: Fontana.

Watson, L.R., Lord, C., Schaffer, B. and Schopler, E. (1989) *Teaching Spontaneous Communication to Autistic and Developmentally Handicapped Children.* Austin, TX: Pro-ed.

Weitzman, E. (1992) *Learning Language and Loving It.* Toronto: Hanen Centre.

Play ideas

Britton, L. (1992) *Montessori Play and Learn: A Parent's Guide to Purposeful Play from 2–6.* London: Vermilion.

Denziloe, J. (1994) *Fun and Games: Practical Leisure Ideas for People with Profound Disabilities.* London: Butterworth Heinemann.

Einon, D. (1985) *Creative Play.* Harmondsworth: Penguin.

Hong, C.S., Gabriel, H. and St John, C. (1996) *Sensory Motor Activities for Early Development.* Bicester, Oxford: Winslow Press.

Jeffree, D. and Cheseldine, S. (1984) *Let's Join In.* London: Souvenir Press.

Jeffree, D. and McConkey, R. (1976) *Let Me Speak.* London: Souvenir Press.

Jeffree, D., McConkey, R. and Hewson, S. (1994) *Let Me Play.* London: Souvenir Press.

Lear, R. (1996) *Play Helps.* London: Butterworth Heinemann.

Matteson, E. (1989) *Play with a Purpose for the Under Sevens.* Harmondsworth: Penguin.

Mcintyre, C. (2002) *Play for Children with Special Needs.* London: David Fulton.

Nash-Wortham, M. and Hunt, J. (1994) *Take Time: Movement Exercises for Parents, Teachers and Therapists of Children with Difficulties in Speaking, Reading, Writing and Spelling.* Stourbridge: Robinswood Press.

National Association of Toy and Leisure Libraries (1989) *Talk to Me.* London: NATLL.

National Association of Toy and Leisure Libraries (1990) *Switch to Play.* London: NATLL.

Rice, M. (1993) *Child's Play.* London: Kingfisher Books.

Riddick, B. (1982) *Toys and Play for the Handicapped.* London: Croom Helm.

Streeter, E. (1993) *Making Music with the Young Child with Special Needs.* London: Jessica Kingsley Publishers.

Self-esteem

Lawrence, D. (1996) *Enhancing Self Esteem in the Classroom.* London: Paul Chapman.

Plummer, D. (2001) *Helping Children to Build Self-esteem.* London: Jessica Kingsley Publishers.

Roberts, P. (2002) *Self Esteem and Early Learning.* London: Paul Chapman.

Sher, B. (1998) *Self-esteem Games.* Chichester: John Wiley and Sons.

Sensory integration disorder

Anderson, E. and Emmons, P. (1996) *Unlocking the Mysteries of Sensory Dysfunction.* Arlington, TX: Future Horizons.

Kranowitz, C.S. (1998) *The Out of Sync Child: Recognizing and Coping with Sensory Integration Dysfunction.* New York: Skylight Press.

Trott, M.C. with Laurel, M.K. and Windeck, S.L. (1993) *Understanding Sensory Integration.* Tuscon, AZ: Therapy Skill Builders.

Siblings

Lobato, D. (1990) *Brothers, Sisters and Special Needs.* Baltimore, MD: Paul H. Brookes.

Meyer, D. (ed.) (1997) *Views from our Shoes: Growing Up with a Brother or Sister with Special Needs.* Bethesda, MD: Woodbine House.

Powell, T. and Gallagher, P. (1993) *Brothers and Sisters – A Special Part of Exceptional Families.* Baltimore, MD: Paul H. Brookes.

Sleep management

Durand, V.M. (1988) *Sleep Better! A Guide to Improving Sleep for Children with Special Needs.* Baltimore, MD: Paul H. Brookes.

Ferber, R. (1986) *Solve Your Child's Sleep Problems: A Practical and Comprehensive Guide for Parents.* London: Dorling Kindersley.

Quine, L. (1997) *Solving Children's Sleep Problems: A Step by Step Guide for Parents.* Huntingdon, Cambs: Beckett Karlson Publishing.

Special needs

Cowes, A. (1994) *Taking Care.* York: Joseph Rowntree Trust.

Greenspan, S.I. and Wieder, S. with Simons, R. (1998) *The Child with Special Needs: Encouraging Intellectual and Emotional Growth.* Reading, MA: Merloyd Lawrence.

Hannaford, C. (1995) *Smart Moves: Why Learning is Not all in your Head.* Arlington, VA: Great Ocean Publishers.

Knight, A. (1996) *Caring for a Disabled Child.* London: Straightforward Publishing.

Serfonteirn, G. (1990) *Hidden Handicap: How to Help Children who Suffer From Dyslexia, Hyperactivity and Learning Difficulties.* New York: Simon and Schuster.

Tanguay, P.D. (2000) *Nonverbal Learning Disabilities at Home.* London: Jessica Kingsley Publishers.

Woolfson, R. (1991) *Children with Special Needs.* London: Faber and Faber Ltd.

For children

Thompson, M. (1992) *My Brother Matthew.* Bethesda, MD: Woodbine House.

Toilet training

Wheeler, M. (1999) *Toilet Training for Individuals with Autism and Related Disorders: A Comprehensive Guide for Parents and Teachers.* London: Jessica Kingsley Publishers.

Visually impaired

Coleman, M. (2001) *Play it Right.* London: RNIB.

Fullwood, D. (1988) *A Start to Independence for Your Visually Impaired Children.* Melbourne: Royal Victorian Institute for the Blind.

Haughton, L. and Mackvicius, S. (2001) *I'm Posting the Pebbles.* Melbourne: Royal Victorian Institute for the Blind.

Holbrook, M.C. (1996) *Children with Visual Impairments: A Parent's Guide.* Bethesda, MD: Woodbine House.

Lear, R. (1998) *Look at it this Way: Toys and Activities for Children with a Visual Impairment.* London: Heinemann.

Mencap and RNIB (1995) *Play it My Way: Learning Through Play with Your Visually Impaired Child.* London: Mencap and RNIB.

RNIB (2000) *Setting Out.* London: RNIB.

For children

Carter, A.R. (1998) *Seeing Things My Way*. Chicago, IL: Albert Whitman and Company.

Horgan, D. (1988) *Charlie's Eye: Pops Out All Over the Place*. Harmondsworth: Penguin.

Litchfield, A.B. (1977) *A Cane in her Hand*. Chicago, IL: Albert Whitman and Company.

White, P. (1998) *Think About Being Blind*. London: Belitha Press.

Wilson, J. (2001) *Take a Good Look*. Harmondsworth: Penguin.

VOLUNTARY ORGANISATIONS OFFERING SUPPORT FOR PARENTS OF CHILDREN WITH SPECIAL NEEDS

Listed below are national organisations which provide support and information for parents of children with special needs. Both mainstream and alternative organisations are listed. I have focused on a few of the many services provided, so contact the organisations for full details.

There are also many excellent local organisations and help groups which it is not practical to list here. Your local library, social services, health visitor, Citizens Advice Bureau or telephone directory may be able to provide details.

Most organisations provide information to parents free of charge even if they are not members. However, since membership costs are usually fairly nominal, it is well worth joining the organisation relevant to your child. Many of the organisations have comprehensive mail order catalogues and so are a good source of relevant books.

If your child has a disability not included in the lists consult *The CaF Directory of Specific Conditions and Rare Disorders in Children with their Family Support Networks* (most public libraries have a copy) which lists many more organisations.

Action for Leisure

c/o Warwickshire College
Moreton Morrell Centre
Moreton Morrell
Warwickshire CV35 9BL
Tel: 01926 650195
Email: enquiries@actionforleisure.org.uk
Website: www.actionforleisure.org.uk

Promotes play and leisure with and for children with disabilities. Offers
resources centre containing equipment, toys, books and videos (to try out
equipment before buying it), an information service, training and a
database of local opportunities for disabled people in the UK. Sells some
toys and leisure items and a range of books.

Action for Sick Children

c/o National Children's Bureau
8 Wakley Street
London EC1V 7QE
Tel: 020 7843 6444

Campaigns for high quality health care for children. Campaigns for
services that are child-centred, needs-led and delivered in the appropriate
environment. Supports parents and professionals, offering advice and
information.

Advisory Centre for Education

1C Aberdeen Studios
22 Highbury Grove
London N5 2DQ
Tel: 020 7354 8318
Advice line: 0808 800 5793 (Monday–Friday 2–5 p.m.)
Email: enquiries@ace.dialnet.com
Website: www.ace-ed.org.uk

Provides help, legal advice and information – publications and freephone
– for parents. Produces a range of publications on school and education
including *Special Education Handbook* on statutory assessments and how to
appeal.

AFASIC Association for all Speech Impaired Children
50–52 Great Sutton Street
London EC1V 0DJ
Tel: 020 7490 9410
Helpline: 0845 355 5577
Email: info@afasic.org.uk
Website: www.afasic.org.uk

Supports children with language and communication impairments, their parents and carers. Has a helpline, provides support locally and works to improve services for children. Provides training for parents and professionals. Produces publications and activity books to support your child's language etc.

Arthritis Care
18 Stephenson Way
London NW1 2HD
Tel: 020 7380 6500
Helpline: 0808 808 2000 (under 26s)
Website: www.arthritiscare.org.uk

Young Arthritis Care is for the under 45s. Provides information, advice and publications on diet, exercise and pain management, etc. Has a nationwide network of contacts, including Parent Contacts, who can give support. Local groups also meet up and share information. Also runs confidence-building courses for older children.

Association for Spina Bifida and Hydrocephalus
ASBAH House
42 Park Road
Peterborough PE1 2UQ
Tel: 01733 555988
Email: postmaster@asbah.org
Website: www.asbah.org

For individuals with spina bifida and/or hydrocephalus and their families. Provides advice, advocacy, information and other services. Publishes a magazine and publications on statementing, school, etc. Specialist advisers give individual advice to families concerning continence, education, mobility, benefits and medical issues.

The Bobath Centre for Children with Cerebral Palsy
250 East End Road
London N2 8AU
Tel: 020 8444 3355
Website: www.bobathlondon.co.uk

Treats children in accordance with Bobath principles to enable them to maximise functional independence. Provides training to parents and therapy professionals in Bobath.

Brainwave Centre
Huntworth Gate
Bridgwater
Somerset TA6 6LQ
Tel: 01278 429089
Email: brainwavetherapy@hotmail.com
Website: www.brainwave.org.uk

For brain injured children. Designs individual tailored programmes of rehabilitation therapy which are carried out at home. Regular assessments are held at the centre.

British Association of Behavioural Optometrists
c/o Greygarth
Littleworth
Winchcombe
Cheltenham GL54 5BT
Tel: 01242 602689
Email: greygarth@compuserve.com
Website: www.babo.co.uk

Provides a list of accredited members.

British Deaf Association
1–3 Worship Street
London EC2A 2AB
Tel (voice): 0870 770 3300
Tel (textphone): 0800 6522 965
Videophone: 020 7496 9539
Email: helpline@bda.org.uk
Website: www.bda.org.uk

Campaigns for deaf sign language users. Offers the following services: education and youth, information, health promotion, video production and community services. Operates a helpline and publishes a newsletter.

British Epilepsy Association
New Anstey House
Gate Way Drive
Yeadon
Leeds LS19 7XY
Tel: 0113 210 8800
Helpline: 0808 800 5050
Email: epilepsy@bea.org.uk
Website: www.epilepsy.org.uk

For people with epilepsy and their families. Provides information, publications and videos. Supports a network of branches. Offers newsletters, free insurance scheme and access to helpline.

British Heart Foundation
14 Fitzhardinge Street
London W1H 6DH
Tel: 0207 935 0185
Heart information line: 0870 600 6566
Website: bhf.org.uk

Funds research. Provides information for children with heart conditions and publishes books and videos to promote healthy lifestyles.

BIBIC The British Institute for Brain Injured Children
Knowle Hall
Bridgwater
Somerset TA7 8PJ
Tel: 01278 684060
Email: info@bibic.org.uk
Website: www.bibic.org.uk

For children with learning difficulties. After an assessment a programme of exercises and activities is devised for parents to conduct with their children at home. Parents are supported by the centre and progress is monitored.

British Society for Music Therapy
25 Rosslyn Avenue
East Barnet
Herts EN4 8DH
Tel: 020 8368 8879
Email: info@bsmt.org
Website: www.bsmt.org

For those with an interest in music therapy. Provides information on music therapy and how to find a music therapist. Holds workshops, produces journals and has a catalogue of books on music therapy.

Brittle Bone Society
30 Guthrie Street
Dundee DD1 5BS
Tel: 01382 204446
Helpline: 08000 282459
Email: bbs@brittlebone.org
Website: www.brittlebone.org

Promotes research into brittle bone diseases and provides support and advice to sufferers and their families. Organises meetings and conferences for the exchange of ideas. Produces a newsletter and advises on grants, education, equipment and genetics. Can sometimes help with equipment and financial needs.

Carers UK
20–25 Glasshouse Yard
London EC1A 4JS
Tel (admin): 020 7490 8818
Carers line: 0808 808 7777 (Monday–Friday 10–12 and 2–4)
Email: info@ukcarers.org
Website: www.carersonline.org.uk

Provides information to carers about the services and support available to them. Campaigns for greater awareness of their needs and for action to support them. Has a network of branches and produces publications on benefits, combining caring and work, etc.

Centre for Studies in Inclusive Education
New Redland
Frenchay Campus
Coldharbour Lane
Bristol BS16 1QU
Tel: 0117 344 4007
Website: www.inclusion.uwe.ac.uk and www.csie.org.uk

Aims to increase the number of children with special needs who are educated in mainstream schools. Produces a range of publications on the theory and practice of integrating children.

The Child Brain Injury Trust
The Radcliffe Infirmary
Woodstock Road
Oxford OX2 6HE
Tel: 01865 552467
Email: info@cbituk.org

For children with acquired brain injury, their families and professionals. Provides advice and information on brain injury and special schools. Has regional groups. Supports research and has a hardship fund.

Children's Legal Centre
University of Essex
Wivenhoe Park
Colchester
Essex CO4 3SQ
Tel: 01206 873820 (general advice – Monday–Friday 10–12.30 and 2–4.30)
Tel (education advice line): 01206 874807
Tel (admin): 01206 872466
Email: clc@essex.ac.uk
Website: www.childrenslegalcentre.com

Runs a free legal advice and information service covering all aspects of the law and policy affecting children. Provides representation to parents in education disputes with a school or LEA. Produces a range of information sheets and guides.

The Children's Trust
Tadworth Court
Tadworth
Surrey KT20 5RU
Tel: 01737 365000

For children with profound disabilities and complex medical needs and those with acquired brain injury who require rehabilitation. Offers rehabilitation, transitional, continuing and palliative care, respite care and outreach. Services are run by an interdisciplinary team including medical staff, therapists and teachers.

CLAPA Cleft Lip and Palate Association
235–237 Finchley Road
London NW3 6LS
Tel: 020 7431 0033
Email: info@clapa.com
Website: www.clapa.com

Provides support for those affected by cleft lip and/or cleft palate. Offers training, information, telephone helpline and support through local branches. Organises children's camps and publishes a children's magazine.

CLIMB
The Quadrangle
Crewe Hall
Crewe CW1 6UR
Tel: 0870 7700 325
Email: info@climb.org.uk
Website: www.climb.org.uk

For children and families affected by metabolic diseases. Provides advice, support, information and publications, a helpline and befrienders.

Contact a Family
209–211 City Road
London EC1V 1JN
Tel: 0808 808 3555 (helpline – Monday–Friday 10–4)
Tel (admin): 0207 608 8700
Email: info@cafamily.org.uk
Website: www.cafamily.org.uk

For families of children with any type of special need. Provides advice and information and has a network of local and national support groups. Provides a service of linking up parents of children with very rare diseases and conditions. Publications include *The CaF Directory of Specific Conditions and Rare Disorders*, magazines and fact sheets.

Cystic Fibrosis Trust
11 London Road
Bromley
Kent BR1 1BY
Tel: 020 8464 7211
Email: enquiries@cftrust.org.uk
Website: www.cftrust.org.uk

For people with cystic fibrosis (CF), their families and professionals. Provides support through helplines and information. Funds research and clinics and raises awareness. Has a mail order list of publications on CF and physiotherapy, diet, financial help, school, genetics etc.

DDAT: Dyslexia, Dyspraxia and Attention Deficit Disorder Treatment Centre
Camden House
St Johns
Kenilworth CV8 1TG
Tel: 0870 737 0011
Email: info@ddat.org
Website: www.ddat.org

For children with dyslexia, dyspraxia and/or ADHD. The approach is based on the idea that the cerebellum can be stimulated with specially designed exercises. Children are assessed at the centre and then given a programme of exercises to be done at home.

DELTA Deaf Education through Listening and Talking
PO Box 20
Haverhill
Suffolk CB9 7BD
Tel: 01440 783689
Email: enquiries@deafeducation.org.uk
Website: www.deafeducation.org.uk

Provides support, information and advice for parents of deaf children trying to help their child develop speech and live independently within a hearing society. Branches hold meetings and events. Runs conferences and courses including summer schools for parents.

Disability Sport England
Unit 4G
784–788 High Road
London N17 0DA
Tel: 020 8801 4466
Email: info@dse.org.uk
Website: www.disabilitysport.org.uk

Provides opportunities for people with disabilities to participate in and enjoy sport and recreation. Organises sports events. Gives advice and information on aspects of sports provision. Has local offices.

Disabled Living Foundation
380–384 Harrow Road
London W9 2HU
Tel: 020 7289 6111
Helpline: 0845 130 9177
Email: dlfinfo@dlf.org.uk
Website: www.dlf.org.uk

Provides information and advice on equipment for disabled people by email, telephone or letter. Has a centre displaying equipment for people to try out. Produces a range of fact sheets, lists of manufacturers and suppliers of disability equipment e.g. 'children's play equipment'.

Down's Ed: The Down's Syndrome Educational Trust
The Sarah Duffen Centre
Belmont Street
Southsea
Portsmouth
Hants PO5 1NA
Tel: 023 9285 5330
Email: enquiries@downsed.org
Website: www.downsed.org/

Aims to promote development of children and young people with Down's. Funds research, provides direct services to families and disseminates information through publishing and training activities. Provides publications, training events (e.g. early development, behaviour management), psychological assessments, consultancy, a catalogue of books and educational materials.

Down's Syndrome Association
155 Mitcham Road
London SW17 9PG
Tel: 020 8682 4001
Email: info@downs-syndrome.org.uk
Website: www.downs-syndrome.org.uk

For people with Down's Syndrome, their parents and professionals. Campaigns to improve awareness and to uphold the rights of people with Down's Syndrome. Provides information and support, specialist advisors

on health, education, benefits, etc. Produces a newsletter by and for young
people with Down's Syndrome. Has a network of local branches.

The Dyscovery Centre for Dyspraxia, Dyslexia and Associated Learning Difficulties

4A Church Road
Whitchurch
Cardiff CF14 2DZ
Tel: 029 2062 8222
Email: discoverycentre@btclick.com
Website: www.dyscovery.co.uk

Provides an interdisciplinary assessment and treatment service to meet the
needs of each child with dyspraxia, dyslexia or associated learning
difficulties. Provides training courses and publications including 'Play
Activities for the Infant School Child', 'Scissor Skills' and 'Helping the
Child with Dyspraxia at Home'.

Dyspraxia Foundation

8 West Alley
Hitchin
Herts SG5 1EG
Tel: 01462 455016
Website: www.dyspraxiafoundation.org.uk

Supports individuals with dyspraxia and their families. Acts as an
information and resource centre, offering support and advice to parents.
Promotes rapid diagnosis and treatment and a wider understanding,
especially among health and education professionals. Produces
publications including 'Living with Dyspraxia – Handy Tips', 'Children
with Developmental Dyspraxia: Information for Parents/Teachers'.

Friends for Young Deaf People

FYD Communication Centre
East Court Mansion
Council Offices
College Lane
East Grinstead RH19 3LT
Tel (voice): 01342 323444
Tel (minicom): 01342 312639

Email: fyd.egho@charity.vfree.com
Website: www.fyd.org.uk

Promotes partnerships between deaf and hearing children and empowers
deaf young people to be active members of society. Organises activities,
events, training courses. Produces publicity material.

Hemihelp
215 Balham High Road
London SW17 7BQ
Helpline: 020 8672 3179 (10–1)
Tel (admin): 020 8767 0210
Email: support@hemihelp.org.uk
Website: www.hemihelp.org.uk

Provides support and information for parents and professionals dealing
with children with hemiplegia. Provides newsletters, publications,
helpline, website and workshops.

Henshaw's Society for Blind People
John Derby House
88–92 Talbot Road
Old Trafford
Manchester M16 0GS
Tel: 0161 872 1234
Email: info@hsbp.co.uk

For people with a visual impairment who may have other disabilities and
their families. Based in the north of England. Provides home visits by a
family support officer, parental support groups, training, a resource centre
– including a sensory stimulation room, toy and tape library – and holiday
and social activities. Also provides specialist residential, educational,
rehabilitation and day services.

High/Scope
192 Maple Road
London SE20 8HT
Tel: 020 8676 0220
Email: highscope@btconnect.com
Website: www.high-scope.org.uk

Aims to bring the High/Scope approach to people working with children through support and training. Provides training and information, publications and videos. 'Together We are Special' is a course aimed at giving information and support to parents of children with special needs.

Holiday Care
Second Floor Imperial Buildings
Victoria Road
Horley
Surrey RH6 7PZ
Tel: 01293 774535
Email: holiday.care@virgin.net
Website: www.holidaycare.org.uk

Provides holiday and travel information and support for people with disabilities. Can provide information on accessible accommodation (hotels, B and Bs etc.), visitor attractions, transport, holidays for children with disabilities, respite care, funding etc.

Hyperactive Children's Support Group
71 Whyke Lane
Chichester
West Sussex PO19 2LD
Tel: 01243 551313
Email: web@hacsg.org.uk
Website: www.hacsg.org.uk

For parents and professionals seeking help for ADHD/hyperactive youngsters. Provides support and help for parents and information for professionals, and seeks to raise awareness and undertake research. Provides a resource pack for schools.

I CAN
4 Dyers Buildings
Holborn
London EC1N 2QP
Tel: 0870 010 4066
Email: ican@ican.org.uk
Website: www.ican.org.uk

For children with speech and language difficulties. Offers early years programme, special schools, a mainstream programme, a national training programme and an information service for parents and professionals.

Information Exchange
1A Potters Cross
Wootton
Beds MK43 9JG
Tel: 0845 1275281
Email: flocatalyst@aol.com

For families and professionals living or working with children who have sensory impairments and other complex needs. Produces a magazine with a multi-sensory approach with lots of practical ideas and activities to help children achieve the quality of life they deserve.

IPSEA Independent Panel for Special Education Advice
6 Carlow Mews
Woodbridge
Suffolk IP12 1EA
Tel (admin and fax): 01394 380518
Advice line: 0800 0184016
Website: www.ipsea.org.uk

Offers free and independent advice and support to parents of children with special educational needs. Offers advice on LEAs' legal duties towards children with special needs, home visits where necessary, support and representation for parents appealing to the Special Educational Needs Tribunal and second opinions on a child's needs and the provision required to meet those needs.

ISEA Independent Special Education Advice (Scotland)
164 High Street
Dalkeith
Mid Lothian EH22 1AY
Tel: 0131 665 7080

As IPSEA above but for Scotland.

Kidscape
2 Grosvenor Gardens
London SW1W 0DH
Tel: 020 7730 3300
Helpline: 08451 205 204
Email: contact@kidscape.org.uk
Website: www.kidscape.org.uk

Works to keep children safe. Committed to preventing bullying and abuse. Offers books, videos, leaflets on tackling bullying, a helpline and a training programme for teachers and also for children who have been bullied and need help to restore self-esteem and confidence.

The Lady Hoare Trust for Physically Disabled Children
First Floor
89 Albert Embankment
London SE1 7TP
Tel: 020 7820 9989
Email: info@lhtchildren.org.uk

For children with arthritis and limb disabilities. Has a network of workers to help children and their families with practical support on education, medical treatment and care and with emotional support. Provides some small grants.

Limbless Association
Roehampton Rehabilitation Centre
Roehampton Lane
London SW15 5PR
Tel: 020 8788 1777
Email: stepfwd@limbless-association.org
Website: www.limbless-association.org

For amputees and people with limb deficiencies and their families. Offers information, advice and a network of volunteer visitors. Campaigns for better provision of prosthetic, orthotic and wheelchair equipment and holds events geared towards improving the fitness and mobility of limbless people. Produces a magazine.

The Listening Centre (Lewes) Ltd
Maltings Studio
16A Station Street
Lewes
East Sussex BN7 2DB
Tel: 01273 474877
Website: www.listeningcentre.co.uk

Offers assessment and treatment (listening therapy) for children with autism, ADHD, dyspraxia and epilepsy. Based on the idea that some children have their listening senses distorted, which distorts neurological patterns and exacerbates developmental disorders. Based on the work of Alfred Tomatis, it aims to re-educate the way children listen to improve learning and language abilities etc.

LOOK, National Federation of Families with Visually Impaired Children
c/o Queen Alexandra College
49 Court Oak Road
Harborne
Birmingham B17 9TG
Tel: 0121 428 5038
Email: info@look1991.freeserve.co.uk
Website: www.look-uk.org

Provides support and information for families of visually impaired children. Family support officers offer support and advice regarding education, benefits and eye conditions. Links parents as individuals or as part of local parent groups.

Makaton Vocabulary Development Project
31 Firwood Drive
Camberley
Surrey GU15 3QD
Tel: 01276 61390
Email: mvdp@makaton.org
Website: www.makaton.org

Makaton is a communication system using the spoken word and signs. Created for children and adults with communication difficulties, it aims to give a visual aid prompt alongside speech and symbols. Has a mail order catalogue of publications including books of the signs and symbols, and training materials including parent/carer training pack. Organises courses on Makaton throughout the country given by accredited teachers.

Mencap

123 Golden Lane
London EC1Y 0RT
Tel: 0207 454 0454
Helpline: 0808 808 1111
Email: help@mencap.org.uk
Website: www.mencap.org.uk

For all children with a learning disability and their families. Provides support and help for parents through local societies and family advisors. Campaigns for the rights of people with learning disabilities. Provides advice and support on issues including leisure, holidays and education. Produces a range of publications. Local groups organise Gateway Clubs to offer leisure opportunities to children.

Muscular Dystrophy Campaign

7–11 Prescott Place
London SW4 6BS
Tel: 0207 720 8055
Email: info@muscular-dystrophy.org
Website: www.muscular-dystrophy.org

Provides information and support through local branches for families affected by muscular dystrophy. Offers specialist advice by phone and through family care workers. Provides OT advice on equipment and a fund is available for essential equipment. Publishes newsletters and booklets on physiotherapy, equipment and housing adaptations.

Music and the Deaf

The Media Centre
7 Northumberland Street
Huddersfield HD1 1RL
Tel: 01484 425551
Email: info@matd.org.uk
Website: www.matd.org.uk

Helps hearing impaired people gain access to music and performing arts as performers or listeners and observers. Offers workshops for children, produces a list of performances nationwide which will be signed and a publications list: 'All Join In: Musical Activities for Hearing Impaired Children'.

National Association of Toy and Leisure Libraries: Play Matters
68 Churchway
London NW1 1LT
Tel: 020 7387 9592
Email: admin@natll.ukf.net
Website: www.natll.org.uk

Parent body for over 1000 toy libraries in the UK. These libraries provide good quality, carefully chosen toys for young children and include more specialist toys for those with special needs. Offers a befriending service to parents. Contact above address with an SAE for the address of your nearest toy library. Has a mail order catalogue of books and leaflets on play and special needs.

National Asthma Campaign
Providence House
Providence Place
London N1 0NT
Tel: 020 7226 2260
Helpline: 0845 7 01 02 03
Website: www.asthma.org.uk

Provides information and support to people with asthma, their families and professionals. Promotes and funds research and campaigns to raise awareness. Has a helpline staffed by specialist nurses, a network of local branches and a magazine. There is a Junior Asthma Club for children aged 4–12. Produces a range of publications and runs children's adventure holidays.

National Autistic Society
393 City Road
London EC1V 1NG
Tel: 020 7833 2299
Autism helpline: 0870 600 8585 (for parents and people with autism)
Information line: 020 7903 3599 (for professionals and students)
Email: nas@nas.org.uk
Website: www.nas.org.uk

For people with autism, their families and professionals. Provides information, advice, advocacy and training. Runs a diagnosis and assessment centre and a number of specialist schools. Local branches also offer information, support and other services.

National Blind Children's Society
Bradbury House
33 Market Street
Highbridge
Somerset TA9 3BW
Tel: 01278 764764
Email: enquiries@nbcs.org.uk
Website: www.nbcs.org.uk

Aims to enable children with a visual impairment aged from 0 to 25 to reach their educational and recreational goals. Provides advocacy service, large-print book service, IT advisory service and grants for recreational activities; also has a specially adapted holiday home.

National Centre for Young People with Epilepsy
St Piers Lane
Lingfield
Surrey RH7 6PW
Tel: 01342 832 243
Email: info@ncype.org.uk
Website: www.ncype.org.uk

Provides education, treatment, assessment and care for children with epilepsy. Offers a national assessment service with Great Ormond Street Hospital. Runs a school and training courses for parents and professionals.

National Children's Bureau
8 Wakeley Street
London EC1V 7QE
Tel: 020 7843 6080
Website: www.ncb.org.uk

Promotes the interests and well-being of children through policy development, advocacy, research and the promotion of good practice. Works with professionals in education, social work and health care and promotes multidisciplinary, cross-agency partnerships. Has an extensive library and information service and a programme of conferences and seminars. Publishes books.

National Council for One Parent Families
255 Kentish Town Road
London NW5 2LX
Tel: 020 7428 5400
Helpline: 0800 018 5026
Email: info@oneparentfamilies.org.uk
Website: www.oneparentfamilies.org.uk

Provides information and advice to lone parents on issues like benefits, tax, housing etc. Campaigns nationally to change people's attitudes and government policy.

National Deaf Children's Society
15 Dufferin Street
London EC1Y 8PD
Helpline: 0808 800 8880
Email: helpline@ndcs.org.uk
Website: www.ndcs.org.uk

For families of children with any hearing loss to enable deaf children to maximise their skills and abilities. Has a helpline for information, advice and support. Specialist support provided on audiology, benefits, technology and education. Has a network of regional staff and local groups. Produces a range of publications and a magazine.

National Institute of Conductive Education
Cannon Hill House
Russell Road
Moseley
Birmingham B13 8RD
Tel: 0121 449 1569
Email: foundation@conductive-education.org.uk
Website: www.conductive-education.org.uk

Provides direct services to children with motor disorders, such as cerebral palsy and dyspraxia, and those who have suffered head injuries. Through a system of positive teaching and learning support, conductive education maximises their control over bodily movement. Offers training and has a library of works on conductive education.

National Society for Epilepsy
Chesham Lane
Chalfont St Peter
Bucks SL9 0RJ
Tel: 01494 601300
Helpline: 01494 601400 (Monday–Friday 10–4)
Website: www.epilepsynse.org.uk

For anybody with an interest in epilepsy. Provides an information service through its helpline, support through a network of volunteers and a range of information on medical, psychological and social aspects of living with epilepsy. Funds medical research and campaigns to increase public awareness and runs a range of residential and specialist medical services.

NCH
85 Highbury Park
London N5 1UD
Tel: 020 7226 2033
Website: www.nchafc.org.uk

Aims to improve the quality of life for the most vulnerable children in society, including children with special needs. Runs a range of projects, usually with health, education or social services, including supporting children with special needs in the community, family centres, respite care and residential schools.

Network 81
1–7 Woodfield Terrace
Chapel Hill
Stansted
Essex CM24 8AJ
Helpline: 0870 7703306
Tel (admin): 0870 7703262
Email: network81@tesco.net
Website: www.network81.co.uk

A network of parents working towards properly resourced inclusive education for children with special needs. Offers advice on issues such as choosing a school, inclusive education and education law. Has a system of befrienders who support parents through the statutory assessment process. Produces publications including the 'Network 81 Parents Guide: How to get Support for Your Child with Special Educational Needs'.

Parents at Work
45 Beech Street
London EC2Y 8AD
Tel (helpline): 020 7588 0802
Email: info@parentsatwork.org.uk
Website: www.parentsatwork.org.uk

To help parents balance their work commitments with their home life. Has a Working Parents of Children with Disabilities Project, called 'Waving Not Drowning', which is a forum for those who wish to work to exchange views and experiences. Publishes newsletters and books.

Reach (Association for Children with Hand or Arm Deficiency)
PO Box 54
Helston TR13 8WD
Tel: 0845 130 6225
Email: reach@reach.org.uk
Website: www.reach.org.uk

For families of children with upper limb problems, and professionals. Provides information and publications including a newsletter, advice and support and access to other families in similar situations.

REACH National Advice Centre for Children with Reading Difficulties
California Country Park
Nine Mile Ride
Finchampstead
Berkshire RG4 4HT
Tel (admin): 0118 973 7575
Helpline: 0845 604 0414
Email: enquiries@reach-reading.demon.co.uk
Website: www.reach-reading.demon.co.uk

For parents, teachers and librarians. Aims to help children who have difficulty with reading because of their special needs. Advises teachers and parents trying to encourage their child or who want advice on materials. Produces publications, has a resource centre and provides INSET training for teachers.

Rett Syndrome Association UK
113 Friern Barnet Road
London N11 3EU
Tel (local callers): 020 8361 5161
Tel (national callers): 0870 770 3266
Email: info@rettsyndrome.org.uk
Website: www.rettsyndrome.org.uk

For families of people with Rett Syndrome and professionals. Runs support groups and a contact network, provides information booklets and organises an annual family weekend. Holds diagnostic and management clinics and therapy clinics with a multidisciplinary team of professionals.

Riding for the Disabled Association
Lavinia Norfolk House
Avenue R
National Agricultural Centre
Stoneleigh Park
Kenilworth
Warwicks CV8 2LY
Tel: 024 7669 6510
Email: rdahq@riding-for-disabled.org.uk
Website: www.riding-for-disabled.org.uk

Provides disabled people with the means to ride and/or carriage drive at the level of their ability, choice and ambition. Puts people in touch with their local branch of Riding for the Disabled.

Royal Association for Disability and Rehabilitation (RADAR)
12 City Forum
250 City Road
London EC1V 8AF
Tel: 020 7250 3222
Tel (minicom): 020 7250 4119
Email: radar@radar.org.uk
Website: www.radar.org.uk

For people with physical disabilities and those interested in disability issues. Provides information and advice and campaigns for the rights and needs of disabled people. Produces publications such as 'Holidays', 'Mobility' and 'Children First: A Guide to the Needs of Disabled Children in School'.

Royal National Institute for the Blind
105 Judd Street
London WC1H 9NE
Tel: 020 7388 1266
Email: helpline@rnib.org.uk
Website: www.rnib.org.uk

For visually impaired people, their families and professionals. Provides a range of services including information and advice on education, and will support children in mainstream education. Provides training, specialist assessment and technology services. Produces publications including magazines and information on toys and play ideas, different eye conditions and their treatment and specialist products. Has a mail order catalogue of products and books (see section on suppliers below).

SCOPE
PO Box 833
Milton Keynes MK12 5NY
Tel (cerebral palsy helpline): 0808 800 3333
Email: cphelpline@scope.org.uk
Website: www.scope.org.uk

Offers services focusing on early years, education and daily living. Provides information and support, funds research and campaigns. Has a network of local groups. The helpline provides information, advice and initial counselling on all aspects of cerebral palsy and disability issues.

Sense (The National Deafblind and Rubella Association)
11–13 Clifton Terrace
London N4 3SR
Tel: 020 7272 7774
Textphone: 020 7272 9648
Email: enquiries@sense.org.uk
Website: www.sense.org.uk

Supports and campaigns for the deafblind and their families. Offers advice, help and information, supports families through local branches. Runs holidays for deafblind children, provides education, residential, respite and day services. Has communicator-guides and one-to-one intervener support.

The Signalong Group
North Pondside
Historic Dockyard
Chatham
Kent ME4 4TY
Tel: 01634 819915/832469
Email: mkennard@signalong.org.uk
Website: www.signalong.org.uk

Signalong is a sign-supporting system based on British Sign Language and designed to help children and adults with communication difficulties to express their needs, choices and desires. Runs courses throughout the country, produces signing manuals with over 7500 signs and other visual communication resources including CD-ROM and researches signs for users.

Sound Learning Centre
12 The Rise
London N13 5LE
Tel: 020 8882 1060
Email: pallen@thesoundlearningcentre.co.uk
Website: www.thesoundlearningcentre.co.uk

Offers auditory integration training, lightwave stimulation and neuro-developmental delay programme for children and adults with learning, sensory, behavioural and emotional difficulties. Offers informal briefings to introduce the treatments, demonstrate equipment and present case studies.

Steps National Association for Children with Lower Limb Abnormalities
Lymm Court
11 Eagle Brow
Lymm
Cheshire WA13 0LP
Tel (helpline): 0871 717 0044
Tel (admin): 0871 717 0045
Email: info@steps-charity.org.uk
Website: www.steps-charity.org.uk

For parents of children with lower limb abnormalities. Puts families and children in touch, has a telephone helpline, produces a range of publications on such subjects as splints, plaster and talipes, and supports research.

Sustrans
35 King Street
Bristol BS1 4DZ
Tel: 0845 113 0065
Website: www.sustrans.org.uk

Provides information on traffic-free cycling. Produces a range of guide books on the National Cycle Network.

Thrive
The Geoffrey Udall Centre
Beech Hill
Reading RG7 2AT
Tel: 0118 988 5688
Email: info@thrive.org.uk
Website: www.thrive.org.uk

Aims to enable the disadvantaged, disabled and elderly to participate in gardening. Runs a range of practical garden projects, produces newsletters and a range of information sheets on sensory gardens, designing gardens for children with special needs etc.

Unique – The Rare Chromosome Disorder Support Group
PO Box 2189
Caterham
Surrey CR3 5GN
Tel: 01883 330766
Email: info@rarechromo.org
Website: www.rarechromo.org

Supports people affected by any rare chromosome disorder. Provides information, a comprehensive database, a family matching service, newsletters, an annual conference and a web discussion forum.

VisionAid
106 Junction Road
Deane
Bolton BL3 4NE
Tel: 01204 64265

Provides advice, information and support for visually impaired children, their families and professionals. Offers an information and reference library, specialist toy loan and visual stimulation equipment, hi-tech aid and tactile photocopying. A helpline is available for support and information can be given on such issues as education and benefits.

Wheels for All
1 Enterprise Park
Agecroft Road
Pendlebury
Manchester M27 8WA
Tel: 0161 745 9944
Email: cpnw@cycling.org.uk
Website: www.cycling.org.uk

Has a range of bicycles, tricycles and handcycles for people with disabilities, which it hires out from centres in the north of England.

SUPPLIERS OF TOYS AND EQUIPMENT FOR CHILDREN WITH SPECIAL NEEDS

Child's Play (International)
Ashworth Road
Bridgemead
Swindon SN5 7YD
Tel: 01793 616286

Supplies educational books, games and audio-visual material.

Galt Educational
Culvert Street
Oldham
Lancashire OL4 2GE
Tel: 0161 627 5086
Email: enquiries@galt-education.co.uk

Supplies toys, games and furniture.

Hope Education
Hyde Buildings
Ashton Road
Hyde
Cheshire SK14 4SH
Tel: 0161 366 2900
Email: enquiries@hope-education.co.uk
Website: www.hope-education.co.uk

Supplies toys and equipment for children including those with special needs. Includes fibre optics.

Logic Engineering Concepts Ltd (incorporating PJ Taylor Specialist Cycle Manufacturer)
Nash Works
Nash Lane
Belbroughton
Stourbridge DY9 9TD
Tel: 01562 731355
Email: roger@logicengineeringconcepts.info
Website: www.logicengineeringconcepts.info

Produces a range of specialist bicycles including tricycles, trailers, tandems and a wheelchair/bicycle combination.

Longstaff Cycles
Albert Street
Chesterton
Newcastle under Lyme
Staffs ST5 7JF
Tel: 01782 561996
Email: glongcycle@aol.com

Makes tricycles and tandem-tricycles for children and adults.

Mike Ayres Design
Unit 8
Shepherds Grove
Stanton
Bury St Edmunds
Suffolk IP31 2AR
Tel: 01359 251551
Website: www.mikeayresdesign.co.uk

Supplies soft play and sensory equipment.

NES Arnold
Ludlow Hill Road
West Bridgford
Nottingham NG2 6HD
Tel: 0115 945 2201

Supplies a wide range of toys and equipment to playgroups and pre-schools.

Nottingham Rehab
Ludlow Hill Road
West Bridgford
Nottingham NG2 6HD
Tel: 0115 945 2345

Provides a mail order catalogue, 'Ways and Means', of household products for people with special needs. Includes cutlery and crockery, special scissors and pencil grips. Also has a paediatric catalogue with equipment, games and toys for children with special needs.

Pashley Cycles
Masons Road
Stratford upon Avon
Warwickshire CV37 9NL
Tel: 01789 292263
Email: info@pashley.co.uk
Website: www.pashley.co.uk

Make tricycles, wheelchair tandems, side-by-side tricycles and trailer tricycles.

Peta (UK) Ltd
Marks Hall
Margaret Roding
Dunmow
Essex CM6 1QT
Tel: 01245 231118

Suppliers of scissors, gardening and cooking utensils.

Pyramid Educational Consultants UK Ltd
Pavilion House
6 Old Steine
Brighton
BN1 1EJ
Tel: 01273 609555
Email: pyramid@pecs.og.uk
Website: www.pecs.org.uk

Provides training and consultancy for Picture Exchange Communication System

Quest Enabling Designs
Ability House
242 Gosport Road
Fareham
Hants PO16 0SS
Tel: 01329 828444

Supplies switches and wheelchairs.

RNIB Royal National Institute for the Blind
PO Box 173
Peterborough
Tel: 0345 023153

Provides a toy catalogue and catalogue of products which include games, puzzles and leisure activities for children with a visual impairment.

ROMPA
Goyt Side Road
Chesterfield
Derbyshire S40 2PH
Tel: 0800 056 2323
Email: sales@rompa.co.uk
Website: www.rompa.co.uk

Supplies mail order toys, soft play and multi-sensory equipment for children with special needs.

SpaceKraft Ltd
Crowgill House
Rosse Street
Shipley
West Yorks BD18 3SW
Tel: 01274 581007
Email: enquiries@spacekraft.co.uk
Website: www.spacekraft.co.uk

Supplies multi-sensory equipment.

TFH
5–7 Severnside Business Park
Severn Road
Stourport on Severn
Worcs DY13 9HT
Tel: 01299 827820
Email: tfh@tfhuk.com
Website: www.tfhuk.com

Provides a mail order catalogue of multi-sensory equipment, switches, fun toys and games for children and adults with special needs.

Winslow
Goyt Side Road
Chesterfield
Derbyshire S40 2PH
Tel: 0845 921 1777
Email: sales@winslow-cat.com

Produces a catalogue of resources – games, books, computer programmes and equipment for children with special needs.

Index